DECISION
FOR
DESTINY

Everett Tilson

Women's Division
Board of Global Ministries
The United Methodist Church

Library of Congress Cataloging
Tilson, Charles Everett
Decision for Destiny
Bibliography: p
1. Prophets I. Title
BS1198.T55   224'   .06'6   75-8557

For
Joseph Everett Tilson
and
John, Hazel and Robert C. Lilly

CONTENTS

Foreword vii

I. **The Prophetic Faith of the Prophets'**
   Forerunners 1
   The Divine Deed of Liberation 7
   A Covenant Between Unequals 9
   Israel's Confession of Obligation 11
   The Priority of Purpose over Promise 12
   For Further Study
      The JE Traditions 15

II. **The Search for a Common Denominator** 18
   Did the Prophets Belong to
      Organized Groups? 20
   Who Turned the Prophets'
      Oracles Into Books? 23
   Has Prophecy Ceased? 28
   For Further Study
      What's in a Title? 30
      Were the Prophets Ecstatics? 31
      Were the Prophets Traditionalists? 33

III. **The Test of Israelite Loyalty** 37
   The World of Amos 40
   The Message of Amos 46
   The Real Threat to Israel's Future 48
   The Awful Burden of Divine Election 51
   The Lord's Contempt for
      Thoughtless Religion 53
   The Negative Test of Authentic Worship 55
   The Shocking Reversal of Popular
      Expectation 57

IV. **The Source of Covenantal Life** 64
   The Background of the Prophet 66
   The Compilation of the Book 67
   The Message of Hosea 75

v

V. **The Exaltation of Political Power** 89
   The Literary and Historical Background of
      the Dynastic Oracles 90
   The Lord's Word to the Participants 95
   The Positive Appreciation of Power 103
VI. **The Vulnerability of God's Spokesman** 105
   The Priority of the Divine Claim 112
   The Persistence of the Human Claim 119
VII. **The Rewards of the Lord's Service** 131
   The Mission of God 132
   The Mission of Israel 143
   The Method of the Servant 147
VIII. **The Legacy of the Great Prophets** 156
   The Combination of Apparent Opposites 157
   An Example in Involvement 164

Appendices

   I. JE Materials in Genesis—Numbers 170
   II. The Detection of Secondary Additions to a
         Prophetic Book 172
III. The Absence of Prophetesses from This Study. . 177

Study Guide 180

Bibliography 207

Glossary 215

The Author 223

The Cover 225

FOREWORD

This is a study book on selected prophets of the Old Testament. It was written at the invitation of the Women's Division of the Board of Global Ministries of The United Methodist Church. Throughout its preparation my work was governed by consideration of two things: (1) the desire of my audience to establish clear points of contact between the biblical and modern worlds; and (2) the anticipation that its publication would fall on the eve of the bicentennial observance of the American Revolution. In view of these special influences, it is only fitting that I indicate three of the reasons why the study of Israel's great prophets should hold special significance and relevance for us at this time.

The great prophets were the heirs of a long, vast, complex, and multifaceted heritage. It is widely assumed that the cultural antiquity of Israelite prophetism renders it obsolete for modern humankind; that it, with all its crude simplicities, has no place in our world of intricate and mystifying complexities; and that the representatives of this movement, with their typically one-dimensional approach to life and its problems, have about as much importance for our time as television salesmen would have had in theirs.

If nothing else, the fate of the prophets at the hands of modern interpreters belies these facile assumptions. Were the prophets ancient Israel's counterparts to Protestantism's unremitting and indignant decriers of social and ecclesiastical abuses, unrelated to the cultus and contemptuous of its personnel; cult functionaries, within a hair's breadth, functionally speaking, of the priests; God-appointed lay "loners," propelled onto center stage by an impulse they gladly would have resisted, had they been in control of themselves; or were they, as most recently depicted, the critical transmitters of tribal folk wisdom? At one time or another, and within the lifetime of most of us, each of these portraits of the prophets has won solid endorsement by biblical interpreters of great repute.

This variety of seemingly irreconcilable views stems in part from our shortage of information about prophetic origins. But our lack of data is not the only reason for such amazing diversity. A far more compelling consideration is the incredibly varied and paradoxical character of the data themselves. Used selectively, they may be employed to sustain any one of the above—and, in all probability, any one of several other equally plausible —positions. But should they be used so selectively? I think not. They should be construed, instead, as evidence of the many-sided and paradoxical character both of Israel's prophets and their heritage.

If this be the case, then Israel's prophets found themselves in a dilemma not unlike that facing us, and they were perplexed for much the same reasons that we now find ourselves in the grips of "future shock." Like us, they stood on the brink of social and international disruptions of absolutely shattering proportions. And while they believed, as many of us do about ours, that their heritage, rightly appropriated, could see them through their crisis, they were oftentimes as hard put to it as we are to find just the right handles with which to lay hold of it.

The great prophets were the children of their respective times and places. To be sure, they and their contemporaries were caught, as we are, between the demands of a bold new future for change and the pleas of a rich and hallowed heritage for faithfulness. But let us not oversimplify the connection. Even if we could trace the exact path by which they moved from problem to solution, we could never begin to meet today's challenge simply by following the same route. For while the future beckoning them, like that confronting us, held ominous signs of imminent shifts in the balance of power, our future is clouded by a grim reality with which they never had to reckon—the balance of terror. And, too, our heritage has been vastly enriched and enlarged by the absorption of new elements from a wide variety of sources since it last felt the impact of Israel's prophetic influences. But these additions, far from simplifying our task, have only served to make the hard choices ahead of us even harder than they otherwise would have been. And all this has taken place at a time, mind you, when these hard choices have become all the more urgent and inescapable and dangerous because of the dynamic world in which we shall have to make them.

As we approach these decisions, it is well that we should renew our acquaintance with Israel's great prophets. For they can surely help us, provided we remember that, in view of the differences between their history and ours, they cannot make them for us.

The great prophets can only lead us through these perilous times at the cost of great risk and pain to ourselves. We cannot do for our time what they did for theirs save as we take our stand *where* and *as* they took theirs. And where would that be? That would be astride freedom's saddle, where the battle between the divine will for all humanity and the will of self without regard for the rest of humanity is joined. And how would that be? That would be as single-minded servants of humanity's welfare, despite the tempter's bid to join it in warfare, poised and ready to heed the divine summons to our God-appointed destiny.

If you should read this book solely from the desire to ascertain just how things were in Israel in the days of her great prophets, I would not be displeased, but for at least two reasons I would nevertheless be disappointed. First of all, although this consideration does not greatly disturb me, I would be disappointed because you would be doing an injustice to these great spokesmen of God. The full meaning of their utterances did not begin to be exhausted by the times and circumstances to which they addressed themselves. But secondly, and far more importantly, I would be disappointed because you would be doing yourself an injustice. If you will but get on the divine wave length, they have far more to say to you than thus far they have said to you.

I now mention by name a few persons who have been of special help to me in the preparation of this manuscript. My colleagues, Drs. Robert Browning, Jeffery Hopper, and Donald Mauck, have served me well as literary and theological critics, as has also the Tilsons' good friend, Dr. Ruth Davies. For typing the manuscript I am indebted to Marcia Augspurger, a skilled secretary, and Jean Hopper, whose typewriter reflects the influence of her other vocation as a college teacher of English composition and literature. Finally, Mary Tilson, my wife, has given me many occasions during my work on this project to be grateful for the fact she did her graduate work in English.

Everett Tilson
Methodist Theological School
Delaware, Ohio
January 20, 1975

I

THE PROPHETIC FAITH OF THE PROPHETS' FORERUNNERS

1976 will be the bicentennial anniversary of the American Revolution. Next year the "four score and seven years" of Lincoln's Gettysburg Address will have become two full centuries. That is how long it will have been since our ancestors "brought forth on this continent a new nation, conceived in liberty, and dedicated to the proposition that all men are created equal." [1]

This birthday of the American experiment will be widely celebrated all year long. And that is as it should be. Certainly far less deserving undertakings have triggered "the noise of solemn assemblies." [2]

Yet this celebration could become an occasion for self-adulation and hollow boasting. In fact, we can only avert this calamity by taking stock of what has happened to us since 1776.

Let us look first at the credit side of the ledger. Here there are some clear gains of which we must take note and in which we can also take delight. The "government of . . . , by . . . , and for . . . the people" [3] still has a long way to go before it becomes the government of, by, and for *all* the people. Yet mass participation in the affairs of state is much greater than ever before. The rights of women, children, and minority groups have been recognized in law and extended in practice. The same can also be said for the social obligation of the rich and the human rights of the poor. And we cannot overlook our achievements in the field of public education. No major world power has ever boasted a more widely educated citizenry. Considering the significance and magnitude of these gains, we may justifiably ask whether any great nation in all human history has come so far so quickly.

But there is a debit side to the ledger, and we had better take a close look at its entries, too. For while they may not be as numerous as they are ominous, they are much too dangerous to ignore. Not many of us any longer experience taxation with no representation, but a lot of us are still at the mercy of those who gather capital and power by underpaying taxes and over-representing their case. We have made some progress in the punishment of crime, but we have not learned half enough about *The Crime of Punishment*. [4] Our skill in warmaking has literally skyrocketed, but not our love of peacemaking. Peacemaking continues to be a part-time business in a land of mammoth business and governmental conglomerates. It is easier to secure clemency for conscienceless soldiers than it is to win amnesty for conscientious objectors. There is talk about putting a floor under the poor and weak, but we hear little about putting a ceiling over the rich and powerful. And then there is Watergate, the lawless assault on the order of law by architects of the campaign for "law and order." To say that we hardly needed this reminder of the enormous gap between the ideals of our founders and the achievements of their descendants would be an understatement. Watergate has moved us to question the vitality, if not the validity, of the so-called "American dream."

Looking at this kind of mixed record, marked here by striking accomplishment and there by impressive failure, some people might be inclined to dismiss it as mere evidence of our humanity, but we Americans know that is simply not the case. Why do I say that? Because we feel within us a force that is working to overcome this contradiction. And we feel this presence within us because we have behind us a heritage which

2

emphatically denies that this is what it means to be human.

The glorious truth is that in our search for a new beginning we do not have to begin at the beginning. As we have been aptly and recently reminded: "The . . . ingredients of the vision are already there to anyone who will open his eyes. They are deep in our tradition and our being; they consist of values we have denied and betrayed for too long. Young idealists who profess utter emancipation from the past pour out torrents of words about the values they wish to live by, and lo, they turn out to be . . . updated versions of old values." [5] Unwittingly, they honor our American heritage as surely as did Abraham Lincoln when he—quite wittingly, of course—wrote of Jefferson's generation: "They meant to set up a standard . . . for free society, which should be . . . constantly looked to, constantly labored for, and even though never perfectly attained, constantly approximated, and thereby constantly spreading and deepening its influence augmenting the happiness and value of life to all people of all colors everywhere." [6]

Our chances for success in this venture do not appear to be particularly bright, but we can take courage from the achievement of Israel's prophets. Certainly the odds against them were far greater than those we have to buck. By the time most of them appeared on the scene, the independence of their country had ceased to be the central issue. And for some of them even the question of national survival had likewise disappeared as a live option. All that remained of their ancestral heritage were the religious traditions (the composite of which I choose to designate as Mosaic faith, not because I believe that Moses gave to Israelite faith its final form, but because I see Moses standing at the head of the stream within whose channels the central elements of that faith were given their definitive shape and character) that had awakened and sustained Israel's self-identity as the people of God.

But these traditions were enough to enable the

3

prophets to do their thing. They squeezed from them something more—and something more important—than the inspiration that kept them going when their nation was on the ropes. This more important something was their summons of Israel to a decision for destiny. For more than any other single factor, it was this call that kept Israel going long after, as a nation, it had been counted out.

The details of this summons changed from prophet to prophet, but its main outline remained constant. The key elements in the prophets' "updated versions of old values" never ceased to bear a striking resemblance to the principal ingredients of the Mosiac faith. They would not have hesitated to trace what we call the prophetic faith of Israel to more traditional expressions of Israelite faith. In all probability, they would have explained the prophetic faith as the offshoot of their efforts to keep the Mosaic faith aloft as a "standard constantly looked to" and "constantly labored for."

Despite the popular tendency to think of the prophets as Lone Rangers before the discovery of Texas, their achievements were as much the by-products of their religious heritage as they were the products of their own labors. When the prophets opposed Israel's leaders, as they too often had to do, they did not assail those leaders for supporting the traditions of the people; more often than not, they attacked them for the betrayal of those traditions. In short, they were heirs of the prophetic faith before they became its spokesmen.

Support for this claim of the prophets' dependence on the ancestral faith lies close at hand. In fact, we do not have to look beyond the classical formulation of Israelite faith to lay hold of conclusive evidence of this indebtedness. (See the discussion of the JE tradition at the end of this chapter.) The key elements in this presentation, as my elaboration of them will shortly make clear, bear too close a kinship to the message of the prophets to permit any other explanation. But this exposition must await a brief summary of the process

4

by which Israel's traditions developed from skeletal summaries into a narrative of epic proportions.

Two words keynote this development. They are Exodus and Sinai. Exodus and Sinai stand for the two great climactic events in the formation and growth of Israelite religion. Exodus became a symbol of the liberating deed (construed by the shapers of Israelite tradition as an act of God) that resulted in Israel's release from Egyptian bondage. And Sinai came to stand for the conditions (popularly identified with the Ten Commandments) which, if accepted and met, would enable Israel to secure and maintain her status as the people of God. Originally, these two events may have been unconnected (some scholars are convinced that the traditions of Exodus and Sinai emerged in total independence of each other). If so, time healed this separation, and the tradition of Sinai came to be assimilated to that of the Exodus.

This union set a precedent and a pattern for Israel's other traditions. They too got assimilated to the Exodus chain of narratives. In fact, the Exodus became such a magnet for Israel's religious traditions that "the Exodus event" has come to stand for the Israelite religion in much the same way "the Christ event" has become a virtual synonym for the Christian religion.

This development precludes the simple equation of the Exodus (or, as I prefer to call it, the Mosaic) faith with the religion of Moses and those whom he led out of Egypt. Mosaic faith has a far broader meaning than that. It embraces the activity of all Moses' followers who, inspired by the labors of him and his cohorts, continued their work. It includes the contribution of all those who participated in the tradition-making process that evolved as a commentary on Israel's history from the viewpoint of Mosaic faith and for the sake of its perpetuation. Thus we have a principal reason for the designation of this great work as a "confessional history" of Israel (i.e., the telling of Israel's story in such a way as to bear witness to her faith). Not only were the materials,

5

as a rule, assembled, sifted, updated, and transmitted by religious functionaries, but they were both preserved and altered, in most instances, for use in worship.

This process began with brief creeds (Deuteronomy 6:20-25; 26:5-10, and Joshua 24:2-13 are frequently cited as examples of such formulations) that custodians of the local sanctuaries prepared for recital in festival celebrations. At the appropriate time in the service the worshipers would confess their faith by reciting the story of God's role in their history and of his requirements for their life together. With the increase of leisure and curiosity, the demands on the shrinekeepers grew swiftly. And they responded to the challenge by filling in the details, not only of God's action in bygone days, but of his will for the present time. When tribes united with other tribes, their stories of God's dealings with them became the common property of the entire group, and they were subsequently joined and edited so as simultaneously to reflect this union and to update the obligations of its members before God.

The people of almost every community derive their self-understanding from some document connected with their origin. Not only do succeeding generations hail its formulation as a turning point in their history, but they hark back to it with monotonous regularity. And they hold up the names of those associated with it as models for their children in their untiring effort to link the future to the past in a chain of unbroken glory.

The Declaration of Independence is that community-shaping document for us Americans. Patriotic speakers of all persuasions trace their inspiration to its framers. The account of the career of Jesus of Nazareth forms its counterpart for us Christians. For while we may mock those who claim to speak only as he spoke and to do only as he did, we never relax our efforts to ground what we say and do in what he said and did. The Sinaitic History served the ancient Israelites as their founding document. From it they mined the ingredients of the faith—the dependence on the Lord that turned

6

no people into his people; the covenant with the Lord that made Israel his junior partner; the law of the Lord that alerted Israel to its obligations; the conditional character of the Lord's promise that kept Israel honest— that preserved Israel alive in the face of circumstances that would have devastated most people.

The Divine Deed of Liberation

Passover commemorates the deliverance of Israel from Egypt. Each year, at a crucial point during the celebration of this festival, a recital is made of the events that attended Israel's escape from Pharaoh's bondage. We cannot be sure of the precise age of this custom, but it is undoubtedly ancient. Some scholars hold not only that the practice antedates the biblical narrative of the exodus, but that this narrative itself came into being in response to the need of Passover celebrants for written material to assist them in their worship. In other words, just as the exodus inspired and informed Israel's transformation of Passover from a harvest festival into a celebration of the escape from Egypt, Israel's observance of Passover likewise inspired and shaped its record of the exodus itself.

The form of the biblical account of the exodus certainly lends support to this view. This story does not belong in the category of straightforward historical narrative, in which actions may be traced to the impact of one human on other humans. Quite the contrary, in both chapters of this epic adventure, in the report of the call of Moses to act as deliverer no less than in the report of the deliverance itself, we get a studied, deliberate, calculated disregard of secondary causes and human agents. The key actor in this drama is neither the person Moses nor the people Israel, but the Lord. From beginning to end, whenever an important action is narrated, the Lord is the subject of that action. We are not presented here with a report plus a theological interpretation of what happened. We are given the the-

7

ological interpretation of what happened in the report itself. Hence, instead of labeling this report a simple historical narrative, we should recognize it, instead, as a liturgical historical narrative. It is designed not only to express, but also to call forth, the faith that interprets this entire complex of events, from the emergence of Moses to the escape of Israel, as a divine deed of liberation.

The call of Moses furnishes the prelude and pattern for the emancipation of Israel. In both instances the story hinges on Yahweh's struggle with humanity as Yahweh tries to liberate that humanity from the bondage into which it has gotten itself. Four times Moses meets the summons to serve as the agent of Israel's would-be deliverer with an objection (Exodus 3:11-12, 13; 4:1, 10). In each instance his objection is met with a hint that the power on his side is greater than that arrayed against Israel. And Moses, once his doubts have been removed, yields himself into the service of that power. He now becomes anxious for further instructions concerning his role in Israel's deliverance, but he must wait for a fuller introduction to the power whose agent he has become.

This power, Moses learns, has a name (Exodus 3:15). And that name, Yahweh (although the vowels were not supplied in ancient Hebrew, this is the preferred English transliteration of most scholars), usually translated the Lord, is not the name of one god among many; quite the contrary, it is a name for the God who has the will and power to liberate Egypt's slaves. Yet the Lord's design for Israel, while it includes the offer of political freedom, entails the promise of something more and something better than that. Ahead of all else, it features the promise of a covenant in which the Lord shall become the Lord of Israel and Israel shall become the people of the Lord.

Many obstacles blocked the path of this achievement, but in Israelite memory one of these impediments, namely the "Sea of Reeds," dwarfed all the others into virtual insignificance. Of course, in view of the incomparably

8

superior resources and forces at Pharaoh's disposal, any gambling person present would have quoted absolutely prohibitive odds against Israel. Their chances could hardly have appeared dimmer. Had not a power not of this world come to their rescue, they would have perished. An element in the old ritual for the feast of the Passover (Exodus 13:14f: in this text the festival still gets called by its old name, the "feast of Unleavened Bread") yields interesting testimony in support of this conviction. When children ask concerning this observance, "What does this mean?" their elders are instructed to answer them, "By strength of hand the Lord brought us out of Egypt... For when Pharaoh stubbornly refused to let us go, the Lord slew all the first-born... of Egypt..."

This Passover proclamation is the heart of the Old Testament Gospel. It is also the backbone of Israel's understanding of history. It is not only a sample but the source of the simultaneous stress in Israelite history-writing on the priority of the action of God and the insignificance of human calculations. From it came the reminder with which a great Israelite theologian-historian freed his friends and neighbors from the possibility of rationalizing Israel's choice by God: "It was not because you were more in number than any other people that the Lord . . . chose you . . . ; but it is because the Lord loves you and is keeping the oath which he swore to your fathers, that the Lord has . . . redeemed you from the house of bondage" (Deuteronomy 7:7-8).

In effect, the Deuteronomist was saying to Israel in a fashion that would have pleased the best of the prophets' forerunners: "You have not made the Lord the subject of your liberation because you chose him to be your God; rather, it is because the Lord has chosen you to be the beneficiaries of his liberating deed."

A Covenant Between Unequals

The Deuteronomic view of Israel's inferior status did not enjoy universal support. Many Israelites subscribed to the notion that the health and welfare of the Lord and Israel had become inseparable. They felt that the Lord would be as helpless without Israel as Israel would be without the Lord.

The spread of this conceit appalled the prophets. They were shocked by their neighbors' poor memory. They simply could not understand the widespread neglect of this central affirmation about the election of Israel, so effectively and dramatically symbolized in the exodus: the Lord had cast the deciding ballot.

The older account of the Israelite ceremony for ratifying the covenant (Exodus 24:1-11 contains two versions of this celebration: the first but later appears in vss. 1a, 9-11; the second and older, in vss. 1b-8) leaves Israel without excuse for this oversight. The rite begins with the draining of the blood of the sacrificial animals into two separate containers. As soon as this process has been completed, the blood in the first container is dashed over the altar, symbolizing the presence of the Lord. There follows an interlude in which the "book of the covenant" is read in the hearing of the people. To this rehearsal of their covenantal obligations (the "book of the covenant" probably refers to a code of laws; if the reference is to one of the Old Testament codes, a likely candidate would be an early version of the Ten Commandments) the congregation responds with this pledge: "All that the Lord has spoken we will do, and we will be obedient." Following the offer of this vow, the blood in the second container is thrown over the assembled worshipers.

While the primitive character of this ceremony can scarcely fail to impress us, we must not overlook the underlying conviction of its symbolism. Behind this ritual stands the belief that two parties can become one through mutual association with the vital essence of a third—in this case, the blood of the sacrificial animals. By the enactment of this ceremony Israel dramatizes her faith that she and the Lord, though originally separate, have achieved union.

Yet the terms of the covenant, while they clearly establish Israel's status as the Lord's partner, leave no room for doubt that what we have here is clearly not a partnership of equals. The Lord's status is unconditional; regardless of what happens to Israel, the Lord is and shall continue to be God. Israel's status, on the other hand, is totally conditioned. It can remain the people of God only by making good on its vow to fulfill the requirements of the "book of the covenant."

In taking this vow Israel attests to its awareness and acceptance of this condition. At the same time, by clear implication, if not openly, it likewise acknowledges its relationship to the Lord to be that of subject to ruler. Hence we might describe the ritual of the covenant as a coronation ceremony in which Israel enthrones the Lord as its king.

Israel's Confession of Obligation

Just as in the New Testament law follows Gospel, so in the Old Testament Sinai follows exodus. Israel's ceremonies of renewing the covenant (for which Exodus 24:1-11 may have come to serve as a model) attest to the seriousness with which Israelites took the notion of divine kingship. They knew the Lord of the covenant as one who made demands and exacted obedience. Yet his monarchy was of the constitutional variety. His requirements were not only based on principle, but they were repeatedly defined in law.

According to many scholars, the "Book of the Covenant" (Exodus 24:11) marks one such attempt at translating divine will into law. They are not sure that this particular collection can be identified with any one of the many law codes contained in the Old Testament (such as, e.g., Exodus 20:1-17; 20:22-23:33; 34:11-26; Leviticus 17-26; Deuteronomy 12-26). Yet they feel quite certain that most, if not all, of these law codes originated in a setting of worship. If correct, this would not only mean that they were first expressed as the will of Israel's

11

heavenly king. It would likewise mean that adherence to their requirements was seen as a condition for Israel's survival as the covenant partner of the Lord.

Law in ancient Israel was rooted in quite different premises than those on which modern case law rests. Chief among these would be the following: that the law comes from the Lord of the covenant; that the law defines the duty of the Lord's covenantal partner Israel; that obedience to the terms of the law is necessary if Israel is to remain the Lord's partner in covenant; that disobedience represents a ground for the termination of Israel's membership in the covenant; that Israelite destiny, whether as covenantal member or outcast, hinges on its decision for or against the law.

This conception helps to explain the quantity as well as the diversity of Israel's legal codes. For if their differences attest to the fact that opinion could vary as to what planks Israel should include in the platform of her declaration of dependence on the Lord, their multiplicity bears witness to the conviction that she could not get along without such a declaration.

When the ancient Israelites pledged obedience to the law, they did not view their action at all as some of today's readers of the Old Testament are apt to construe it. They did not see themselves taking an oath against the pursuit of joy and liberty. They saw themselves clearing the high road to survival and freedom. This is not to suggest that the confession of obligation came any easier for them than it comes for us. It is simply to point out that, at their best, the Israelites could conceive of no other way of being or remaining the people of God. Unfortunately, they quickly descended from this lofty plane, and alien notions soon corrupted this idealism.

The Priority of Purpose over Promise

The belief that the Lord has singled out Palestine as the home for Israel is the focus of modern Jewry's bid for a place in the sun in the Middle East. In fact, this notion has become so deep-rooted in Jewish life and hope that "belief" no longer does justice to it. It has become one of today's most powerful "motivational myths." [8] For not only does it provide those who subscribe to it with an "outlook on history and its purpose, (but) by finding a place in (their) feelings and choices . . . , it (moves) them to action." [9]

If one has any doubt on this score, one has only to look at what has happened to Palestine since the establishment there of the state of Israel in 1948. Hundreds of thousands of Jewish citizens of nations from all over the world have forsaken the land of their birth to claim their birthright to a residence in the "land of promise."

This view of Palestine finds expression in almost all of Israel's oldest writings. When Moses appears before the elders, he is instructed to say to them in the Lord's name, "I promise that I will bring you up out . . . of Egypt, to the land of the Canaanites (the name of the pre-Israelite inhabitants of Palestine) . . . , a land flowing with milk and honey" (Exodus 3:17).

But the narrative of Sinai proceeds to attach important qualifications to this promise of land. From the Mount, the Lord calls to Moses, and tells him to say to Israel, "You have seen what I did to the Egyptians, and how I . . . brought you to myself. Now therefore, *if* (!) you will obey my voice and keep my covenant, you shall be my own possession . . . , and you shall be to me a kingdom of priests and a holy nation" (Exodus 19:4-6). The result clause (everything that follows that second comma) of the last sentence in the foregoing passage defines for us the ultimate end for which God has chosen Israel. He chose it, in short, that it might be the Lord's "own possession" and become to him "a kingdom of priests and a holy nation."

Here we have a goal that so far transcends the occupation of land that the latter is at best but a condition for its achievement. Yet the only hope for its realization

13

hinges on obedience to the Lord's commandments and adherence to his covenant. The "if" clause clearly implies that, should Israel fail to meet these conditions, it could neither remain "the Lord's possession" nor become "a kingdom of priests and a holy nation."

In case of such an event, we are forced to ask, what would become of the land? Now that Israel is incapable of realizing the purpose for which it has been given title to the land, will it be permitted to continue to hold title to the land for no apparent purpose? Can the Lord permit an unholy people to continue to occupy the Holy Land? Does not the betrayal of the Lord's purpose by the people to whom he has given the land release him from any promise he might have made to them at the time of this gift? Can the Lord be true to himself if he does not press the search for a more responsible tenant —for one who will view the divine promise as sanction for the pursuit of God's will.

These questions should have posed little difficulty for the prophets' contemporaries. Considering the hedges with which tradition had surrounded the Lord's gift of land to Israel, they should have promptly subordinated the promise of the land to the purpose of the Lord. But this they did not do; in fact, multitudes of them did precisely the opposite. They parlayed the gift of land into a claim of special favor and an excuse for shabby living.

In this chapter I have presented a summary of the message with which the prophets' forerunners confronted Israel. This same outline could be used to capsule the proclamation of the prophets themselves. For while the message of the prophets may have been radical, it was not radically new. All its essential notes had all been sounded before. They had all been heard before. And they had all been ignored before.

By the time the great prophets arrived on the scene, the history of Israelite rebellion was in full swing. Defiance of the Lord had become a national habit. And not all Israel's prophets worked to break it. Some of them actually contributed to the growth and development of apostasy. As we shall have occasion to note in chapter two, some of the history and personnel of the prophetic movement itself threatened the credibility and reception of the great prophets.

For Further Study

The J E Traditions

The J document (so-called because J is the first letter in the spelling of its preferred name for God in the language of the scholars who developed the abbreviations J, E, D, and P for the four documents which were combined to form the first five books of the Old Testament) was the confessional history of all Israel from the standpoint of the tribes of the Southern Kingdom, following the split of the United Kingdom on the heels of Solomon's death. The E document (so-called because E is the first letter of its preferred name for God) was the confessional history of all Israel from the perspective of the Northern Kingdom. Despite their origin in different places and times (J, from the Southern Kingdom in the latter half of the tenth century before Christ; and E, from the Northern Kingdom about 150 years later), the J and E documents are so much alike literarily that at times it is hard to distinguish the one from the other. Theologically, they are so much alike that this distinction seldom matters any way. For this reason, inasmuch as my purpose in the present volume is theological rather than literary, I shall proceed to treat the two documents as if they were one, for in two very important respects they are one: (1) they may be used equally as sources for reconstructing the Mosaic faith as it was known in Israel before the rise of its great prophets; (2) they are in basic agreement as to what constitutes the essential elements of Mosaic faith, and the editors of each were concerned to keep the faith pure.

As you ponder the various elements in the foregoing elaboration of JE theology, compare them with the major themes in the message of the prophets. This exercise should remove any misgiving you may have had about my description of this work as an instance of prophetic religion before the prophets. And it will likewise convince you of the right of its editors to be called the prophets' forerunners, both in terms of their faith and their time in history.

The four subheads of this chapter provide at most a sort of thematic guide to JE theology. They only hint at the wealth of materials embodied in the contributions of the J and E writers. A detailed breakdown of the passages generally assigned to each of these collections appears in Appendix I. By reading all the passages in Genesis through Numbers designated in this list as belonging either to J or E, but taking care to exclude all others, you can doublecheck my interpretation of their thought. Better still, you can get a feel for the sweep and the majesty of their achievement that you could not hope to match from a third-party introduction to them.

The JE emphasis on the Exodus-Sinai narratives (some scholars employ "the Sinaitic History" as shorthand for this complex of materials) spotlights their central place in Israel's faith and history. Even though they do not stand at either the beginning or the end of Israel's tradition-making process, they nevertheless furnish the angle of vision from which prophetic faith surveyed the whole of Israel's traditions in its search for the definitive clue to its life, death, and destiny. They define the people-shaping convictions to which Israel must constantly go back before it can with a sense of direction and confidence go forward.

FOOTNOTES

[1] From the Gettysburg Address, the text of which is reprinted in a volume edited by G. B. deHuszar, H. W. Littlefield, and A. W. Littlefield, *Basic American Documents* (Ames, Ia.: Littlefield, Adams & Co., 1956), p. 205.

[2] Title of a book by Peter Berger (Garden City, N.Y.: Doubleday & Co., Inc., 1961).

[3] See deHuszar, Littlefield, & Littlefield, eds., *Basic American Documents,* p. 205.

[4] Karl Menninger (New York: The Viking Press, Inc., 1969).

[5] John W. Gardner, *The Recovery of Confidence* (New York: W. W. Norton & Co., Inc., 1970), p. 94.

[6] A quote from Lincoln in the volume edited by J. A. Garraty & Peter Gay, *The Columbia History of the World* (New York: Harper & Row, 1972), p. 763.

[7] Ignatius Hunt, *Understanding the Bible* (New York: Sheed & Ward, 1961), p. 98.

[8] Quoted by Conrad Cherry, ed., *God's New Israel* (Englewood Cliffs, N. J.: Prentice-Hall, Inc., 1971), p. 21.

[9] *Ibid.*

II

THE SEARCH FOR A COMMON DENOMINATOR

Prophetism has been defined as "simply a particular way of looking at history. The *meaning* of history is to be found only in terms of God's concern, purpose, and . . . participation in history." [1] Given this definition of prophetism, we must do better by the producers of the JE history of Israel than merely acclaim them as "the prophets' forerunners." At the very least they were the prophets' tutors in the Mosaic faith. In fact, the basic message of the great prophets may even be described as the renewal and extension of the covenantal theology of the JE writers.

Unfortunately, though, not all of those on whom Israel pinned the title of "prophet" neatly fitted this classification. In Israel, as elsewhere, the prophets worthy of the adjective great were not the rule but the exception.

The appearance of Amos in the royal sanctuary at Bethel illustrates the confused meaning in Israel of the term "prophet." When Amaziah the priest ordered Amos, whom we recognize as the first of Israel's great prophets, never again to prophesy in Bethel, Amos disowned the prophetic title, saying, "I am no prophet, nor a prophet's son; but . . . a herdsman, and a dresser of sycamore trees" (7:14). Whatever else this denial may have meant, it clearly indicated Amos' displeasure at having his name linked with the current crop of prophets. By the time the first truly great prophet arrived on the scene, the institution of prophecy had degenerated to the point that he preferred not to be known as a prophet.

No doubt, given our tendency to think of prophetic faith as the most sublime expression of religion, we are perplexed by this refusal. And our bewilderment is probably compounded by the assumption that, if you want to study the origins and pinpoint the concerns of prophetic faith, you have only to trace the growth and development of the prophetic movement in Israel. This assumption suffers from two basic oversights. Not only does it wrongly equate the prophetic faith with the popular religion of Israel, but it obscures the minority status of the spokesmen for this faith within the ranks of the prophets themselves. A scene from the Deuteronomic history of Israel corrects this impression with a vengeance. According to its report of a head-to-head encounter between opposing prophets, the prophet of the Lord is outnumbered four hundred to one (1 Kings 22).

The ratio was not always so one-sided, yet the succession of persons who gave to prophetic faith its definitive stamp seldom exceeds ten. The names of Amos, Hosea, Isaiah, Micah, Jeremiah, and Ezekiel almost never fail to crash this select group of contributors to the Old Testament scriptures. On the other hand, the names of the prophets Daniel, Haggai, Joel, Jonah, Malachi, Nahum, Obadiah, and Zechariah only rarely make it, even though the framers of the Old Testament canon of scriptures viewed them as authors of prophetic writings.

This fact alone illustrates the difficulty of trying to reduce the prophetic movement in Israel to a common denominator. Yet we ought to take note of these other indications of the great complexity and diversity of Israelite prophecy: the title of prophet had a long past before it came to be applied to the prophets who gave to it its deepest meaning; the differences in function and thought between the earlier and the great prophets were sometimes so marked as to call forth amazement at their designation by a common title; the great prophets themselves exhibited considerable variety in message and method; the title of prophet, because of a demonstrated or assumed likeness in one or more respects to the great prophets, was applied retrospectively to several Old Testament figures whose contemporaries did not know them as prophets; Israelites continued to bestow the title of prophet on their contemporaries long after it had undergone radical shifts in meaning. Such considerations make it impossible neatly to trace the evolution of Israelite prophecy. We simply do not have the necessary information for fitting its developments into a chronological framework. About the best we can hope for is to indicate the diverse patterns of prophetic conduct and communication and try to determine their compatibility with the behavior and speech of the great prophets. This approach may at first incline us to exaggerate the number of their relatives, but close examination will convince us, in most instances, of the remoteness of their kinship. If nothing else, it will prove that, while social destiny may have inclined persons like Amos and Isaiah to join the prophetic movement, it was personal decision that made them the kind of prophets they became.

Did the Prophets Belong to Organized Groups?

Since the Old Testament clearly witnesses to the presence of organized bands of prophets, the existence of such prophetic groups in Israel lies beyond dispute. The big question concerns the relationship of the great prophets to the members of these professional communities. Were the great prophets members of such bodies? Or if not, in what ways, if at all, do they reflect their impact?

At least two types of such prophetic groups, court and cult, made their presence felt in Israel for the entire period of its existence as an independent national state. While the great prophets can scarcely be identified as card-carrying members of any of these groups, their message and activity were doubtless influenced by all of them. Due to our inability to fix dates, the lines of connection between them have to be drawn broadly, but even this outline should be sufficient to indicate some of the principal similarities and primary differences between them.

Associations of cult prophets played an important role in the religious life of the Ancient Near East from the second millennium onward. In Israel these groups did not mark the simple extension of their Near Eastern counterparts, yet they continued to resemble them in various ways, particularly at the organizational level. It is generally agreed, for example, that such prophets functioned in Israel as members of a regularized staff at the local shrines and, very probably, at the single sanctuary after Josiah's centralization of worship in Jerusalem; that they performed cultic duties in a professional role; and that some of their descendants were absorbed into the Levitical orders responsible for temple worship after the return from exile.

There is less agreement as to which Old Testament prophets, if any, served as cult functionaries. Reports of the performance of semi-priestly duties by some of the early prophets lend credence to the assumption of such connections for a number of them. But the alleged evidence in support of the membership of Isaiah and Jeremiah, and possibly others of the great prophets, in cultic associations has attracted more attention than followers. Yet there is no longer serious doubt that cult prophetism had a sometimes positive impact on the great prophets. Contrary to the view of older scholars, many of whom saw the great prophets as uncompromising foes of all cultic worship, interpreters now agree that what these prophets sought was not the eradication but the transformation of the cultus. Since the cult was so central to Israel's faith that "Israel could be Israel only cultically," it doubtless served them, like other Israelites, as their original instructor in the faith. From it they derived their demand for "justice and righteousness," for "these were qualities of . . .the character and demand of the very God upon whom the whole cultus" was focused.[2] And from its ritual some

21

of them—in addition to the minor prophets Nahum, Habakkuk, and Joel, this group includes the great Second Isaiah (author of Isaiah 40-55)—even borrowed the literary forms for the communication of their message.

To express doubt about the membership of the great prophets in the professional groups of cult prophets is not to deny the impact of the cult (i.e., formal worship) on their life and work. The fact and dimensions of their indebtedness to the cult are much too great for that. They were the beneficiaries of its worship. From it they absorbed their knowledge of Israel's traditions. By it they were nurtured in the theology of their ancestors. And from it they derived the stimulus and standards for their criticism of the excesses and distortions, the externalities and banalities, of Israelite life and worship. My reluctance to identify the great prophets as cult prophets is simply a way of acknowledging the absence of convincing evidence, despite the undeniable influence on them of the cultus, that they were related to it in a professional capacity.

The evidence concerning the activity of the court prophets and their relation to the great prophets is similarly unclear. Several important questions still go unanswered. Nobody questions that there were groups of prophets who functioned at court (1 Kings 22:6), but the question of sponsorship continues to be debated. Did these prophets render their service as members of the king's staff, or were they simply members of the staff of a sanctuary located in the royal city? If as members of the staff of a sanctuary, did they confine their activity solely to political issues? Or were they generalists whose counsel was sought by the king because of their demonstration of special talent for—or, more likely, the proper bias in—the resolution of political issues? And if they were enlisted by the king because of their expressed political views, why did they voice support for the king? Did they adopt this stance in quest of personal and professional advantage? Or did they do it in the hope of winning royal support for a

22

narrowly conceived understanding of religion in their struggle against rival religious leaders? We must not jump to the conclusion that all the prophets who functioned at court were mere court prophets. Even if they prophesied only at royal command, that fact in itself would not prove that they were always docile instruments of the crown. After all, some of the great prophets issued some of their most scathing denunciations (see, e.g., Jeremiah 21:1-10 and 37:3-10) of national policy in response to the king's request for "the word of the Lord" concerning its outcome.

On at least a few occasions, some of the prophetic forerunners of the great prophets, who sometimes get classified as court prophets, acted with courage and insight. They took positions vis-á-vis not only the king and national policy but the Lord and his supremacy over the crown (see the account of the activity of Ahijah, 1 Kings 11:29-39; Shemaiah, 1 Kings 12:22-24; Jehu, 1 Kings 16:4, 7, 12) that complicate our effort clearly to distinguish them from the great prophets who stood on their shoulders. Yet the forerunners, as a class, were more unlike than like the great prophets. For while the great prophets frequently addressed themselves to political issues, they normally did so with sovereign disregard for the opinion not only of the head of state, but of other prophets.

Who Turned the Prophets' Oracles Into Books?

A century of disproportionate scholarly attention to prophetic literature has not produced universal agreement concerning the processes of its origin, growth, development, and canonization. Even such elementary questions as the forms of prophetic speech and the origins of prophetic collections, not to mention the compilation of separate scrolls under the names of individual prophets, continue to be the subject of vigorous debate. Consequently, while the views I shall here express concerning the collection, preservation, and transmission of the prophetic materials enjoy wide support, they nevertheless deal with issues where there is much room for differences of opinion.

Prophetic communication has been narrowly defined as a form of "messenger speech" in which "the transmission of a speech . . . depended entirely on its retention and repetition by the appointed messenger." [3] This description may be applicable to some of Israel's earliest prophets, but at best it has limited value in interpreting the activity of the great prophets. At least a few of them probably wrote down some of their proclamations before delivering them.[4] Besides, given their commitment to the Mosaic faith and its application to their time and situation, it is unthinkable that they could have imitated the form of "messenger speech" without stretching its boundaries beyond recognizable limits. And even more importantly, given their sense of distance between God and humanity, they could not have thought of themselves as God's messengers in quite the same sense as others saw themselves as the messengers of a secular king.

No matter what the original model of prophetic proclamation, the great prophets did not allow themselves to be imprisoned by it. They did not hesitate to appropriate verbal forms from all spheres of Israelite life. They were no more reluctant to embrace new forms for the delivery of their utterances than they were to credit the Lord with the inspiration of their own revisions of Mosaic faith. Their freedom expressed itself professionally as well as theologically. Just as their faith would not permit them to become mere slaves of "the faith," they were kept by a feel for art as well as a sense of mission from unthinkingly adopting inherited forms. [5]

This is not to credit the great prophets with either the creation or use of all the verbal forms and literary types that appear in the prophetic books. Inasmuch as the final editions of these works embody additions from periods two to four centuries later than the activity of the prophets whose names they bear, some of these

24

forms and types had not yet come into being. But it is to credit these prophets with employment of most, if not all, of the rhetorical and literary patterns in common usage at the time of their activity. Even more importantly, it is to find in their attitude toward the problems and challenges of communication ample precedent for the expansion of their words and work by later hands. To them communication was basically a matter of substance rather than form. Since they borrowed from the literary and theological traditions of their predecessors, they would hardly have objected on principle to the expansion of their utterances by others.

Granted the lapse of a long period of time between the activity of the great prophet and the final compilation of his book of prophecies, questions arise concerning the preservation of his words. What was the connection between the prophet himself and those responsible for the original collections of his words? And what, if any, was the relationship of these collectors to the persons who amassed the final compilation of his book?

Some interpreters have found the clue for solving the historical puzzle enfolded in these questions in Isaiah 8:16-18. In this passage the prophet gives the order for a group of "disciples" (rendered by RSV as "those who are taught") to preserve a copy of his utterances as a witness to the integrity of his message and mission. Taking this statement at face value, they have concluded that a group of the prophet's own disciples were responsible for the first step in the process that ultimately issued in the book of Isaiah.[6] Inasmuch as the author of Isaiah 40-55, who lived two centuries after Isaiah of Jerusalem, twice refers (50:4) to himself as a member of a group of "disciples," at least one of these interpreters has concluded not only that an ongoing community of the disciples of Isaiah of Jerusalem continued to flourish two centuries after the great prophet's death, but that Second Isaiah not only was—but wanted to be—numbered among them.[7] This same commentator proceeds to ask whether, in view of "the remarkable unity pervading its various . . . sections," despite their composition by different writers from widely separated periods of time, the book of Isaiah "in its present form does not constitute an effective testimony to a long-continuing discipleship to the prophet." [8]

Even granted the existence of a band of Isaiah's disciples across so many centuries, a case has hardly been established for a similarly "long-continuing discipleship" to Amos or Jeremiah or any of the other great prophets. Certainly most of "their" books do not always exhibit sufficient unity in thought or style for us to employ it as an argument for the ongoing existence of such a group. But what of the assumption that, unless these collections reflect sameness of style and substance and form, they could not have come from ongoing circles of disciples? Does it not suggest a kind of slavish dependence on the person and teaching of the great prophets which an Amos or an Isaiah would not have accorded anyone? And does it not overlook the fact that, even if these prophets had consciously worked to instill such an attitude among their followers, they would have thoroughly undermined such efforts by their example of creative improvising and rugged independence? In short, could the persons who preserved the collections of the great prophets really have been their disciples (or "learners": in Greek the word from which "disciple" is derived has the root meaning "to learn"), had they been content merely to be their parrots?

If we answer this last question in the negative, as I believe we must, we may safely credit disciples of the great prophets with not only the collection and the preservation but also the transmission of their words, all the way from the time when they were first uttered to their ultimate incorporation into the prophetic corpus. But we must take care to define discipleship in far broader and looser terms than do the aforementioned interpreters. For while their role may have owed much to the charismatic figure whose disciples they fancied themselves to be, they too, in all probability, felt a stronger obligation to the faith than to the group and to the Lord of heaven and earth than to either the founder or the leader of their prophetic band. In other words, just as the word of the Lord did not move from tradition to the great prophets without engaging their whole persons, neither did it proceed from them to their disciples without reflecting the changed and changing circumstances of the latter's environment. Or to put it differently, the preservers and transmitters of the words of the prophets flattered their teachers in the sincerest manner possible. They duplicated their mentors' refusal to become anybody's passive agents, the prophets themselves not excepted.

The Mosaic faith did not continue to be a vital force in Israelite life, because the custodians of the prophetic teaching slavishly adopted their masters' formulations of tradition. It retained its dynamic power and became a stimulus to renewal because they internalized its demand for personal obedience to the living God. And they did it amidst all the perplexities and uncertainties and dynamics of historical existence. That their adaptations and revisions of the utterances of the prophets greatly complicate our attempt at the recovery of the prophets' words there can be slight doubt. But had they made no attempt to relate the oracles of the prophets to their day, our loss would have been incalculably greater. For had that happened, both the message of the prophets and the faith for which it appealed would have vanished from the earth.

This view of Hebrew prophecy has more to commend it than its portrayal of Israelite prophets as real, sure-enough, flesh-and-blood, alive and breathing persons. It has the further advantage of enabling us to approach the prophetic books for what they are: the complex records of a living tradition with a long history. Despite the presence of an overarching theological unity throughout the period of the growth of the prophetic material, variety marked every aspect of its development. Various people contributed to the collection assembled in each prophet's name. And while the disciples who transmitted and canonized these materials may not have been as creative as the prophets and their first disciples, they were by no means passive conveyors of an unexamined tradition. They left their marks on the various collections that went into the formation of each of the prophetic books. First, minor collections, linked together because of similarity in sound, style, substance, or occurrence in time, and major collections, similarly organized, were joined. Still later, on the basis of time, quality or theology, these composites were brought together to produce the canonical books of the prophets. Even after that, as post-exilic Jews came increasingly to anticipate the judgment of their enemies between the time of the imminent punishment and the ultimate salvation of Israel, users of the prophetic books felt free to rearrange the materials of these collections in line with their own outlook.

To call these makers of the prophetic books—the preservers and collectors and transmitters and canonizers—joint authors with the prophets would be to say too much. Yet to call them anything less than creative editors would be to say too little. Not only did they enlarge the prophets' utterances to make room in them for their own ideas, but they sometimes altered them to fit the needs of a different time or place.

Has Prophecy Ceased?

Ever since Josephus, a Jewish historian born shortly after the death of Jesus of Nazareth, popular tradition has treated prophecy and law as successive eras in the history of the Lord's dealing with Israel. According to this view, prophecy had a quite precise end, which Josephus dates to the reign of Artaxerxes of Persia (464-424). Needless to add, this interpretation likewise minimizes the connection between the preexilic prophet and the postexilic scribe into virtual nonexistence. Not only does it obscure the fact that "the decisive impingement of the Lord upon history" [9] was the most distinctive characteristic of Israelite prophecy, but it also overlooks the extent to which the prophetic interpretation of history marked the point of departure for the activity alike of both the legalists and the apocalyptists, the two principal groups of interpreters of Israel's traditions during the postexilic period.

Granted the dynamic, flexible, creative and unpredictable understanding of prophecy set forth by me, the postulation of an authentically "prophetic" tradition that dates at least from the time of Moses can scarcely be disputed. At the same time, and for similar reasons, we must reject out of hand the notion that essential prophetism came to an end in the fifth century before Christ. Certainly the burden of proof falls on whomever would deny that the statute of the scribe or the vision of the apocalyptist, any less than the oracle of the prophet, was intended to serve any other purpose than to actualize the divine will in the history of Israel.

So long as prophecy gets defined by the activity of the persons to whom the title of "prophet" was applied in the Old Testament, it is a simple matter to date its beginning and determine its end. As soon, however, as we begin to date it on the basis of the stance and thrust of Israel's great prophets, the task becomes vastly different and far more difficult. Not only does it make it impossible any longer to speak of the eclipse of prophecy, but it makes it at least as difficult to pinpoint the decline of prophecy as it does to trace its origins. And it compels us to ask about the candidacy of a host of other claimants to the title of prophet. May we not quite legitimately apply it to all the upright and courageous proclaimers of biblical faith who, irrespective of their appearance in time, adopted the style and stance of the great prophets? And why, since the hallmark of the great prophet was his readiness, on the basis of the fresh examination of the ancestral faith, to call his generation to a decision for its God-appointed destiny, should we not hail as prophet any person who does for our sacred traditions what the great prophet did for Israel's?

Our search for a common denominator among Israel's great prophets has yielded no readily detectable similarity in either personal or professional demeanor. Nevertheless it has produced a most encouraging result. It has located their genius in a disposition towards God and neighbor that brings their achievement within reach of each of us. By the same token, it has turned the wildly enthusiastic exclamation of Moses (Num. 11:29), "Would that all the Lord's people were prophets!" into not only a prayable but a plausible prayer for all of us.

For Further Study

What's in a Title?

Many scholars have sought the clue to the meaning of prophecy in the origin of the Hebrew word for prophet. Their search has yielded three top candidates as the probable root of this title, but the significance of this discovery leaves considerable room for debate. This fact becomes clear in the evaluation of these candidates' respective claims by a scholar who attaches much importance to the history of linguistic forms.[10] He dismisses the first possibility, "derived from a verb meaning 'to bubble up,'" because "it is hardly applicable to the great prophets." His misgivings about the second, which comes from a root "meaning 'to announce' or 'to speak,'" likewise stem from its dubious applicability to the manner and method of the great prophets. He expresses his strong preference for a word derived from an Akkadian root, meaning "one who is called (by God)" or one who "has a vocation (from God)." Why? Because "it is sound linguistically" and, in addition, because it is "undeniably in accord with the great prophets' own understanding of their nature and mission." [11]

Despite the foregoing commentator's obvious desire to leave a quite different impression, his argument owes

30

little to linguistic considerations. It derives almost entirely from side glances to the history of Israelite prophecy. And these are not directed, as you would expect, at its earliest but at its most refined—and, incidentally, later— manifestations.

Of course, given the fact "we simply do not know and cannot now determine the original . . . root of (the) word" [12] for prophet, dependence on historical considerations in the examination of this issue is inescapable. But evaluation of the evidence ought to be weighted in favor of the oldest rather than the highest expressions of prophecy. This approach would yield just the opposite conclusion from that drawn above. Since the verb "to prophesy" is first used in the Old Testament to describe rapturous speech or frenetic behavior (see, e.g., 1 Samuel 19:18-24), it would seem to dictate the choice of the first and not the last of the above candidates. In any event, the above writer's explanation of his choice of root errs in casting the great prophets into an altogether too instrumental a role. To portray them as divine mouthpieces is to convey "a very false, misleading picture. The prophets have nothing of an instrument about them, not even an instrument of God." [13] They did not view divine inspiration as an alternative to human freedom, but as the precondition for its valid exercise.

Like most common words with a long history, the Hebrew word for prophet not only confronts the interpreter with several plausible roots from which it could conceivably have been derived, but it presents him with a history that "is at least as important as the word study. The history of the word 'prophet' is of the essence here. It is necessary that we see the prophet as he appeared and functioned in the community of ancient Israel." [14]

Were the Prophets Ecstatics?

Many older interpreters of the prophets concentrated their studies on prophetic behavior. They paid special attention to the conduct of prophecy in its

31

initial phases. Two factors prompted several of these investigators to conclude that ecstasy holds the key to the meaning of prophecy.[15] One is the occasional designation of the early Hebrew prophet as "seer,"[16] a title that suggests a strong kinship to soothsayers. Secondly, and more importantly, several of Israel's early prophets are described as acting in frenzied fashion in response to artificial stimuli (see e.g., 1 Samuel 9:1-10:16; 16:13ff; 1 Kings 18:1-46).

Today's interpreters do not challenge the accuracy of this description. They would quickly acknowledge the susceptibility of early prophecy in Israel, as elsewhere, to such seizures. They might even concede the vulnerability of an Isaiah or Ezekiel to occasional attacks of this sort. But they would just as promptly downgrade its importance as a clue to the genius of biblical prophecy at its best. They would contend that, in the case of at least the great prophets, it was hardly more crucial for their basic function than is a whistle to the navigation of a steamboat.

Before leaving the phenomenon of ecstasy, note should be taken of the scholars who have redefined its meaning in such fashion as to reduce the offense of claiming the prophets as its subjects.[17] According to this definition, the accent does not fall on the suspension of one's rational faculties, rendering mind and body alike subject to alien power(s). Instead, it falls on the heightening of one's powers of concentration until the whole self, mind and body and will, gladly becomes the agent of another.[18]

No careful student of the great prophets would challenge their capacity for this sort of mystical union with God. But while ecstasy, thus defined, may take us closer to their hallmark, it too fails to take us to the heart of the matter. What set them apart from others—from other prophets no less than from other people—was not some esoteric and ecstatic gift, whether of the magical or mystical variety, beyond the knowledge of ordinary mortals. It was something as available as the best in tradition and the best in humanity. It was their singularly unique capacity for combining ethical discernment and theological analysis in the creative appropriation of Israelite tradition in the context of decision. Or to put it more simply, it was a gift as rare as the courage, in simple obedience to God, to commit oneself to the service of neighbor without regard for personal status or fear of public reaction.

Were the Prophets Traditionalists?

Tradition has a variety of meanings. It may refer to a set of inherited beliefs, the employment of an inherited pattern of action, or to the transmission of the received tenets of faith (quite often, particularly in biblical studies, transmission means the passing on of tradition via oral communication). Since I have already said a good deal about this subject in earlier connections, here we need pause only long enough to assemble our findings with respect to each of these understandings of tradition and bring them into focus, with special reference to the activity of the great prophets.

Already I have had occasion to hint at the close proximity of the beliefs of the great prophets to those of such shapers of Israelite tradition as the authors of the JE theology. This similarity forced me to conclude with a great Old Testament scholar that, if we would trace the basic and abiding thrust of Hebrew prophecy to its source, "we must tread the way of the history of Israel's faith from the beginning, and investigate how on this way that essential core develops." [19]

It is now generally agreed that, just as the great prophets drew upon a body of inherited beliefs, they likewise employed inherited patterns of behavior. Few scholars would any longer dispute the susceptibility of at least some of them to the phenomena of ecstasy, audition, vision, and divination, not to mention the disposition to speak in oracles and preface them with a "Thus saith the Lord." Yet no great significance is attached to this susceptibility. For while it may have helped the public to distinguish the men who were prophets from those who were not, these phenomena were of slight help in distinguishing one prophet from another. The real differences among them, those differences which prompt us to classify certain ones of them as "great" and others quite differently, come to light only as we compare them at a much deeper level. The great prophets have not achieved distinction because they enjoyed special access to unique media of religious experience. They owe their acclaim to the fact that they subordinated the religion both of themselves and their society to the judgments of a righteous and holy God.

Claims for the originality of the Hebrew prophets have taken a realistic and modest turn under the impact of modern studies. The discovery of important precedents alike for their beliefs and behavior has prompted the belated recognition that they were by no means wild-eyed revolutionaries. But neither were they merely the preservers and transmitters of a body of inherited wisdom. Had they been that, they would have missed the goal of all their instruction, which was nothing more nor less than the personal "experience of the terrible and gracious presence of God." [20] Hebrew prophecy achieved a unique quality because Israel's great prophets spoke on the basis of a truth they had experienced personally.[21] This is why Israelite faith, though continuously nourished by a common tradition, never ceased to vary from age to age and person to person. Just as the ancestral faith shaped the setting of the children's (the most vital and perceptive of whom we know as prophets) experience of God, so the children were prompted by their experience of God to scrutinize, correct, and update the faith of their fathers.

God did not speak to Israel's prophets as a dead God from a dead past. God spoke to them as the Lord of the Here and Now. He was as alive as they were to the changes that made their situation different from that of their ancestors. God knew that they wanted to address him and him to address them about the problems pecu-

34

liar to their time and place and circumstance. And God knew, too, that the hopes and expectations with which they entered into his presence concerned the destiny of their children to a much greater extent than they concerned the fate of their ancestors. And God spoke to them accordingly.

If the prophets were "unique" because they spoke on the basis of personally experienced truth, then the word of the Lord to the prophets must be conceived in historical terms. An interesting bit of support for this view appears in the reluctance of one prophet ever literally to reproduce the words of another prophet. Considering the absence in antiquity of laws against plagiarism, there must have been a reason for this aversion for repeating another's words. A clue as to what that reason was appears in Jeremiah 23:18, 30. "For who among them," Jeremiah asks of the "false" prophets, "has stood in the council of the Lord to perceive and to hear his word, or who has given heed to his word and listened? . . . I am against the prophets, says the Lord, who steal my words from one another."

One who does not speak for God in one's own words cannot speak God's Word, and one who presumes to do so is worse than a fraud; he or she is a thief. That is the plain implication of Jeremiah's indictment. And that is the inescapable conclusion of the pooled witness of the collection of prophetic writings. Even in cases where the direct influence of certain canonical prophets on others has been alleged, the language of the later prophets offers no trace of literal dependence. The following examples are typical: The God of Amos is the God of Isaiah, but the words of Amos in Bethel are not repeated by his younger contemporary in Jerusalem. The God of Jeremiah is the God of Ezekiel, but the words of Jeremiah are never repeated by his younger contemporary.

The Word of the Lord to the prophets was concrete, particular, and personal. It was a form of personal communication. It never went from the ancestors to the prophets without engaging their personalities at the very

35

core of their being. Consequently, even though they longed to be able to root their teaching in the traditions of their people, they were even more determined to find its ground and goal in the will of the Lord. They refused to accord to tradition the place that belonged to God alone.

FOOTNOTES

[1] B. D. Napier, *Prophets in Perspective* (New York: Abingdon Press, 1962), p. 13.

[2] *Ibid*, p. 38.

[3] Claus Westermann, *Basic Forms of Prophetic Speech,* trans. Hugh C. White (Philadelphia: The Westminster Press, 1967), pp. 98-100.

[4] Ernst Sellin and Georg Fohrer, *Introduction to the Old Testament,* trans. David Green (New York: Abingdon Press, 1965), p. 359.

[5] In *Ibid.,* p. 356, we are told that the traditional prophetic literary types were simply not "sufficient . . . for the great prophets; they needed other forms for their message."

[6] For an elaboration of this theory, see R.B.Y. Scott, "Introduction and Exegesis to the Book of Isaiah," *Interpreter's Bible,* V, pp. 157-60.

[7] Napier, *Prophets in Perspective,* p. 53.

[8] Martin Buber, *The Prophetic Faith* (New York: The Macmillan Co., 1949), pp. 203 ff.

[9] Napier, *Prophets in Perspective,* p. 59.

[10] J. P. Hyatt, *Prophetic Religion* (New York: Abingdon Press, 1947), pp. 48 ff.

[11] *Ibid.*

[12] B. D. Napier, "Prophet, Prophetism," *Interpreter's Dictionary of the Bible,* ed. G. A. Buttrick, K-Q, 1962, p. 896.

[13] Claus Westermann, *A Thousand Years and a Day* (Philadelphia: Fortress Press, 1962), p. 182.

[14] Napier, "Prophet, Prophetism," p. 897.

[15] E. g., G. Hoelscher, *Die Profeten* (Leipzig: J. C. Hinrichs'sche Buchhandlung, 1914).

[16] See I Sam. 9:9; cf. II Sam. 24:11; II Kg. 17:13; Is. 29:10; 30:10; Am. 7:12; Mic. 3:7.

[17] Johannes Lindblom, *Prophecy in Ancient Israel* (Philadelphia: Muhlenberg Press, 1963), pp. 216 ff., says the state of prophetic activity is better described as an example of "elevated inspiration" than of ecstasy.

[18] Harold Knight, *The Hebrew Prophetic Consciousness* (London: Lutterworth Press, 1948), p. 96.

[19] Buber, *The Prophetic Faith,* p. 2.

[20] Sellin and Fohrer, *Introduction to the Old Testament,* p. 358.

[21] *Ibid.*

III

THE TEST OF ISRAELITE LOYALTY

The great prophets did not represent the majority of Israelites. In fact, they did not even speak for the majority of Israel's prophets. For while they shared a common heritage with the rank-and-file prophets, they recognized a loyalty that transcended Israel's heritage. Not only did they put the will of the Lord before Israel's heritage, they put the will of the Lord before Israel itself.

At no point did this shift in loyalties reflect its transforming influence more graphically than in the change it effected in the prophets themselves. To gauge its impact, we have only to compare the great prophets with their professional forerunners, not to mention their more conventional contemporaries. The great prophets continued to speak in oracles, but they did not deliver them in a state of frenzy. They continued to enlist disciples, but they did not resort to artificial stimuli in the effort to induce in them the state of prophecy. They continued to give oracles at the sanctuaries, but they did not proclaim them as spokesmen for the official cult. They continued to advise heads of state, but they abandoned the role of royal soothsayer for that of theological critic of official policy. In short, they sought to revitalize and make relevant to their day the relationship, if not the terms, of the Sinaitic covenant. They called for the application of the equal rights principles of the Mosaic covenant in a more sophisticated and complex socio-economic order.

The final severance of Israel's vocation as the people of God from Israel's destiny as a national state or an ecclesiastical community marks the most outstanding achievement of Israel's great prophets. They checked the tendency to shrink the Lord's role to that of Israel's indulgent sponsor or sentimental patron. They proclaimed his imminent appearance in judgment against Israel as well as against Israel's enemies. One by one, the prophets challenged all the main props—blood, cult, soil—with which their neighbors sought to turn the Lord into Israel's junior partner in a parity covenant. By reactivating concern for the Lord's role as judge, a by-product of their renewed emphasis on the ethical obligations of the covenant, they indirectly confronted Israel with the possible loss of statehood. Some would contend that, in so doing, they dwarfed their own influence on their contemporaries. If so, it was only to magnify their impact on succeeding generations. For once history had vindicated their grim outlook for Israelite nationalism, the Israelite survivors of that calamity turned to their words with deference and anticipation. They scrutinized their utterances in search of a new foundation on which to restore the covenant and the people of Israel.

In this chapter we shall focus our attention on only the first of the prophetic contributors to this renewal of the faith and people of Israel. Yet this great prophet, namely Amos, anticipates almost all the major presuppositions that one day will get top billing in the program of the postexilic workers for Israel's reform and restoration.

Before looking at the elements in the message of Amos, let us recall our prior discussion of the growth of tradition that took place between the prophetic movement in Israel and the inclusion of "The Prophets" as the second of the three divisions of the Hebrew Bible. We have already seen how the complexity of this development undercuts the common tendency to treat the prophets of Israel in splendid isolation, as if they neither stood nor were carried on the shoulders of people of comparable stature. Awareness of this intricate history has not only raised the possibility that we may have credited a prophet with the oracles of his disciples, but it has greatly complicated the task of separating the secondary material (that added by a disciple or later editor) in a prophetic book from the primary material (the work of the original prophet). In short, full appreciation of this process has had a twofold and somewhat ambiguous effect. For while it has aggravated the difficulty of distinguishing the words of the prophet by whose name a biblical book is known from those added by later hands, it has simultaneously tended to mute the significance of this distinction.

One can be confident of the identification of secondary material in a prophetic book only when it comes from an obviously different time or in a vastly different style from the work of the original contributor. In fact, we must take care not to be overly impressed by stylistic likenesses. Certainly, similarity of style alone cannot be taken as proof of the singularity of authorship. In view of the persistence of literary types in the Psalter, where Psalms of lament and thanksgiving from widely separated centuries exhibit oneness of form and many stylistic similarities, it would be absurd of us to question the ability of the disciple of a prophet to imitate the theme and form of his master in the delivery of oracles. Therefore, even though the terms primary and secondary will be retained in the present work, they will be given a slightly modified meaning. Primary will be used to designate the portions of a prophetic collection which, because of date and view and style, may with reasonable confidence be assigned to the period and circle within which the major prophet carried out his ministry; all other material will be regarded as secondary. This distinction will be further stretched in the case of those collections that yield conclusive evidence of multiple prophetic authorship. Instead of labeling the works of these later prophets as secondary, they will be identified by prefixing the appropriate ordinal ("First" or "Second" or "Third," as the case may be) before the name of the book in which they appear (whether Isaiah, Zechariah, or some other).[1]

The World of Amos

Two passages (the first appears in 1:1; the second, in 7:10) in the book of Amos have special significance for determining the date of his activity. In 7:10 we get a recollection of the prophet's defamation by the priest of the royal sanctuary at Bethel during Jeroboam's kingship over Israel. Since 1:1 not only confirms this identification of Jeroboam as the king of Samaria (another name for North Israel, also called Ephraim, or simply Israel), but further identifies this Israelite king as the contemporary of Uzziah, king of Judah (783-742 B.C.), Israel's king during the time of Amos must have been Jeroboam II (786-746 B.C.). In fact, save for 9:8b-15, we may safely assume these dates for the careers of almost all the prophetic contributors to the Amos collection. Therefore, if they seem to speak as "with one mouth," they do so not only because they speak from a common faith and under the influence of Amos' person and words, but also because they presuppose a common background and address themselves to common problems.

Jeroboam II ruled Samaria as if, after making a careful study of the reigns of the ablest kings in Israel's history, he had set out to put together an administration in which the virtues of all of them might be put on simultaneous display. Capitalizing on a combination of economic genius and a rare gift for astute diplomacy, he outlined for Israel a program of recovery and advance which seems to have envisioned the establishment of some sort of partnership with Judah. At any rate, thanks to the timely emergence of Uzziah, a truly great king of Judah (783-742), he was able to negotiate and maintain a peaceful and mutually advantageous relationship with the Southern Kingdom. As a consequence, Palestine once again became the spawning ground of imperial dreams and large hopes in the minds of others besides crackpot politicians.

The historical account of the reign of Jeroboam II consists of only seven verses (2 Kings 14:23-29), yet it crowds into this brief space a broad hint at the scope and magnitude of his achievements. It reports his restoration of Israel's borders to their farthest limits—"from the entrance of Hamath as far as the Sea of the Arabah" (vs. 25)—since the days of Solomon (1 Kings 8:65). Fortunately for the historians of the period, the details of this achievement, as well as other aspects of his reign, can be amplified from other sources, biblical (e.g., see Hosea 1:1; Amos 7:9-11) and archaeological.

External threats from nearby enemies combined with an uninterrupted series of inept rulers to relieve him of the need for anxiety about Assyria. The other probable source of foreign interference in the affairs of Samaria, Syria, had likewise fallen on hard times. The combination of Assyrian preoccupation with eastern enemies and Syrian weakness gave Jeroboam II his opportunity, and he pressed it decisively and immediately. He committed Samaria's revitalized army to a showdown against the Syrians, and his soldiers, vindicating his confidence in them, soon forced the fall of Damascus. Then, demonstrating that he knew when not to wage war as well as how to wage war, Jeroboam II made a successful bid for the renewal of good relations and mutually profitable economic arrangements with both Phoenicia and Judah. After that, with Samaria either in control or friendly with those who were in control of the entire territory from "the entrance of Hamath as far as the Sea of Arabah," he directed his and his people's energies to more peaceful and more profitable pursuits.

Having extended Israelite holdings in land to the fullest limits of reasonable expectation, Jeroboam II of Samaria and Uzziah of Judah proceeded to give the lie to the saying that the only thing history teaches us is that humans learn nothing from history. Instead of squandering their energies and resources on a fratricidal duel for sovereignty, they concentrated their efforts on a program of economic development. While we have no evidence that they functioned as an international team in their varied and many undertakings, their accomplishments compel us to credit them with the achievement of a remarkably harmonious and supportive relationship. Taking advantage of their control of the important trade routes, they levied tolls on travelers and goods passing through their land. As a result of Judah's reconquest of Elath, they regained access to sea trade with Africa via the Red Sea and with Asia Minor via the Mediterranean. They likewise generated a sweeping industrial revival, headlined by the industries in dyeing, weaving, and copper. Archeological excavations at several sites in Samaria and Judah have removed any lingering doubt that this period marked "the height of . . . power and prosperity" [2] for the two kingdoms of Israel. The buildings at these sites, and especially the ivory inlays, [3] offer impressive witness to the grandeur of Palestine's material civilization during the time of Jeroboam II and Uzziah. The two kingdoms of Israel had never produced anything more splendid, and at least some of the Israelite people lived in hitherto unmatched luxury.

But if the few had never had it so good, the many still did not have it good at all. And that disconcerting fact offered a more reliable clue of things to come than did the apparently promising economic and political picture.

Peace and prosperity, far from relieving Samaria and Judah of all their problems, simply confronted them with problems of a different sort. For example, in the area of religion, the big question was not whether the Mosiac faith would experience serious rivalry, but whether the principal threat would come from external competition or internal corruption. As it turned out, the challenge emanated from all directions, and it swept within its

42

vortex all areas—the theological, the economic, the moral, the ecclesiastical—of Israelite life.

Sixty-three inscribed potsherds (pottery fragments) from Samaria, which date from 778 to 770, witness to the superficiality of Samaria's theological commitment to the Lord of Israel. [4] These pieces of pottery contain lists of agricultural goods received by government officials from subjects in outlying districts. Both the senders and receivers of the goods frequently bear compound names, with the name or the title of the deity often serving as one element. The name of the most prominent god of the Canaanites, Baal, appears as the divine element in almost a third of the occurrences of this usage. While this fact may be construed as evidence that the named persons were of Canaanite background, it may just as naturally be read as an indication that many Israelites by birth became Canaanites by faith.

Scholars have yet to determine whether the goods itemized on the ostraca (potsherds) of Samaria represented taxes on private property or produce from crown lands, but there is widespread agreement that, in either case, they may be taken as evidence of the concentration of land holdings in the hands of the privileged few in defiance of the Israelite law concerning the inviolability of the family title to land (Numbers 27:5-11; 36:5-9; Deuteronomy 19:14; 27:17; cf. Exodus 23:10-11; Leviticus 25). Amos testifies to the further aggravation of the plight of the poor by sharp loan practices (2:6-7; 4:6-9; 5:10-12; 8:4-6). Famines and droughts forced them to turn to money lenders in an effort to bail themselves out of hock with the internal revenue service or to deliver their families from starvation. When the anticipated crops failed and no relative showed up to pay off their debt, the interest-greedy lenders enacted foreclosures on their mortgages. And the judges, displaying singular contempt for both the requirements of the ancestral faith and the claims of justice, sustained the lenders in their exploitative action, provided the beneficiaries of their chicanery were not above the payment of a bribe.

43

Thus inordinate wealth and capricious power came increasingly to be concentrated in the hands of the very few and the very rich. Left with little to fight with and even less to fight for, the masses responded to bids for unity and calls to arms with growing skepticism and declining enthusiasm. Why should they work to preserve a society that had plundered them? Had not the monarchs of Samaria and Judah, by subtly shifting the basis of social obligation from the covenantal community to the bureaucratic state, effectively undermined the foundations of economic democracy and group solidarity? Had they not unwittingly committed Palestine to economic policies that could scarcely fail, despite the many evidences of affluence, to trigger deep social cleavages and, ultimately, national disaster?

If Amos thought and proclaimed this to be the case, that is not to impute to him the gift of clairvoyance. It is merely to credit him with an understanding of the human dimension of prosperity and progress. He fully appreciated the connection between economics and ethics or, to put it more militarily, between morale and morality. That is why, despite the optimistic predictions of his contemporaries, he confronted his neighbors with threats of economic depression and foreign invasion. Others were too impressed with what prosperity was doing for the country to ask what it might be doing to the people, but Amos was too appalled by what it was doing to the people to be impressed by what it might be doing for the country.

Hand in hand with the raising of economic success above the divine will went a corresponding decline in the Hebrew sense of right and wrong. Once again the unity and interdependence of the Israelite community hung in the balance. Loss of a sense of obligation for neighbor closely paralleled the shrinking regard for the Lord as sovereign and righteous judge. As the distance between deity and humanity narrowed, that between persons widened. The more God became like people, the less human people became. The worship of a domes-

44

ticated deity produced undomesticated people. They esteemed their neighbors for instrumental rather than intrinsic reasons. They treated them more as means than ends. Consequently, in the view of Amos, God would "not judge them (the people of Israel) for their iniquity against him, but for their iniquity against each other." [5]

The reception accorded Amos at Bethel attests to the fact that Palestinian ecclesiastical life did not enjoy immunity from these corrupting influences. Just as success and security had once turned the prophets from spokesmen for the Lord into royal parasites (in 1 Kings 22, only one of 401 prophets warns King Ahab of the trouble in store for him in the battle of Ramoth-Gilead, in which he lost his life; all the others, as "with one mouth," assure him of a happy ending to his proposed venture), so prosperity and domestic tranquility have now converted the official religious functionaries of the prophet's time into arrogant chauvinists or, worse, hired agents of the crown. Not only does the chief priest in the Samaria of Jeroboam II speak no word of judgment against royal policies in the Lord's name, but he assumes the duty of silencing anybody bold enough to voice such an utterance (note, e.g., the eviction order by the priest Amaziah to the prophet in Amos 7:10-13). As if the disallowance of criticism by the foremost priest in all Samaria, namely Amaziah, were not sufficient evidence of the bankruptcy of the land's ecclesiastical life, the foremost prophet in all Judah offers additional proof of its degradation. When Amaziah refers to him as a "seer" and "prophet" in ordering him to leave Samaria and return to his native land of Judah, Amos spurns the alleged connection with contemporary prophets. Why? Because they have ceased to be the nation's conscience, judging its achievements and defining its goals in light of the ancestral faith. Those who have not degenerated into time-serving, fee-splitting agents of wealthy sponsors have betrayed the Mosaic faith by their silence. By failing the prophetic obligation to sensitize their neighbors to God's demand for the dispersion of power and property, they have aided the process of internal corruption and decay. They have aggravated the dangers of injustice by allowing irresponsible wealth and power in the midst of spiraling poverty to go unchallenged. And while they may have managed to take themselves off the spot by spurning the invitation to debate, they have left their neighbors with no warning of the fate in store for them. In short, by making dissent all but intolerable, they have made disaster all but inevitable.

By the end of Jeroboam II's reign, the very existence of Israel as a people hung precariously in the balance. Only a new model of the JE theologian could forestall the loss of covenanthood and, with it, the loss of identity. Happily for the people of the covenant and for us, such a person did appear on the scene, and he answered, as we all know by now, to the name of Amos.

The Message of Amos

Amos' analysis of the situation in Samaria leaves out of account the most obviously impressive achievements of Jeroboam II's reign. Bypassing its political and economic triumphs, he concentrates his attention wholly on its consequences for human relations and for the relationship between the Lord and his people, and the verdict he returns against it is highly negative. Economic prosperity has exacted a frightfully exorbitant toll in human values. Not only has it aggravated the hopelessness of the dispossessed masses, but it has nourished the irresponsible preoccupation of the bureaucrats and wealthy merchants with their own private gain. It has put distance between persons, and it has not closed the gap between the common life and common worship. In fact, only one thing exceeds the indifference of the advantaged to the plight of the wretched. That is the participation of the elite in all the appointed religious celebrations.

Yet the boldness of Samaria's transgressions does not exceed the boldness of the prophet's indictment. Both its content and the place of its delivery stamp Amos as an enemy of the establishment. Refine his accusation as you may, the twin charges of inhuman insensitivity and blasphemous piety can still be neither denied nor excused. His verbal firing evokes a predictable response, considering his unlikely choice of the king's royal sanctuary in Bethel as the site for its delivery. [6]

Amaziah, in reporting the prophet's crime against the crown to the king, charges Amos with proclaiming death for the monarch and dispersion for his subjects. Then, in language equal to his fury at the prophet's outrageous presumption, Amaziah revokes Amos' license to prophesy in Bethel on the spot. "O seer," he cries, "go, flee away to the land of Judah, and eat bread there, and prophesy there, but never again prophesy at Bethel, for it is the king's sanctuary, and it is a temple of the kingdom" (7:12-13).

Amos' reply (7:16f) calls in question the royal priest's assumption of the right to pass on the credentials of those who would speak for God in the Bethel sanctuary. After reminding Amaziah of his prohibition of further prophetic activity there by the native of Tekoa, Amos proceeds to include Amaziah in the prophecy of doom he has earlier pronounced on the king and the nation. And he leaves little doubt that a cause-and-effect relationship exists between his own rebuke at Amaziah's hands and the imminent judgment of Amaziah at God's hands. Whereas the future remained open for Amaziah until his countermand of the Lord's order for Amos to prophesy in Samaria, he has now brought on himself the judgment of the disobedient. Amaziah's punishment shall be of a piece with the Lord's judgment of the king and the kingdom because he and they have committed a common crime. All alike have spurned the word of the Lord.

The crucial issue in the controversy at Bethel is neither a personality conflict nor a professional conflict. At the heart of the controversy is the question of sovereignty. [7] To whom is a prophet answerable, and who can certify his credentials? Amaziah's revocation of Amos' right to speak in the temple at Bethel attests to his belief in the immediate authority of the priestly personnel at the royal sanctuary over the prophet. At the same time, in view of his condemnation of Amos' words as a piece of declamatory sedition, he tacitly acknowledges the ultimate authority of the state over the prophet. Having already demolished the latter claim in his prior remarks, Amos proceeds to do the same for the former claim in his reply to Amaziah. He proclaims the Lord's visitation of the ultimate punishment upon the priest: for his blasphemous intrusion of intermediary authorities between the word of the Lord and its bearer, God will consign Amaziah to death in an "*unclean* land" (7:17). Amos' words on this occasion repeat his earlier and more eloquent statement concerning the accreditation and accountability of the prophet. In this passage (3:3-8) Amos links the vocation of the prophet to the sovereignty of God by making him the servant of the Lord's compelling, if not irresistible, word:

Do two walk together,
  unless they have made an appointment?
Does a lion roar in the forest,
  when he has no prey? . . .
The lion has roared;
  who will not fear?
The Lord God has spoken;
  who cannot but prophesy?

Despite the rhetorical character of these words, they cannot be dismissed as mere rhetoric, for they only underscore the central presupposition of Amos' entire message. All its various elements are but different ways of asserting and accentuating the sovereign power and goodness of the Lord.

The Real Threat to Israel's Future

Twice Amos draws on the Exodus tradition (3:2; 9:7)

48

in his address to Israel.[8] But he does not on either occasion enlist Israel's memory of this event in support of the idea that the Lord has singled Israel out for preferential treatment. In each instance he invokes this tradition for a quite different purpose: in the first, as a reminder of Israel's special liability to punishment (3:2); and in the second, as a denial, vis-à-vis this event, of Israel's right to exercise an exclusive claim to the Lord's intervention in history (9:7).

The latter reference holds special significance for raising, if only fleetingly, the possibility of the Lord's origination of the peoplehood of other groups besides the Israelites. Unfortunately, Amos does not go on to pursue this latter suggestion to the farthest limits of its logical implications. But he does draw out some of the implications of his notion of Israel's peculiar susceptibility to divine judgment. After charging Israel with the perpetration of grossly inhuman crimes against its neighbors (2:6-16), he threatens it with destruction from the face of the earth (9:8a). Once he even confronts it with the prospect of the Lord's use of a foreign nation to oppress it from its northernmost to its southernmost limit (6:14), presumably a veiled reference to Assyria, yet Amos never makes the explicit identification of this power. While this omission could have been quite accidental, I am inclined to view it otherwise. I see this exercise in vagueness as a way of lending force to his conviction that history turns, in the final analysis, on theological rather than political considerations. It was Amos' way of reminding Israel that the issue with which it must come to terms, and the only issue with which it *must* come to terms, is not the international primacy of Assyria but the righteous sovereignty of the Lord.

When Senator J. William Fulbright rebuked the United States of America for the display of what he called *The Arrogance of Power*,[9] he was addressing himself to an attitude not unlike that at which Amos directed his efforts. Despite the length of the intervening years, this similarity gives us no ground at all for surprise, inasmuch as we got this "favored people" idea from reading the Bible of the Israelites. About the only flaw our ancestors found in the biblical version of divine election was the name of the elected. And they lost no time in correcting that oversight. They quickly substituted the New Israel for the Old, and they promptly identified America as God's New Israel. And they laid claim for it to all the rights and privileges and immunities which the popular prophets had claimed for the original Israel.

From this notion we have evolved a lofty and, at times, perverse view of American destiny under God. Typical expressions of this faith have entailed these two basic obligations: (1) to provide the rest of human kind with an example; (2) to extend and safeguard democratic ideals throughout the inhabited world.

To say that great peril attends the acknowledgment of these responsibilities would be an understatement. For proof of this fact we have only to take a close look at our national history. If awareness of our role as an example to the nations has prompted us to make claims for ourselves that have dwarfed our achievements, consciousness of our status as God's missioner has worked even more serious mischief. Not only has it moved us to believe that we have a higher destiny than other nations, but it has nourished in us the conceit that we are entitled to determine God's will for others as well as ourselves. And to it we can likewise trace "the muscular imperialism that cloaks American self-interest with platitudes about saving the world for democracy, a racist myth that justifies American actions abroad because of 'Anglo-Saxon superiority,' etc." [10]

Thus far "God's New Israel" has been spared the judgment due such presumption. For this deliverance we are much indebted to the appearance among us of Amos-like figures—such as Michael Wigglesworth, Thomas Jefferson, Abraham Lincoln, Horace Bushnell, Washington Gladden, Reinhold Neibuhr, John Kennedy and Martin Luther King, Jr.—who have ever kept before us these two reminders about our destiny under God:

50

(1) that it is no different from that intended by God for all other members of the human family; and (2) that we cannot imperil the God-given destiny of others without jeopardizing our own destiny under God. President Kennedy capsuled these reminders in a 1962 July Fourth address to the nation's governors. He told the chief executives that our attempt to live up to the destiny disclosed in the Declaration of Independence imposes two requirements on us. These are, he declared, "the encouragement . . . of national independence, and a contribution to the cooperative interdependence of nations." [11]

Kennedy's language to the governors was more secular than Amos' deliverances at Bethel. Yet the American President's words, no less than those of the Tekoan prophet, add up to this simple assurance: our destiny as human beings hinges less on what others can do to us than on what we do for others.

The Awful Burden of Divine Election

Amos did not challenge the Lord's selection of Israel for a peculiar relationship with himself. Yet he interpreted that choice as an expression of God's concern for the realization of his holy purpose. The simple logic of this understanding led inevitably to the conclusion that if Israel should ever veto the Lord's purpose the Lord would be obligated to terminate this relationship. Although Amos must have found the confrontation of his people with this possibility distasteful in the extreme, he nevertheless performed his painful duty. In fact, he proclaimed the disruption of Israel's preferred status not as a distinct possibility for some future rebellion, but as a moral necessity for past disobedience. And he did not shrink from drawing a cause-and-effect connection between Israel's transgression of the divine will and her imminent punishment (3:1-11). For while he left the historical agent of this judgment unidentified, he left no doubt that the Lord would be its ultimate source.

51

Amos recognizes that vulnerability, as well as responsibility, varies according to privilege. Therefore, declares Amos, because "you only have I known of all the families of the earth; . . . I will punish you for all your iniquities" (3:2). Amos does not question the Lord's election of Israel, but he refuses to let Israel view it in separation from God's purpose for Israel. He cannot revel in the reassuring knowledge of Israel's privileged status before God for recalling and proclaiming the terrible burden of Israel's holy mission to the world. Nor can any of the other great prophets after him. In fact, this transcendent vision of Israel's destiny, and the courage to pursue it without swerving or support, this is the quality which, more than any other, sets these prophets apart, not alone from fellow Israelites, but from the comfortable pious of every generation.

Few American presidents have been as conscious of the hand of God at work in our history as was Abraham Lincoln. Yet Lincoln never allowed even the passions of war to turn him into a holy jingoist (nationalist). With no less readiness than he credited our blessings to the love of God, he interpreted our reverses as punishment by God. His Second Inaugural offers a typical expression of his viewpoint in this regard:

> And whereas, when our own beloved country, once, by the blessing of God, united, prosperous and happy, is now afflicted with faction and civil war, it is peculiarly fit for us to recognize the hand of God in this terrible visitation, and in sorrowful remembrance of our own faults and crimes as a nation and as individuals, to humble ourselves before Him, and to pray for His mercy,—to pray that we may be spared further punishment, though most justly deserved. . . .[12]

Lincoln held unfalteringly to the conviction that "a just God, in His own good time, will give . . . the rightful result,"[13] but he never claimed the capacity to ascertain that result in advance of its occurrence. With characteristic modesty, a modesty we would do well to

52

imitate, he never presumed to say when that time would come or what its consequences might mean for him and his people.

The Lord's Contempt for Thoughtless Religion

The reproof of Israel by Amos contains no hint of the neglect of ecclesiastical niceties by the subjects of Jeroboam II. Quite the contrary, it assumes the most studied and painstaking observance of the appointed festivals at the appointed times in the appointed places. In fact, only two things seem to impress Amos more than his people's slavish performance of their formal religious obligations. The first of these is their indifference to human misery; and the other, their insensitivity to the fact that they have provoked the anger of God by their unconcern for people. Although the prophet's reaction to this phenomenon is important for getting at his estimate of current piety, it is equally important for the clue it gives us to his view of authentic worship.

So now, we ask, "When, according to Amos, does worship become valid?" To this our prophet would answer, "When it moves people to substitute service to neighbors in need for attempts at the appeasement of an angry deity." Then, so as to make his point concrete, he might add, "Acts of piety by perpetrators of cruelty, whether by hateful deed or thoughtless inaction, are not only hypocritical (5:21-24); they are also blasphemous." Amos compounds his assault on the significance of ritualistic practices with a challenge of their pedigree. In a question (5:25) about Israel's religious observances during the wilderness period, which some scholars construe as "a rhetorical question demanding a negative answer," [14] he asks whether it then brought "sacrifices and offerings" to the Lord (5:25).

Conceivably, we do have here a rejection of the prevailing worship in principle. Yet we must not jump to the conclusion that Amos was opposed to all cultic worship in principle. At least two variables aggravated the hostility and intensity of his reaction to the religious ceremonialism of his day. In addition to concentrating on the mechanics of liturgy, without regard for its ethical connections and human consequences, it tended to become the private indulgence and showplace (3:15; 6:4-6) of unscrupulous exploiters.

Had this not been the case, and cultic worship in Israel had not become an excuse for leaving the weightier matters of the law undone, would Amos still have welcomed its denial? Would he have opposed all cultic practices even if the public worship of God had been attended by the just treatment of people? This hypothetical question, though the frequent recipient of a simple answer, really defies a simple answer. Why? Quite simply, because the situation in which the matter came to Amos' attention was by no means a hypothetical situation.

What appalls Amos—and, according to Amos, what revolts the Lord—is the fact that temple worship flourishes while simple justice wanes. We cannot say what his attitude towards the cultus would have been if it had not become a shield for immorality. Amos did not address himself to the situation as it might have been. He addressed himself to the situation as it was. We cannot be at all sure that Amos, had he been able to shape Israel's response to God according to his own design, would have dispensed with all cultic worship. We can only be sure that Amos, confronted by a cultus, unmarked by human concern, viewed it as the encouragement of mere pious busyness, and he called for its destruction.

When Christian worship failed to come to the aid of Blacks in the civil rights struggle of the sixties, Martin Luther King, Jr., blasted white church members for standing "on the sideline" and mouthing "pious irrelevancies and sanctimonious trivialities." [15] Yet his reproof came forth as an expression of bitterness mingled with sorrow. "In deep disappointment," he wrote, "I have wept over the laxity of the church. But be assured that my tears

54

were tears of love. There can be no deep disappointment where there is not deep love." [16]

King did not indict churchgoers for their cultivated attention to the details of public worship, but for their thoughtless disregard of the victims of oppression and exploitation. What troubled him was not so much what they were doing in the sanctuary as what they were failing to do in the marketplace.

If Amos had left behind as extensive writings as those we have from King, I have no doubt but what we would know Amos, like we know King, as a prophet who could rail against the church only because he had wailed for the church. I am likewise convinced that his contempt for thoughtless religions would, like God's, be mixed with a wounded love for its unwitting practitioners.

The Negative Test of Authentic Worship

The Old Testament has two sets of terms for worship. One comes from a verb meaning "to bow" or "prostrate oneself," as before an altar, where one engages in specific acts of formal worship. The other comes from a root that means simply "to work" or "serve," and its derivatives may be used to describe either activity directed towards one's neighbor or an enterprise undertaken in behalf of the deity. The persistence of this latter usage throughout the Bible attests to the inseparable connection between the worship of God and service to people.

Amos played a key role in this humanization of worship. His challenge of any service to God that bypassed the claims of people forced Israel to ponder anew the requirements of divine worship. Do they include, for example, acceptance of firsthand responsibility for the achievement of social justice?

Amos' answer to this question would surely have been an emphatic yes. But would he also have held that the just treatment of people marks the sufficient worship of God? Personally I think not. Amos did not, as this question seems to assume, substitute the worship of God in daily life for the formal worship of God. Genuine worship for Amos may be defined as personal communion with God the Father in the contemplation and advancement of his purpose for all the members of his family. Since this purpose, like God's family, includes not only the whole of mankind but the whole life of all of us in each aspect of our being, we can neither truly serve the neighbor without indirectly worshipping God nor truly worship God without indirectly serving the neighbor.

In other words, even though justice and worship are not identical terms in the vocabulary of Amos, they nevertheless bear an almost inseparable connection. For while Amos might concede the possible existence of justice—which may best be defined, according to Amos, as the reflection of God's will for the human community in the conduct of daily life, with special emphasis on economic considerations—in the absence of genuine worship, he would deny the possibility of rendering authentic worship without the simultaneous practice of true justice. Try as he may, and he does not greatly exert himself in the effort, Amos simply cannot veil his contempt for preoccupation with the details of elaborate worship without a corresponding concern for the demands of simple justice. Bethel's urbanites betray the principles of community inherent in the Mosaic faith by their overweening attention to matters of ritual. In the prophet's view, unless they have defined their mission in relation to their neighbors, they have failed their mission in relation to the sanctuary. Or to state the issue squarely and plainly, as Amos would doubtless have us do, any worship of God that goes unattended by service to persons is not merely inadequate; it is counterfeit.

Many of our nation's founders subscribed wholeheartedly to the broad view of worship espoused by Amos. Some carried this tendency so far that they even referred to magistrates as "God's ministers."[17] Yet Samuel West, the pastor of a church in Dartmouth, declared in 1776: "If magistrates . . . pursue measures . . . destructive of the public good, they cease being God's ministers. . . ."[18] With these words West not only updated but extended the application of Amos' negative test of authentic worship. Whereas Amos had focused his challenge on the service of God within the sanctuary, West addressed his to the service of God that takes place outside the sanctuary.

The Shocking Reversal of Popular Expectation

The entire message of Amos found its focus and thrust in his original proclamation concerning "the day of the Lord." For while he followed tradition's use of this term as a symbol for divine visitation in the future, he stood the usual interpretation of this doctrine on its head.

Amos' pronouncements concerning this day derive from such aforementioned assumptions as the following: responsibility varies in proportion to privilege; Israel has been privileged above all peoples; if Israel does not repent, its punishment shall exceed that of all peoples. Analyzing the situation from a perspective informed with these presuppositions, Amos can turn "the day of the Lord," a symbol of hope, into a threat of doom. But the seemingly unambiguous character of his annunciations of judgment notwithstanding, the logic of his position leaves room for doubt that he believes Israel's doom is inevitable. Since the rebellion of Israel underlay his reversal of the usual meaning of the day of the Lord, would not a change in its character have altered the ground and, therefore, the outcome of its judgment at the Lord's hand?

The answer to this question often turns on the interpretation of a series of visions. Although these visions have come to be known by the objects which inspired them, all of them are, in reality, verbal portraits of the day of the Lord's imminent appearance in judgment against a rebellious Israel. A vivid imagination converts sight of an ordinary object or event, except in the case of the final vision—locusts (7:1-3), a summer drought (7:4-6), a plumb line (7:7-9), a basket of summer fruit (8:1-3)—into a vision of calamitous consequences for Israel. The last vision (9:1-4) reports the prophet's sight of the Lord, standing beside the altar, calling for the slaughter of Israel to begin.

The prophet intercedes after each of the first two visions, and we are told that the Lord "repented" of his decision. The absence of any hint at such a change in the account of the subsequent visions is often taken as evidence that Amos eventually came to believe that nothing could forestall Israel's doom. This interpretation overlooks the fact that, for Amos, "the word of God (whether communicated via vision or otherwise) was the occasion for self-judgment . . . , whether it contained a prediction of ineluctable (inevitable) national catastrophe or an exhortation to . . . repentance. The prophet's obligation was to provide this occasion, for it was always an invitation to obedient response." [19]

Here we get the suggestion that Amos used "a prediction of ineluctable national catastrophe" as a prod to the reformation of life and society. I have not the slightest doubt that this represents a correct analysis of the motivation behind the prophet's proclamation of "the word of the Lord." This interpretation is supported by the fact that the Lord is the subject of the active verb which brings each of the objects seen by the prophet within the range of Amos' imagination. It is further corroborated by the fact that the prophet's explanation of each vision is reported as a message from God (7:3, 6, 7; 8:2; 9:1). Thus the vision, as employed in Amos, must be seen as simply another vehicle for the communication of God's word, which had but one purpose. And that purpose was, no matter how presented, to move the members of the prophet's audience to a decision before and for God.

Interpreted biographically, the apparent shift of the

58

prophet's attitude in a more hopeless direction after his first two visions could easily be explained as a reflection of the gap between the hoped-for and actual results of his prophetic activity. According to this exegesis, God's not carrying out the first two visions would represent Amos' anticipated outcome for his ministry, and the unrelieved promises of disaster in the latter visions would stand as testimony to the vanity of Amos' hope for a favorable response to his call for repentance. Instead of the impossibility of turning aside doom, they should be read as indications of Israel's failure to do what was necessary to turn it aside; or, to change the figure, as signs of Israel's tragic inability to read the signs of the time.

In defense of the unrepentant Israelites, it can hardly be said that they were without excuse. Jeroboam II's reign provided them with a multitude of grounds for tuning out the hair-shirted pessimistic prophets in their midst.

During the reign of Jeroboam II, as noted earlier, Israel went from victory to security to greater prosperity in all the spheres of its common life. Economically speaking, it had not fared better since the days of Solomon. Internationally speaking, with Assyria in the twilight of a long nap, Judah under its thumb, and Syria a recent victim of its military machine, dreams of Israelite rule over the whole of the Near East could not be dismissed as delusions of grandeur. Religiously speaking, the keepers of the sanctuaries had never had it so good; no doubt, after leading Israelite royalty and commoners in prayer and sacrifice, they reassured their parishioners and one another with repetitious reminders of the Lord's approval of Israel. "If the Lord were not pleased with our worship," we may imagine them asking rhetorically, "then why would Israel now enjoy such prosperity or such power?"

As if their question permitted only one answer, they translated their confident hope for an ever-expanding future into a figure of pious shorthand. Anticipating the dawn of the ultimate in Israelite power and prosperity, tears of joy accompanied their cry for "the day of the Lord."

Amos strolled into this sleek atmosphere with the stride and reserve of an earth-mover. And he left it that way, too—its mountains of ostentation and shallow piety as denuded and level as a midwestern suburb. "What," he chided Israel (in effect, if not fact), "you praying for the day of the Lord! Believe me, if you knew that for which you were asking (5:18-20), you would ask for something else. Or if not, you would change your ways, beginning now."

Amos' reversal of the popular expectation concerning "the day of the Lord" would be understandable if the prophet had grounded it in a counterspy's report on recent economic, political, and military developments in Assyria. Or if he had rejected out of hand the belief in God's choice of Israel. But he based it on neither. He based his awareness of imminent calamity for Israel on a careful analysis of the state of affairs in Israel. And he accepted as unquestionable fact God's choice of Israel, but his agreement with the popular notion of a special, unique, distinctive relationship between God and Israel entails only superficials. In fact, the question, "Who is Israel?" is the real point at issue between Amos and his contemporaries.

After Amos, when you run across approving references to Israel in prophetic literature, pause and ponder the question: To whom is the speaker referring? The members of a national state, the worshipers at the royal sanctuaries, and the observers of the official traditions? Or the members of a God-centered and neighbor-serving fellowship whose members, though identifiable by God alone, bear witness to their faith by the imitation of God's gracious dealing with their ancestors in their relations with their neighbors?

Because the God of Amos, who chose Israel after the flesh only to enable it to become Israel after the faith, is Lord of everything and everybody everywhere and all the time, the prophet can see no hope for an Israel directed by secular economic, social, political, and ecclesiastical goals. Indeed, since God's righteousness is the final power with which we must come to terms and his power is a match for his goodness, God must, "for his name's sake" (though Amos does not use this phrase, the idea is present), chasten and discipline and, if necessary, disperse his rebellious and wayward children. Amos scoffs at the popular notion that God could not be God without Israel, "his chosen people," as his instrument. God was God, he maintains, before he chose Israel to be his people, and if his chosen ones become unfaithful he can achieve his purpose through others. The choice of God stands firm only so long as the chosen of God remain faithful. The irrevocable factor in God's relationship to Israel is not the choice of Israel but the purpose of God.

Amos, in his single-minded preoccupation with the person and the purpose of God as his exclusive center of concern and reference, reveals the hallmark of Hebrew prophecy. Since this God is one with the God of the Exodus and Moses, Amos does not fancy himself an innovator. Since his will is for the practice among humankind of his own outgoing concern, Amos must proclaim for neighbor-flouting Israelites a message of impending doom if they do not heed his summons to repent. Since God's sovereignty knows no boundaries, neither his future nor his concern can be limited to Palestine. Since he once redeemed Israel from bondage and turned a people who were "no people" into "his people," there is no reason why, Israel willing, he cannot again redeem Israel; or, should Israel be unwilling, that he cannot achieve his redemptive purpose for humankind through non-Israelites.

Either expressly or implicitly, all these ideas find expression in the prophecies of Amos. By the same token, they all represent logical deductions from the Tekoan prophet's message about "the day of the Lord." A day that shall be what it shall be because the Lord is who he is!

America's modern counterparts to Amos may put less stress than did he on the prospects of natural or national calamity as punishment for disloyalty to God, yet they view it as an utterly grave matter. King's proclamation of judgment on the church illustrates the change. "But the judgment of God," he declared, "is upon the church as never before. If today's church does not recapture the sacrificial spirit of the early church, it will lose its authenticity, . . . and be dismissed as an irrelevant social club with no meaning for the twentieth century." [20] This possibility notwithstanding, King did not despair of the future. Though he seemed hardly more confident that Christendom would "come to the aid of justice" [21] than Amos had been that Israel would do so, still he did not despair of the future. For just as Amos had believed that God's purpose could survive the collapse of Israel, so King believed that it could survive the fall of the church.

Amos and King taught us to ask ourselves, if concerned about our loyalty to God, not whether the Lord is on our side, but whether we are on the Lord's side.

FOOTNOTES

[1] If you are interested in the criteria for distinguishing the secondary additions to a prophetic book, consult the appendix on "The Detection of Secondary Additions to a Prophetic Book." There the book of Amos will be treated as a test case.

[2] G. Ernest Wright, *Biblical Archeology* (Philadelphia: The Westminster Press, 1957), p. 157.

[3] James B. Pritchard (ed.), *Ancient Near Eastern Texts Relating to the Old Testament* (Princeton: Princeton University Press, 1955), pp. 129, 214f., 332; cf. Am. 3:15; 6:4; Ps. 45:9.

[4] G. A. Reisner, C. S. Fisher, and D. G. Lyons, *Harvard Excavations at Samaria* (Cambridge: Harvard University Press, 1924), pp. 227-46.

[5] Buber, *The Prophetic Faith,* p. 97.

[6] J. Morgenstern, *Amos Studies,* I (Cincinnati: Hebrew Union College Press, 1941), pp. 3-179, attaches great importance to Bethel as the site of Amos' prophecy.

[7] James M. Ward, *Amos and Isaiah: Prophets of the Word of God* (New York: Abingdon Press, 1969), pp. 23-27.

[8] The prophet continues to address the inhabitants of Samaria as the "people of Israel," despite the division one hundred fifty years earlier of the kingdom of Israel into the nations of Samaria and Judah; since the great prophets never cease to judge both countries by their common religious heritage, such confusion is not only inevitable but, from the standpoint of the prophets, necessary.

[9] (New York: Random House, Inc., 1966).

[10] Cherry, *God's New Israel*, p. 23.

[11] *Ibid.*, p. 312.

[12] Quoted in William G. Wolf, *The Religion of Abraham Lincoln* (New York: The Seabury Press, 1963), p. 121.

[13] *Ibid.*, p. 167.

[14] Ward, *Amos and Isaiah: Prophets of the Word of God*, p. 139.

[15] *Letter From Birmingham Jail* (Nyack: The Fellowship of Reconciliation, 1963), p. 14.

[16] *Ibid.*, p. 15.

[17] From a sermon reprinted in *The Light in the Steeple: Religion and the American Revolution* (New York: National Council of Churches, n.d.), p. 14.

[18] *Ibid.*

[19] Ward, *Amos and Isaiah: Prophets of the Word of God*, p. 58.

[20] *Letter From Birmingham Jail*, p. 16.

[21] *Ibid.*, p. 16ff.

IV

THE SOURCE OF COVENANTAL LIFE

Unlike Amos, who left his native Judah to become a troubler in the Northern Kingdom of Israel, Hosea was an inside agitator. A younger contemporary of the Tekoan prophet, he was born in Samaria, and there he prophesied from the last years (about 750 B.C.) of the reign of Jeroboam II to the time immediately preceding the fall of Samaria to Assyria in 721.

Hosea's message holds great significance for its contribution both to Jewish theology and the Christian faith. But our examination of its various elements must await a prior look at the background of his activity and the compilation of the book of Hosea—and, before either of these, at the assumptions underlying my interpretation of Hosea.

The interpretation of Hosea's career and message presented here will reject out of hand the widely held assumptions that (1) we know a great deal about Hosea's personal life, and (2) that his marriage holds the clue to the interpretation of his message.[1] The first of these notions founders on our inability to name a single member of his family save his father (1:1), identify the locale of a single one of his public appearances, describe the makeup of a single audience to which he ever addressed himself, trace his connection with the institutional prophecy of his day, or, prior to that, his connection with other occupational or vocational groups.

The validity of the second supposition, and perhaps its importance as well, may be quite accurately measured by the failure of scholars to reach a consensus as to how we should answer the most elementary questions about the women in Hosea's life.[2] Not only do they reach different conclusions about the morality and religion of these females; they cannot even agree as to whether the prophet was married once or twice.

Not surprisingly, the interpretations of the prophet's career which attach primary significance to the accounts of his marriage(s) confront us with no less confusion. This fact would be understandable if the utterances of Hosea were similarly obtuse and muddled, but they are not. His oracles (4-14) present us with a relatively clear, generally consistent, and quite cogent picture of both the prophet and his proclamation. What is more, they form a literary and theological unit; unlike the narratives in chapters 1 and 3, they do not leave the interpreter with the feeling that he must consult additional material before being able to ascertain their meaning.

However much the accounts of the prophet's marriage(s) may have facilitated the communication of his message, Hosea's problem with women played a far less prominent role in his and his first disciples' development than it has in the commentaries on the book of Hosea. For while personal experience and Mosaic faith may have combined to produce his social analysis, there can be little doubt as to which enjoyed priority, in time or influence. The movement almost never proceeded from personal experience to theological insight. In virtually every instance, alike from the standpoint of time and importance, the dialectic ran in exactly the opposite direction. It was much less a movement from prophetic experience to communal faith than it was a movement from communal faith to prophetic experience. In other words, Hosea—or, conceivably, the disciple(s) responsible for the narrative material in either chapter 1 or 3, or perhaps both—interpreted his domestic life in the light of his prior reflections on Israelite tradition. And he or they effected this achievement well before undertaking the reinterpretation of that tradition on the basis of the prophet's own marital experience.

The Background of the Prophet

The book of Hosea contains few data of autobiographical significance. Yet it holds much importance for the historian. Not only does it yield decisive clues to the political breakdown in Samaria during the quarter century immediately preceding its fall to Assyria, but it also provides him or her with documentable evidence for detailing the course and progress of the internal decay of the Northern Kingdom. And it is one of the chief sources for tracing the vitality as well as the intensity of the encounter of the Mosaic faith with Canaanite Baalism, the chief Palestinian rival to Israelite religion.

The evidence for dating Hosea to the period between 750 and 721 B.C. consists of two sorts: references to historical figures or occurrences, of which we have three (1:1; 1:2f; 1:4); and the presupposition, in numerous places, of identifiable events and circumstances in Palestinian history. These latter passages mirror Israel's movement from a situation of stable affluence (2:2-15; 4:1-5:7) under Jeroboam II, through a long decade of stormy regicide and anarchic violence (5:10; 7:5-7; 8:4), into the period of impulsive opportunism that reduced it to the sorry status of a tribute-paying vassal (5:13; 7:11; 8:9; 9:3; 6; 10:6; 11:5, 11; 12:1) and, in the course of time, to its tragic demise.

Granted this setting for Hosea's ministry, the prophet's despair of Israel's transformation in time to avert national disaster gives little occasion for surprise. We would even be justified in asking what else a prophet of the Lord might have offered such a wayward people.

As shown by Hosea, he could have offered them a great deal else. He could have offered them his faith in the unquenchable love and unconquerable power of the Lord. In addition, he could have offered them a theo-

66

logical basis for interpreting and triumphing over their dismal situation. And that, as we shall presently see, was exactly what Hosea did offer them.

The Compilation of the Book

The book of Hosea falls into two principal divisions, chapters 1-3 and 4-14. The first division contains, in addition to the title (1:1) and an allegory of the Lord's relationship with Israel (2:2-23), two narratives—one biographical (1:2-9), the other autobiographical (3:1-5)—of Hosea's marriage. While these first three chapters form a literary unit, they were not only appended to the collection of Hosea's oracles in the second division (4-14) of the book, but they were joined in such fashion as to underscore and illustrate those utterances. For these reasons, as well as because of the confusion that has resulted from beginning the other way around, I shall launch my analysis of the book with an examination of Hosea's oracles (references will occasionally be made to 1-3 in my discussion of Hosea's oracles, but such allusions will only be for the illustration of points made in 4-14).

Although the term "covenant" appears only twice (6:7; 8:1) in Hosea's description of the relationship of the Lord with Israel, his utterances may nevertheless best be described as an expression of covenantal theology. But it is covenantal theology in a new key. Both partners to the covenant are portrayed in deeply personal terms. And so, too, is the history of their relationship. Just as Hosea depicts God under the figures, respectively, of father (11:1-4) and husband (2:2, 7, 16), so he casts Israel in the role of son (11:1-4) and wife (2:2-17). Yet the partners to this covenant are by no means equals. For while Hosea's God is not without the warmth and intimacy of a modern father or husband, he nevertheless retains the ascendancy and authority associated with these roles in ancient patriarchal society. He exercises compassion without the loss of sovereignty, and he

67

effects judgment without the sacrifice of mercy. And it is good for Israel that he does. For if covenant breakers could make God the victim of their rebellion, Hosea could not proclaim the Lord as the ground of Israel's hope for redemption.

This combination of power and grace furnishes our prophet with his clue to the vitality and renewal of the covenant. From beginning to end, no matter what the issue under discussion, whether the requirements of God or the centers of Israelite politics and worship, the source and target of Hosea's plea is Israel's adoption of God's faithfulness as the model for the conduct of her life with both the Lord and her neighbors.

When Hosea enumerates the requirements of God (2:19; 4:1, 6; 6:4, 6; 12:6; 14:2), he normally employs relational terms. In other words, the senior partner (the Lord) demands that the junior partner take on the stance and the attitudes of the senior partner. From this union there develops a relationship in which God's partners in covenant spontaneously reproduce his affections and actions. That this requires of us a pretty clear idea about what God condones and approves Hosea has not the slightest doubt. And he has equally little doubt that we must so organize our lives and society in terms of this relationship that nobody can plead ignorance of God's demands as an excuse for unfaithfulness to the Lord. But the primary thing in such obedience is not knowledge of the law (even though the Ten Commandments as reflected in 4:2, 12, 17, 19; 5:13, 7:11; 8:1, 4ff.; 10:1-2, 6, 8; and 11:5, figure prominently in Hosea's indictment of Israel), but the "knowledge of the Lord." And this, in Hosea's vocabulary, is an equivalent for "faithfulness," the prophet's shorthand for personal loyalty to the divine-human partnership.

Hosea's intensely personalized view of the relationship between God and God's people comes through most clearly in his description of the centers, cultic and political, of Israel's most flagrant offenses against God. Place after place (4:13-15; 5:1-2, 8; 6:7-9; 13:16) be-

68

comes a notorious memorial to Israel's deception and betrayal of the Lord. Hosea's accounts of what transpired at these sites almost never accentuate mere legal infractions. They spotlight, instead, the crime of personal disloyalty. In them Hosea characteristically levels two charges against Israel: it has spurned the Lord's love with contempt, and it has courted the favor of the Lord's rivals without anxiety or distinction. Even though these spots stand as landmarks to specific transgressions by Israel, they are best remembered by Hosea as witnesses to the flawed character in which its treachery took root and grew.

Hosea's portrayal of the relationship between God and Israel as "a living dialogue of love and loyalty between committed persons" [3] marks one of the most innovative [4] and significant developments in all Israelite theology. He adds depth to Israelite law by the simple, yet revolutionary, device of personalizing his understanding of not only the demander and his demands but also of the offender and his offenses. When he articulates the Lord's requirements, he simultaneously draws the boundaries of the joy of God and the purpose of God's people. By the same token, when he details Israel's transgressions, he forges an inseparable connection between human judgment and divine anguish. By the simple expedient of substituting familial patterns for legal categories, Hosea lifts the concept of the covenant to a new level. He elevates it from the plane of the formal and objective to that of the personal and subjective.

But Hosea does not become the dispenser of cheap grace in the process. For just as he insists that Israel, though a treacherous harlot and a delinquent child, continues to be the object of God's love, he likewise contends that God, though a forgiving husband and a gracious father, continues to be the Lord and Judge of Israel. In short, even though his oracles do give covenantal theology a personal dimension and meaning, they do not sentimentalize it.

The difficulties in making sense of the narratives (1:2-9

and 3:1-5) about the women and children in Hosea's life are real, but they are not insurmountable. We can hold them to manageable proportions by keeping these three reminders before us: (1) that the oracles hold the key to the meaning of the narratives, and not vice versa; (2) that the book of Hosea is an anthology of the words of the prophet and his disciples, and that some of the disciples put all of its parts together; and (3) that the makers of this book did not include accounts of these domestic incidents for their own sake, but for their value in illuminating Hosea's view of the relationship between the Lord and Israel.

Approached thusly, the place to begin our examination of these materials is by recalling that this understanding of the covenant rests on a very bold assumption. It presupposes the kind of living dialogue between the Lord and his people that makes it impossible to describe one apart from the activity of the other. The divine action may be described in terms of grace and judgment, hinging on the nature of Israel's response to the Lord's deeds. And Israel may be called a victim of habit or an apostle of freedom, depending on whether it heeds the orders of its so-called leaders or the commands of God. Yet the connection between the two never becomes entirely mechanical. For no matter how just God's judgment of his people, Israelite disobedience cannot finally thwart his grace. And no matter how gross Israel's indulgence of its bad habits, it can no more terminate its own freedom by refusing to exercise it than it can destroy God's grace by spurning it.

Despite Hosea's emphasis on interaction between the Lord and Israel in the analysis of his people's present situation, he does not chart Israel's future simply by looking at her past. For Israel's long and shameful record of shocking infidelity notwithstanding, the prophet relates its history as a movement from grace to rebellion and back again. As in the past the Lord made Israel his people in name by an act of unwarranted grace, in the future he will remake Israel his people in character by a second act of unwarranted grace. Thus Hosea, because of what he knows about the Lord and in spite of what he knows about his people, anticipates from twice-redeemed Israel a faithfulness to God (2:14; 3:5; 14:4-7) for which the experience of once-redeemed Israel provides no basis at all.

If I am correct in reading the accounts of Hosea's domestic experience as a parable of Israel's religious history, the two narratives may be assigned, respectively, to the immediate future (1:2-9) and the more distant future (3:1-5). And for theological considerations, even though it may date from a later time, the biographical narrative in the first chapter must be given prior attention.

The third-person account of Hosea's marriage to Gomer in 1:2-9 reflects the prophet's strongly negative assessment of Israel's character. Gomer represents Israel in her dual role as wife and mother. Just as she has betrayed Hosea and seduced his children into the repetition of her infidelity, Israel has betrayed the Lord and lured the children of his covenant into the worship of repulsive deities and the performance of deeds to match, both politically (2:8, 13, 17; 9:10; 11:2; 13:1) and cultically (5:1f., 8-15; 7:3-7; 8:8-11; 9:15). Assuming an inseparable connection between a people's character and its destiny, as Israelite tradition's heavy stress on retribution inclines Hosea to do, the prophet can find nothing in either Israel's past or its character to justify his hope for the diversion of God's judgment of wrath against it. Accordingly, he proclaims imminent disaster as God's punishment of Israel for its rejection of him. To this prophecy he gives added weight by bestowing symbolic names on all three of his children by Gomer. Jezreel, the name of the first child, requires an explanation. He is called Jezreel on divine command, "for," says the Lord to Hosea, "I will punish the house of Jehu for the blood of Jezreel, and I will put an end to the kingdom of the house of Israel" (1:4). Jeroboam II was the last king of the dynasty of Jehu, who came to power in a bloody massacre that made the fields in the valley of Jezreel

71

flow red with blood. Thus Jezreel enshrines Hosea's belief not only that the houses of Jehu and Israel will perish in a common judgment, but that the death blow will fall at the very same spot where the house of Jehu made the house of Israel a party to its crime. The names of Gomer's other two children simply reinforce Hosea's dim outlook for the covenant: "Not my people," the name of the third child, stands as a reminder that Israel's rejection of the Lord as God will be followed by the Lord's rejection of Israel as his people; "Not pitied" serves as a warning against weeping over Israel's loss, since it will have come about as the result of its and not the Lord's faithlessness.

The autobiographical narrative in 3:1-5 relates the prophet's redemption of an anonymous adulteress. After being instructed to "love her as . . . the Lord (loves) the Israelites," despite their religious harlotry (vs. 1), he proceeds to put her in isolation for a period of time. The confinement not only suggests the fate in store for Israel, but it also hints at its possible use as an opportunity for reflection and repentance. Inasmuch as this harlot, like Gomer, represents not only the faithless Israel against whom Hosea rails but the beloved Israel for whom the Lord laments, she and Gomer should probably be viewed as one and the same person. In any event, the crucial item in this autobiographical fragment does not concern the identity of the woman, but the unconditioned—and, potentially, redemptive—love of the faithful man. And its significance lies in the fact that the latter stands for the Lord in his relationship with Israel. The hope of the prostitute's transformation, like Israel's, does not hinge on her faithful response to her husband's love, but solely on his unyielding and invincible love for her. Yet this hope never ceases to be problematic. For while the Lord's love for Israel does not vary with Israel's whims and caprice, neither does it become compulsive or coercive.

The narrative of 3:1-5 itself offers clear support for my refusal to locate its meaning in the prophet's domestic experience. Surely its authors, had this been the focus of their concern, would have related the outcome of Hosea's deathless love for this faithless woman. The very fact that they leave her in her relationship to the prophet at precisely the point where Israel stands in its relationship to God—in the throes of a decision on which the entire future of their covenantal union hangs squarely in the balance—furnishes additional proof of the improbability of their or Hosea's discovery of a parable of the Lord's union with Israel in the prophet's tragic marriage. Rather, we have here another indication that, instead of the prophet's own experience providing them with the clue to the relationship of the Lord and Israel, "the bittersweet story" [5] of the Lord's love for Israel gave them their clue for interpreting Hosea's domestic life.

If this interpretation be correct, then the offense of Hosea's wife should be construed as participation in Canaanite fertility worship. This view is supported not only by the representation of Israel as a harlot in the poetic allegory in chapter 2, but by the fact that, in chapters 4-14, Hosea repeatedly describes Israel's harlotry in religious terms—in short, as submission to Canaanite influences.

It may be lamented that this interpretation minimizes the influence of marriage and the family in the development of biblical faith. If so, it more than atones for this loss by spotlighting the impact of serious theology on Israelite reflection concerning domestic relationships.

The oracles of 4-14, in which Hosea anticipates certain doom for Israel in the short run but its possible deliverance in the long run, mark the point of departure for tracing the development of the book of Hosea. Looking backward, the prophet is both awed by the Lord's unwarranted love in Israel's creation and appalled by Israel's thoughtless ingratitude ever since. Looking ahead, he both foresees the repetition of the Lord's gracious deliverance of Israel and anticipates Israel's grateful obedience to the Lord. Yet he stops short of denying the possibility of Israel's repetition of its apostasy. Even though the oracles themselves do not explicitly identify the Lord and Israel as husband and wife, one can scarcely read their depiction of the relationship between the two without being tempted to translate it into a story of his fidelity and her harlotry.

Chapter 2:2-23 effects the complete translation of this relationship into personal terms in a fanciful piece of poetic allegory. The harlotry of Hosea's wife represents the idolatry of Israel, for which she must stand discipline at the Lord's hands. Following this judgment, the Lord's aggressive love, presented under the figure of Hosea's loving pursuit of the mother of his children, will renew and fulfill his people. But this will happen only if Israel freely and faithfully appropriates the Lord's love as a model for herself.

The relationship of this allegory to the remainder of the book of Hosea may be asserted with some confidence. Its use of the first person suggests familiarity, if not common authorship, with the autobiographical narrative in 3:1-5. By the same token, the plea of the offended husband for his children to press his cause with their faithless mother points to prior acquaintance with the contents of 1:2-9. Previously we have identified the prophet's reassessment of Israelite tradition as the probable source of the presentation of his domestic life as a parable of the union between the Lord and Israel. If correct, the domestic parable of 1:2-9 and 3:1-5 may be viewed as the product of reflection on Hosea's oracular proclamations, and the religious allegory in 2:2-23 as a cryptic summary of the prophet's oracles on the basis of symbolism borrowed from the domestic parable. Thus chapters 1-3 of Hosea may be regarded as a highly personalized introduction to the collection of oracles in the remaining chapters (4-14) of the book. In fact, it might even be viewed as a miniature edition of the oracular division of Hosea. Not only does it resemble the oracles in the portrait it paints of the history of Israel's relationship to the Lord, but it likewise

74

anticipates their alteration of words of accusation with words of encouragement.

As was the case with other prophetic collections, that of Hosea underwent various changes at the hands of the compilers of his works. These editors, judging by the way they modified (as, e.g., in 1:10-2:1) and interrupted Hosea's thought, seem to have felt free to adapt and reformulate his words in any combination that would enhance their witness without destroying his. If at times they pretty effectively blunted or distorted Hosea's message, we are neverthless indebted to them for a great deal else besides the continuing relevance of Hosea's words. In all probability, had it not been for them, the prophet's words would not even have remained in circulation.

Thomas Jefferson did not have the compilers of the traditions amassed in the names of the great prophets in mind when he wrote that the makers of our constitution should provide for its revision every "nineteen or twenty years . . . , so that it may be handed on, with periodical repairs, from generation to generation." [6] Yet the view of tradition embodied in his words did little more than translate into theory their practice of treating tradition with great respect, but with respect of a sort that could not be confused with "sanctimonious reverence." [7]

Some people contend that the power thus to amend tradition will eventually spell its end. But they have yet to demonstrate how any other view of tradition can be reconciled with either dynamic religion or political democracy.

The Message of Hosea

Hosea's message to Israel has ceased to be read as a corrective to Amos' onesided emphasis on the divine justice. There are two reasons for this change. One is the growing conviction that Amos' proclamation presupposes a far broader grasp of the covenant than used to be assumed. The other is the recognition that, while Hosea does lay special stress on the divine mercy, he shows hardly less concern for the fairness of God than does Amos.

Yet the middle term in Hosea's view of the divine-human relationship is not the fairness of God, but his faithfulness. And while the faithfulness of God does not permit him to ignore the faithlessness of Israel, neither does it require his abandonment of Israel. In fact, it does not even permit his abandonment of Israel, its endless line of rebellion notwithstanding. Israel's acts of defiance against God do not alter God's warm feeling for Israel. On the other hand, God's tender regard for Israel could, and hopefully, will elicit from it action of a very different sort. Thus Hosea's description of the God-Israel union after the analogy of the man-woman relationship has a future as well as a past and present reference. It entails hope for their reunion as well as the fact of their marriage and subsequent separation.

The Faithfulness of God

Hosea declares his view of God in eloquent, if indirect, terms. This characterization applies particularly to his indictment of Israel for its offenses, the description of which runs more than half the length of all his oracles put together. He inveighs (rails) against idolatry with special scorn and passionate vigor (4:13; 7:4ff.; 9:1; 10:1-2, 8). His attack could scarcely fail to elicit grave doubts about the validity of the worship of any God but the Lord even by non-Israelites. Yet Hosea does not translate the implications of this assault on idolatry into an emphasis on the universal sweep of the Lord's rule. He subordinates awareness of the Lord's exclusive power to concern for his unmatched character, Hosea's understanding of which is best rendered by the Hebrew word most adequately translated as "faithfulness." In the prophet's understanding this term comprehends both the mercy that initiates the covenant and the morality that gives it stability and character. Hence the concept of the divine faithfulness enables Hosea to assert his confidence in the sovereign goodness of God without sacrifice of his belief in the sovereign love of God.

Apart from the mercy of God, Hosea had nothing to which he could point in support of his hope for Israel. Certainly no change had transpired in Israel's external situation between his activity and Amos' earlier appearance at Bethel to justify any such optimism. If anything, the situation had grown worse. Political uncertainty, aggravated by Assyrian aggression, had triggered anxious concern about the stability and future of the Israelite economy. Upon shifting his gaze for an examination of Israel's inward parts, Hosea found equally little ground for assurance. Instead of loyalty to the Lord and obedience to his commandments, he discovered, instead, the frenetic pursuit of idols (4:12, 17; cf. 8:4ff.; 13:2f.; 14:3) and patent contempt for the Lord's most elemental requirements (4:2; 8:1; cf. 10:13; 12:1, 7).

Hosea searched the character and the society of Israel for some ground on which to plead the case for the Lord's gracious treatment of it, only to discover that there was none. But its moral and spiritual and political and economic and social bankruptcy notwithstanding, Hosea did not cease to claim for Israel the gracious favor of the Lord. Like Amos before him had done, he utterly confounded popular expectation. Just as Amos had voiced despair in the midst of material prosperity, Hosea expressed hope on the eve of national calamity. Whereas Amos had subordinated the facts to his faith in God's judgment, Hosea subordinated the facts to his faith in God's mercy. But this distinction aside, each paid unswerving allegiance to this first principle of prophetic logic: instead of deriving its clues about God from the contemplation of Israel, it derives its clues about Israel from the contemplation of God.

Hosea balances his stress on the Lord's mercy for Israel with the demand that Israel return his covenantal faithfulness with the "knowledge of God." His articulation of this requirement reflects his deeply personal view of God's relationship to Israel. The Lord's love for Israel is not mechanical. Just as Israel cannot destroy God's love by failing to return it, neither can Israel advance the mission of God except by embodying and revealing his love in its relationship with both him and its neighbors. Short of the internalization of his love, God himself can neither protect Israel from itself nor deliver it from the consequences of abusing its God-given freedom.

Yet the Lord remains able, even after judgment has begun to exact its stern toll of his covenantal partner, to continue in communication with it and, granted its repentance, to renew his covenant with it. As illustrated in the temporary confinement of the prophet's wife in the autobiographical narrative, punishment does not destroy either the personhood of the victim or the possibility of restoring the relationship of that person to another, especially if the Lord be the partner in question. Inasmuch as his love serves simultaneously as both the source and the norm of true morality, every act of discipline may, with equal cause, be viewed either as an act of judgment or an opportunity for reconciliation. As important as it may be to acknowledge that the love of the Lord is corrective because it is creative, it is no less important to recognize that it is creative because it is corrective. The mercy and morality of the Lord do not function at cross purposes. Not only does his mercy operate morally, but it initiates social and historical change by working moral renewal within its beneficiaries.

What prompted Hosea to anticipate renewal while others despaired was the same thing that had led him to proclaim judgment while others were relaxed. In both sets of circumstances the decisive consideration for him was the divine faithfulness.

Twenty-six centuries later Abraham Lincoln not only resurrected Hosea's belief in the regenerating power of God's mercy, but he enlarged upon it. He forecast the renewal of this nation on the ruins of a war that he viewed as an act of divine judgment. "He," declared

Lincoln, speaking of God, "will compel us to do right . . . because . . . he means to establish justice. I think he means that we shall do more than we have yet done in furtherance of his plans, and he will open the way for our doing it." [8]

The Faithlessness of Israel

Hosea devotes considerable attention to his people's breaches of the rights of their neighbors. Yet his analysis of these offenses directs the spotlight not on the crime but on the criminal. For while he provides ample material for producing a catalogue of Israel's transgressions, alike of the mortal and garden varieties, he tends to view all such misdeeds as symptoms of a more fundamental ailment. For him the primary choice with which God confronts man is not the choice between good and evil, but the choice between faithfulness and faithlessness. Sin is much less a moral than a religious category. And religion is much less a matter of beliefs than of relations. Accordingly, what whets Hosea's anxiety about Israel's future are not particular infringements of the divine law, but the betrayal of the Lord's person to which these violations bear witness. Just as dedication of the whole self, in affection and action, to the person and purpose of the living and all-sufficient Lord of history defines for him both the supreme good and the supreme goal of Israel, he deplores, ahead of all else, the absence of this commitment. Consequently, even though he finds evidence of Israel's faithlessness on all sides, Hosea directs his big guns against the brazen independence—most callously placarded, in the prophet's view, in Israel's shameless disregard of God's will in its political activity and cultic practices—that permit his people to conduct their life as if the Lord were not their and history's final arbiter.

Hosea's pronouncements on political matters betray slight interest in the survival of political institutions for their own sake. He eschews the usual political norms in gauging their worth and assessing their future. His interest in them begins and ends with their impact on the character and mission of the people of the covenant. But for this very reason, oracles of far-reaching and devastating political import proceed from him with considerable regularity. And while they hardly qualify him for designation as the stateman's statesman, his deliverances on the two issues of foreign alliances and the monarchy alone give us ample reason for calling him the theologian's statesman.

Hosea's attitude concerning foreign alliances leaves slight margin for question. Not only does he predict a disastrous outcome for Israel's attempt to secure her borders in reliance on a foreign protector (5:13), but he brands her participation in the game of international diplomacy as a proof of rebellion against the Lord (7:11ff.). Although the grounds of the prophet's opposition to this involvement never quite get fully articulated, he leaves no room for doubt that it represents a faithless and fateful breach of the Mosaic faith.

In sharp contrast with his castigation of Israelite diplomacy, Hosea's condemnation of the monarchy does not omit the specifics. Along with major responsibility for the aforementioned bankrupt diplomacy, he charges the monarchy with the perpetration of wanton bloodshed (7:3-7; cf. 1:4-5), the encouragement of blatant apostasy (5:1f.; 7:7-16) and flagrant idolatry (8:4, 8-11), the sanction of crippling oppression (5:10f.), the dissipation of treasure on lavish castles (8:14), and the enlistment of popular confidence in fortified cities.

This bill of particulars lends plausibility to the view that Hosea opposed the monarchy on performance rather than principle,[9] yet several items deserve mention in support of the contrary position. No reference to the policies or deeds of an Israelite king, past or present, in any authentic oracle by Hosea can be termed favorable. Not only is king-making denounced as an alien intrusion into Israelite life, but it is broadly hinted that a Lord-approved king and an authentic idol represent equally live options for Israel (8:4). Twice Gibeah, the site of the royal residence of Israel's first monarch (1 Samuel 22:6; 23:19; 26), is singled out as a landmark in the history of Israelite rebellion (9:9; 10:9). In authentic prophecies of Israel's restoration, the prophet's hope does not focus on the head of the state but on the Lord of the covenant. But putting aside the number and weight of these arguments for viewing Hosea as an unqualified opponent of the institution of monarchy, the fact remains that Hosea never debated this kind of abstraction. Whenever he addresses himself to the question of kingship, he discusses it from the standpoint of historical facts and not in terms of theoretical possibilities. He does not argue that the monarchy could not have been good for Israel. He merely contends that it has not been good for Israel. It has been so faithless to the ideals for which it was established that Hosea discounts the institution of monarchy—and, for that matter, every political alternative to it—as the key to Israel's destiny.

Hosea's attitude towards the cultus shifts back and forth between unrelieved contempt and joyful approval. It all depends on whether his gaze is directed towards the existing cultus or the one that will be celebrated in the new era upon the renewal of the covenant between the Lord and Israel. For the existing cultus, which has its focus and center in the system of sacrifice, the prophet has neither kind words nor hopeful expectations. But he expects much from the coming cultus, for it will be marked by "offerings . . . of words, including the confession of sin, the acknowledgment of the sole sovereignty of the Lord as God, and the grateful acceptance of his mercy," in lieu of "material offerings and blood rites of atonement." [10]

The prophet does not leave determination of the grounds of his disenchantment with the prevailing worship to our imagination. He details them for us repeatedly. And, in spite of the personal pain with which they afflict him, he leaves them as clear as they leave him bitter. What they all add up to is an uncontrollable epidemic of idolatry: where the Canaanite cult has not wholly replaced that of the Lord, it has been allowed to subvert it into an intolerable caricature of its authentic self. Israelite apostasy runs the gamut from the unabashed adoration of Canaanite deities (2:8-17; 9:10; 11:2; 13:1) to the celebration of feasts in their honor (2:5-16). While Hosea finds no ground whatever for comfort in this apostate worship, he is even more appalled by the wholesale assimilation of the motifs and motivations of Canaanite religion to the cult of the Lord. Such defection is attested not only by a drastic increase in the use of erotic language (2:1-3; 1; 4:10-5:3; 9:1) and perhaps even erotic practices in public worship (2:10-13; 4:13-18; 7:14; 8:4-13; 9:1-3; 10:1-2; 13:1-6), but also by the use of such worship as a tool for securing agricultural and commercial benefits. In the prophet's view, even where the names of other deities have not displaced that of the Lord in the ritual, Israel worships the Lord as God in name only. Even where Israel continues to implore the Lord as God, it is in support of the goals of Canaanite religion. Concern for the ethical has been superseded by stress on the erotic, and lofty personal concerns have yielded place to shrewd prudential calculations. That leaves Hosea with no alternative but to conclude that the distinction between the cult of the Canaanites and that of Israel marks a distinction without significant difference. And our prophet responds accordingly: he announces the imminent end of Israelite worship, as of its Canaanite counterpart, without apparent reservation or regret.

When Israel under God established its political and ecclesiastical institutions, it was for the purpose of safe-guarding the rights of people and insuring the purity of divine worship. Upon seeing the custodians of these institutions grow indifferent to these goals, Hosea began to announce their overthrow as the necessary prelude to the renewal of the covenant. Yet the primary thing behind his proclamation of doom was not the faithless-ness of Israel, but the faithfulness of the Lord. What triggered his anxiety for his people was of a piece with the fear Thomas Jefferson once expressed for America. Conscience-stricken by our sanction of the inhumane system of slavery, Jefferson declared, "I tremble for my country when I think that God is just." [11]

The Lordship of God

The faithlessness of Israel was doubtless abetted by ordinary human unruliness and self-centeredness, but other factors were also at work. One of its chief causes was of a special theological sort. By the time Hosea arrived on the scene, the war between Mosaic faith and Canaanite religion was in full swing, and the outcome of this struggle was by no means a foregone conclusion. The Lord waged "his battle against Baal (the most important deity in the Canaanite pantheon of gods) for the soul of Israel" [12] through Hosea, one commentator has noted.

This contest spotlighted the question of sovereignty. The religious traditions of Israel emphasized control over history; those of the Canaanites, control over nature. In fact, the religion of Canaan, popularly known as Baalism, may best be described as a vegetation cult. Its divinities were personifications of the weather cycle. And its worship, featuring erotic rites in which its leaders sought through imitative magic to elicit the favor of the appropriate gods, had as its goal the rebirth and renewal of nature.

In all probability, the Israelites would have dismissed this religion as unquestionably inferior to their own, had it not been for one thing. The Canaanites, in whose midst and land they had settled, were better farmers than the Israelites. Not content merely to ask why this was so, the Israelites proceeded to ask what they should do about it. Many resolved the issue by substituting worship of the gods of nature for that of the God of history. Others took the less drastic—but, in Hosea's view, probably no less offensive—step of altering their traditional worship of the Lord to make room in it for the adoration and solicitation of the fertility deities.

Hosea did not merely inveigh, though he certainly did do that, against such defection and accommodation to Baalism. He rejected out of hand the simple choice implicit in the traditional emphases, respectively, of the Israelite and Canaanite religions. He undercut the appeal of the Baals by claiming the spheres of their alleged control for the sovereignty of the God of Israel. By thus asserting the lordship of God over the gentler as well as the more violent forces of nature, Hosea both enlarged and enriched Israelite theology, yet he did not effect this achievement at the expense of Israel's traditional emphasis on the lordship of God over history. In some respects, as we shall have occasion to observe after we have taken a closer look at the prophet's assertion of the Lord's control over nature, he refined and deepened this concept as well.

Hosea's epithets against Baalism's attempts to induce fertility of the soil raise doubts about the propriety not only of nature worship but of the divine interest in nature (e.g., 13:1-2; cf. 2:1-8). One would scarcely be surprised, in the light of these indictments, if the prophet should proceed to exclude nature from the control of God, or if he should put under the ban the pursuit of nature's gifts through the worship of God, yet he does neither. Instead, he sweeps the whole of nature, taking special care to pinpoint the things normally credited to the beneficence of the Baals, under the umbrella of God's dominion (2:8, 15; 14:4-8). For this reason, he ridicules the recourse of the Baalists to imitative magic, especially as illustrated in their performance of sexual union as a religious observance, and he fits the punishment to the crime. For seeking nature's gifts from other gods, the Lord will put an end to procreation in humankind and nature. He will make the people sterile and their land infertile.

Hosea combats the chief rival of Mosaic faith on home ground. Despite its traditional overweening stress on the Lord's control over history, he emphasizes his unrivaled and absolute lordship over nature as well. And he does it in such a way that, in addition to giving depth and emotion to Israelite religion, he offers its proponents something better than a club with which to oppose its rivals.

At no point does Hosea's interpersonal view of the covenant come into clearer focus than in his understanding of history. The prophet's interpretation of history is of a thoroughly dialogical sort. For while it is finally subject to the control of the Lord, it is nevertheless susceptible to human influences. Hosea avoids a hard-and-fast choice between God and humans as causal agents in historical developments. Normally he makes the Lord the subject of the imminent judgment of Israel. At times, however, he depicts such judgment as the inevitable outcome of Israel's own policies or those of some national neighbor (8:3; 10:14f; 11:16; 13:15). And while the Lord's mercy keeps him from seeking a judgment of wrath for Israel, his integrity will not allow him to exempt Israel from the judgment of wrath it has brought on itself.

If now we consider Hosea's conviction of Israel's culpability and God's justice, paying special attention to the prophet's prior belief that history takes shape under the pressure of dynamic interaction between the Lord's initiative and Israel's response, we could say of Israel's judgment that it is either heaven-sent or self-imposed. Yet we should take care to safeguard the priority of God's role as causal agent. For while Hosea lays special stress on human freedom, he limits its operations to a sphere whose boundaries are drawn by the Lord. Hosea reiterates Israel's traditional stress not only on the Lord's action in history but on the significance of that action for determining the course of history.

If we may again invoke the husband-wife analogy in our study of the past of the God-Israel union, this "marriage" may most accurately be described as the union of a persistent and loyal lover on the one side and an incorrigible and undiscourageable prostitute on the other. If faithfulness be the word for telling the story of the Lord's relation to Israel, faithlessness is the only word for telling the story of Israel's relation to the Lord. Israel defiled the bridal chamber even before its escape from the wilderness. And since then it has so ardently pursued the path of infidelity that it has become helpless to envision, much less follow, any other course. Repeatedly the Lord has sent prophets into its midst to recall it from its faithlessness, but to no avail. It has indulged the harlot's role until it has fallen victim to the harlot's habits and, consequently, it has sealed for itself the harlot's judgment.

Although the wary reader cannot help but be struck by the scarcity and vagueness of Hosea's expressions of hope for the future, a few of Hosea's oracles (11:8-9; 14:1-8) do anticipate the kind of deliverance for Israel that is foreshadowed in the autobiographical narrative (3:1-5). This coming redemption, like Israel's deliverance from Egypt, will likewise be set in motion by divine action. Beyond this point, becoming more hopeful than assertive, the prophet hints at a breakdown of the analogy: as did not happen in wake of the Exodus-Sinai event, Israel will crown her coming emancipation with full acknowledgment of her dependence on the Lord.

If I have hedged the description of Hosea's hope for Israel, it is because of the text itself. I have been motivated by the desire accurately to mirror what seem to be genuinely ambiguous elements in the prophet's expectations concerning Israel's future. While this should not be construed as a denial of Hosea's proclamation of hope for the future, the prophet's explicit utterances concerning Israel's future offer slight basis for crediting him with a message of encouragement. The grounds of his hope for the future must be sought, instead, in the implications of his more general pronouncements. In support of this brief for the articulation by Hosea (used corporately here to include all those who in any way contributed to the anthology of prophecies contained in the book of Hosea) of a theology of hope, the following four items deserve special mention: (1) Hosea's repeated bids (2:2; 5:4; 6:6; 10:2) for repentance would mock Israel with false hopes, were his hearers constitutionally incapable of a favorable response to such calls; (2) his consistent depiction of the Lord as a God of grace and mercy in his dealings with Israel's rebellious ancestors could scarcely fail to trigger the hope of similar treatment at his hands by Israel's rebellious children; (3) his portrayal of Israel at the time of its adoption by the Lord as a forlorn orphan (11:1-11) cannot fail to raise the question of whether the Lord might not be able to work a similar miracle of transformation on a wanton woman; (4) the apparent ascription of redemptive power to his love for his faithless wife argues against interpretation of the foregoing reflections of hope as mere rhetorical devices.

Although the foregoing considerations provided ample foundation for the construction of a full-blown hope for the future, Hosea left its development to others. Why he bypassed this opportunity we cannot be certain, but a probable explanation readily suggests itself. That was the fear that prophet-quoting nationalists might turn his words into an excuse for maintaining the status quo. And although Hosea longed to comfort the faithful, he pulled a tight rein on his impulse to wax hopeful, lest he become the unwitting masseur of the faithless.

Hosea does not believe in the faithfulness of God because he believes in the future of the covenant. He believes in the future of the covenant because he believes in the faithfulness of God. He believes that, just as God once turned the slaves of Pharaoh into his people, he will one day turn faithless Israel into faithful Israel and out of disobedience bring obedience. If he does not despair of the possibility of the rebirth of covenantal life for Israel, it is because he remembers how little Israel had to do with its birth. Though Israel may have forgotten, he remembers that the covenant had its sources in the creative work not of Israel but of the Lord.

FOOTNOTES

[1] The best recent commentaries, and the best commentaries on Hosea are recent, have dropped these assumptions. See especially James M. Ward, *Hosea: A Theological Commentary* (New York: Abingdon Press, 1966), pp. 3-71; cf. James L. Mays, *Hosea* (Philadelphia: The Westminster Press, 1969). The German commentaries by H. S. Wolff (1961), A. Weiser (1963), and W. Rudolph (1966) take a similar stand in regard to these matters.

[2] L. W. Batten, "Hosea's Message and Marriage," *Journal of Biblical Literature*, 48 (1929), 257-73; cf. R. Gordis, "Hosea's Marriage and Message: A New Approach," *Hebrew Union College Annual*, 25 (1954), 9-35.

[3] Mays, *Hosea*, p. 13.

[4] J. L. McKenzie, "Knowledge of God in Hosea, "*Journal of Biblical Literature*, 74 (1955), 22-27.

[5] Ward, *Hosea*, p. 70.

[6] Quoted in H. S. Commager (ed.), *Living Ideas in America* (New York: Harper and Brothers, 1951), p. 440ff.

[7] *Ibid.*, p. 439.

[8] Quoted in Wolf, *The Religion of Abraham Lincoln*, p. 146.

[9] James M. Ward, "The Message of the Prophet Hosea," *Interpretation*, 23:4 (1969), 396-400.

[10] *Ibid.*, 394ff.

[11] Quoted in Will D. Campbell, *Race and Renewal of the Church* (Philadelphia: The Westminster Press, 1962), p. 56.

[12] Mays, *Hosea*, p. 1.

V

THE EXALTATION OF POLITICAL POWER

A former chief executive officer of the World Council of Churches, addressing the Riverside Church in New York City, declared:

We are by all odds the wealthiest people that have ever lived, yet less than a mile from this church are rat-infested tenements, a ghetto of the poor, that would be a disgrace to a poor nation or a bankrupt people.

I am weary of comfortable Americans using partisan political and economic arguments as excuses why nothing should be done. . . .

. . . The time is long overdue to change the economic rules of our society so that pockets of abject poverty are eliminated. . . .

Unless the American people begin to press . . . government leadership to treat poverty as a moral issue, our culture and our nation will ultimately collapse in a swamp of greed and crime.[1]

Within less than a month after that pronouncement, our thirty-sixth President gave what may be described as a seconding speech in support of the motion to hold government responsible for the health and welfare of its citizens. In that address he declared:

In a land of great wealth, families must not live in hopeless poverty. In a land rich in harvest, children . . . must not go hungry. In a land of healing miracles, neighbors must not suffer and die untended. In a land of learning and scholars, young people must be taught to read and write.[2]

The similarities between the sermon of the preacher and the address by the politician extended even to the reaction which they elicited. Both attracted mixed responses. The churchman was accused of mixing politics with religion; the politician, of mixing religion with politics.

When the latter proceeded to draft a legislative proposal to match his rhetoric, his critics accused him of having fallen victim to a piece of "utopian nonsense." To that charge a Scrips-Howard editorial writer gave the definitive rejoinder. These were his words:

If, in this sense, "utopia" is a dirty word, so is "humanity." If there is any purpose in humanity, then there is purpose in striving to erase the blights which make humanity meaningless to so many of its members. [3]

If words mean anything, this writer was ready to join the drive to hold government responsible for the distribution and guarantee of justice. Apparently he would even support the rewriting of the rules by which we play the game of hide and seek with the Internal Revenue Service.

Christians have widely acclaimed the aforementioned trinity for their support of social change through political action. But they have not credited them with the dissemination among us of any terribly novel political ideas. And for good reason they have not done so. For what are they doing, we might ask, but pleading for the view of political responsibility set forth 27 centuries ago in the oracles that appear in Isaiah 9:2-7 and 11:1-10.

The Literary and Historical Background of the Dynastic Oracles

There are widely differing views of both the setting

90

and the authorship of these oracles. The one adopted here will construe them as liturgical productions, quite possibly by Isaiah of Jerusalem himself, for use [4] in a ceremony of either inauguration (most probable) or annual enthronement (less likely) of a late eighth-century king of Judah. While this interpretation leaves some important questions unanswered, it gives us some important clues to Isaiah's understanding of the nature and importance of political responsibility. And even more importantly, it brings us face to face with the notion of kingship that informed the social criticism of Israel's great prophets.

Certainly Isaiah of Jerusalem (who, together with his disciples, usually receives credit for the collections of prophecies contained in chapters 1-39; hereinafter, following common practice, he shall be referred to simply as Isaiah) had ample opportunity and incentive for penning such pieces. The title (or, as it is more technically called, the superscription) of his book (1:1) removes all room for doubt on this score. It dates his career to the reigns of Kings Uzziah, Jotham, Ahaz and Hezekiah, whose combined rule over Judah ran from 783 to 687. While few scholars would date any of Isaiah's oracles before Uzziah's death in 742 or as late as the final decade of Hezekiah's reign, there is no ground for challenging the essential accuracy of this date for the prophet's activity. Most scholars hold that specific oracles can confidently be assigned to the reign of each of the heads of state named in the superscription, and that any of the last three of them could have been the subject of dynastic oracles by our prophet.

Before turning our attention to these oracles, let us remind ourselves that the title's description of the prophet's activity in relation to the careers of the chief political figures of his day is neither accidental nor without significance. It indicates that Isaiah's public prominence came about through his connection with the power brokers and involvement in the political developments of his day. In all probability, Isaiah would have denied the charges against him of political irrelevance by saying that he was simply enlarging the context of political debate to include theology. Satisfying solutions to political problems can never be discovered, he would have argued, until they are analyzed from the perspective of God's will for humankind and the nations.

The unconventional character of his political advice should not be construed as evidence that he would have resented the description of himself as a "meddler in politics." Given his assumption that politics and theology are inseparable, he would likely have challenged the credentials of any prophet who denied firsthand responsibility for addressing himself to the political issues of his day. In fact, several commentators subscribe to the view that on at least two occasions Isaiah, having concluded that Judah's political leaders either could not hear or would not heed the word of the Lord, temporarily abandoned its proclamation.[5] By implication, these interpreters are raising the question if Isaiah did not believe politics to be as much the presupposition of significant prophecy as he believed prophecy to be the source of good politics. By so doing, they probably attribute to Isaiah too mundane an understanding of prophecy. If so, they more than atone for this excess by doing full justice to his sublime understanding of politics.

The dating of Isaiah's career by mention of the kings under whom he prophesied leads us to anticipate from this spokesman for the Lord pronouncements of great importance for conduct of the affairs of state. And this son of Amoz (1:1), whoever he was, fully vindicates our expectations, and most especially in the dynastic oracles.

Most scholars seem ready to concede that these passages were prepared for use in some kind of royal celebration, yet they agree that several questions concerning their interpretation have still to be resolved. Granted their creation for use in such a celebration, were they intended to hail the birth of a king, to mark his accession to the throne, or to commemorate his enthronement? Did the same royal figure—and, if so, which one—inspire both oracles? And were they—despite their generally hopeful outlook and their equally non-Isaianic disposition to offer unconditional salvation—put together by Isaiah of Jerusalem?

Once we recognize the literary type of these passages as that of the dynastic oracle or royal psalm (after which they were at least patterned), such questions fade into comparative unimportance. The Royal Psalms (2, 21, 72, 89, 110, 132), which hail the Lord's adoption of Israel's king as his own "son" (see especially Psalms 2:7) and mark some of the outstanding dynastic oracles in all Israelite literature, clearly reflect the tendency in this literary type to employ language that is conventional, stereotyped, ritualistic and hopeful. Given these characteristics of the dynastic oracle, we have small occasion for surprise at the failure of Isaiah 9:2-7 and 11:1-9 to yield a well-rounded, full-orbed version of the prophet's theology. In any event, since they cannot with confidence be assigned to any other prophet and no harm is done either to the words themselves or to Isaiah by ascribing them to him, we shall proceed to interpret them as expressions of his thought and viewpoint.

Given the recent appreciation of the cultic role of Israel's prophets and, in particular, Isaiah's closeness to both temple and crown, there is no good reason why this prophet should not have been asked to compose liturgical pieces for use in the celebration of the king's installation or enthronement. But if he did, and if we have these productions in the passages under consideration, we must take care not to interpret them as if they had originated spontaneously in response to situations of crisis. Instead of reading them as Isaiah's address *to* the people, we should read them as Isaiah's address *for* the people. Restrained and guided by both the occasion and the liturgies and traditions connected with its observance in the past, he would naturally have downplayed his role as judge of the faith of the children of Israel. Construed thusly, these passages should be viewed as an Isaianic version of royal theology and not as a typical expression of Isaianic theology. Or to put it differently, they should be interpreted more as a source than as a summary of the thought of Isaiah and, for that matter, Israel's other great prophets.

Like the royalzion psalms, they interpret the function of kingship in Israel from the standpoint of its covenantal traditions. Hence they describe what ought to be rather than what is. As if the new monarch were sure to do what no king before him has ever done, they delineate the future as if he will satisfy all the conditions for the realization of the Lord's covenant with Israel. This explains the use of darkness and light to pinpoint the utter contrast between the existing and the coming situations or, to put it more politically, the old order and the new (9:2-3). The new monarch, whom the Lord not only adopts as his son (9:6; cf 11:1) but endows with his spirit (11:2), will turn Zion into the center and source of all goodness and blessing (11:9-10). Not only will he establish righteousness and justice within Israel (9:7; 11:4), but he will also bring peace with harmony between Israel and its neighbors (9:5). And not only will he put an end to war and wickedness (11:4), but he will likewise dissolve the enmity between humankind and nature (11:6-9). God will reward this righteous king's efforts by allowing him to rule without end (9:7), and people will hail his achievements with the bestowal on him of divine titles and honorifics (9:6).

Even if these oracles were drafted by Isaiah for use in the coronation of a king of Judah whom we could name, it would still be a mistake to trace their inspiration to that particular king, whether Hezekiah or someone else. They took shape, like the view of the kingship to which they give expression, around the covenantal bond uniting Israel with the Lord. Hence the credit for inspiring them, no less than the covenantal faith from which they derive, must be reserved for the King of kings, the Lord of lords, the God of gods, and for him alone. What sustained Isaiah's confidence in the future was not his faith in Hezekiah or in any other king of

94

Judah. It was his trust in the Lord. And what he sought to do, both in writing and proclaiming these oracles, was to reproduce this same trust and confidence in both the king and his subjects.

The Lord's Word to the Participants

The foregoing description of what the prophet hoped to achieve by these pieces assumes their design for a solemn royal festival. Since every such celebration was simultaneously a political and a religious observance, it became an occasion for the acknowledgment of the union of these two dimensions of life. Normally some prominent religious figure, either priest or prophet, would articulate the connection between God and government. Ordinarily his address of this reminder to the community would take the form of a royal psalm or a dynastic oracle.

At their worst—as, for example, in Psalms 2, 20, and 144 —such deliverances degenerated into nationalistic cries for military success. At their best—as, for example, in Psalm 72 and Isaiah's dynastic oracles—they expressed royal responsibility in terms of the divine purpose.

These formulations turned increasingly into anticipations of what life could be like—indeed, *would be* like —if Israel, king and subjects alike, faithfully discharged their obligations to God and neighbor. Unfortunately, few of Israel's kings and not many of her subjects took their "if" with due seriousness. Yet Israel's prophets left them without excuse for taking it lightly.

In his dynastic oracles Isaiah puts first things first. He subordinates his concern, though real and deep, to bring together the king and people of Israel to his even more pressing determination to bring together the rule of God and the government of humankind. For not only does he put the covenant ahead of the crown, but he ties his promise of the Israelite transformation of society and nature to the following twofold demand on Israel's head of state: (1) that he embody the loftiest personal character;

95

and (2) that he administer public affairs as the agent of the concern and compassion of the Lord of the covenant. But these qualifications of royal power must not be misconstrued. Read fairly, they must be interpreted as a call for humanization of the institution of kingship, and not as a demand for its termination. For while they may be read as a prohibition of the abuse of political power, they can also be read with perhaps even greater justification as a plea for its legitimate exercise.

The King's Duties to God

The king will bear witness to his dependence on God in two principal ways. He will do it, first of all, by the quality of his character, and he will do it as well by the way he interprets and discharges his responsibilities as head of state.

Isaiah, in the second (11:1-10) of his dynastic oracles, describes the king as the dwelling place of "the Spirit of the Lord" (verse 2a). But he does not leave the matter there. He proceeds to characterize the divine spirit as "the spirit of wisdom and understanding, . . . of counsel and . . . of knowledge . . . And his (i.e., the king's) delight," the prophet concludes, "shall be in the fear of the Lord" (verses 2ff.).

Here we should recall that the word translated "fear" can just as accurately be rendered "awe" or "reverence." This makes it easier for us to understand the prophet's summons to take delight in it. It is easier to take delight in him whom we revere than it is to take delight in what we fear. And it likewise explains Isaiah's linkage of the "fear of the Lord" to the "knowledge of the Lord." This is especially true if we pause to recall, as previously noted, that "knowledge" in Old Testament usage is primarily subjective rather than purely objective, more relational than rational, and not purely formal but deeply and intimately personal. To "know" God is much more to hold to God's ideas than it is to hold ideas of God. And it is much less to be aware of God's purposes than it is to share God's purposes. In short, it is a form of interpersonal communion in which a person asserts independence of people by acknowledging dependence on God. It is that act of the whole self in which the human "I," by coming to feel and to love as and what the holy "Thou" feels and loves, proceeds to enact the divine will into human deed.

This understanding underlies the prophet's designation of the king as "Wonderful Counselor, mighty God, Everlasting Father, Prince of Peace" (9:6). He is not thus designated because he is king of Israel. Quite the contrary, he is thus honored in the hope that he will develop a character to match the God in whose name he has been anointed.

But Isaiah does not propose a psychological test as a yardstick for measuring this achievement. For while he has an interest in the king's private habits, he subordinates this interest to his concern for the king's conduct of public affairs. As Isaiah sees it, and in this regard he claims to speak for God as well as himself, the private claim to relationship to God pales into insignificance. What matters is the reflection of this relationship in official action. The masses will not learn of the king's devotion to God from some press secretary's revelation of his daily observance of a quiet hour. They will infer it, instead, from his conduct of the country's thisworldly business on otherworldly terms. "He shall not judge," says Isaiah, "by what his eyes see, or decide by what his ears hear; but with righteousness he shall judge the poor, and decide with equity for the meek . . . Righteousness shall be the girdle of his waist and faithfulness the girdle of his loins" (11:3b-5).

Translated into the idiom of modern politics, what Isaiah's description calls for is a decision-making process that mocks this world's preoccupation with the prejudices of "Mr. Average Citizen"; that eschews the definition of justice in terms of government of the "ins," by the "ins," and for the "ins"; and that, with equal vigor, rebukes our sanctification of the quest for personal

97

advancement, without regard for moral principle or social consequence.

It would appear that Isaiah's fear of the irresponsible exercise of political power is at least matched by his fear of the abdication of responsibility for the proper exercise of political power. For not only does he refuse to limit government's duty to the negative responsibility of restraining evil, but he also credits it with a creative role as the agent of God in the transformation and renewal of society.

Isaiah does not support the idea of the divine right of kings, but he does endorse the idea of the divine responsibility of kings. Or to put it more accurately, he encourages the idea of the responsibility of kings to God.

The ceremony of royal enthronement or coronation, as the case may have been, does more than set the king apart as head of state. It sets him apart as the first among equals in the service of God. The king stands *among equals* because, in the prophet's view, to establish and uphold justice and righteousness is the obligation of every one. But every one does not sit upon the throne of David and feel the weight of the government upon one's shoulders. So the king, by virtue of position, stands *first* among equals. He has a priority of obligation to match his priority of power. Thus he enlists his power—that is, if he exercises it in accordance with the will of the God from whom he derives it—for "the increase of peace . . . . with justice and with righteousness from this time forth and for evermore" (9:7).

When Judah's rulers enlisted their power in quest of causes that were frustrating this pursuit, Isaiah threatened them with disaster at the hands of their enemies. Twenty-five centuries later, when the framers of the Declaration of Independence set forth their case against the King of Great Britain, they justified rebellion against his rule by charging him with the perpetration of numerous flagrantly wicked and unjust acts. In all probability, Isaiah would not have approved the means by which the colonists sought to remedy their situation, but he would surely

98

have endorsed their grounds for attacking the policies of George the Third.

The Consequences of Royal Obedience

From the vantage point of hindsight, imbued as we are with full knowledge of Mesopotamia's rise at the tragic expense of Judah and her Near Eastern neighbors during the last half of the century of Isaiah's principal activity, we are tempted to ask mocking questions of the prophet's apparently serious estimate of royal developments in Judah. With Assyria relentlessly on the march and its Mediterranean opponents biting the dust, one by one, what could possibly have been less important than a ceremony of coronation or enthronement for a king of that inflated little Palestinian state of Judah? What first-rate thisworldly mind could possibly have found anything of consequence in such an apparently foolish and futile "gesture"?

Yet Isaiah of Jerusalem, an unquestionably first-rate mind, discerned in that action something more than a gesture. He glimpsed the shape of a power with which visiting, and probably mocking, dignitaries on hand for the celebration in honor of Judah's king had not come to terms. That was true, no doubt, because their minds, unlike Isaiah's, were entirely thisworldly. But Isaiah, thanks to the demands of the solemn occasion and his role in it, had been forced to come to terms afresh with the traditions of the covenantal community. These spoke to him of one whose coming had taken both Pharaoh and his brick-making slaves by surprise, to mention only the most crucial of that invader's disrupting visits. As it was in the beginning, so it had continued to be. And so, Isaiah became convinced, it still is, and evermore shall be. As when the Lord first came, so will it be when he comes again, and he *shall* come again! He will crash the best laid plans with shocking impact: exalting the debased, and debasing the exalted. He will wrench power from the hands of the tyrants who now wield it, and he will deliver it into the hands of those who now cower in its presence.

Thus shall it be with the advent of "the Spirit of the Lord." This term may properly be construed as a presence and a time. The time is the day of reckoning when the powers-that-be must give account of their exercise of power in the presence of him from whence it comes and by whom it is transferred. In that day surprises will abound on every side. The smug who have ceased to fear will discover their mistake, and so will the humble who have abandoned hope. Proud tyrants will yield up their treasures to marauding savages, and the despised oppressed will go forth to greet their king and ours.

In addition to this sweeping reversal of the unpromising situation facing Judah and the prophet, the last four verses (11:6-10) of the second of the dynastic oracles from Isaiah envision international and natural side effects of absolutely startling proportions. Reversing the order of their mention in the text, let us look first at the consequence for the nations of the emergence in Judah of a Lord-directed monarch.

The anticipated impact of this development is set forth in a single verse. "In that day," we read in 11:10, "the root of Jesse shall stand as an ensign to the peoples; him shall the nations seek, and his dwelling shall be glorious." Two shifts in emphasis distinguish this sentence from the preceding verses: (1) prominence now attaches to the ruler himself ("the root") as well as to the dynasty to which he belongs; (2) attention now focuses, not primarily on the character and issue of government in the new age, but on the adoration of the anointed one by the nations.

These changes in tone have prompted some exegetes to treat verse 10 as a late addition by a postexilic Jewish chauvinist. Certainly, if read alone, it would be hard to give it any other interpretation. And even when read in context, it is still difficult not to be struck by the sudden shift in focus. But when read in context (and this is not to deny the authorship of this verse by a different person from the one who wrote the others, but to suggest that if there were two authors they were, theologically speaking, on the same wave length), verse 10 does not so much contradict as stretch the thought developed in the earlier ones.

Just as the earlier verses herald an inseparable connection between neighbor and neighbor, verse 10 proclaims a similarly unbroken connection between nation and nation. They will be bound together by a common loyalty in pursuit of a common purpose in deference to a common sovereign. To be sure, Judah's king will come in for disproportionate acclaim, but a good face can even be put on this adulation for him, if we will but take care to interpret verse 10 in context. For granted the anointed one's dependence on the spirit described in verses 2-3a and his exercise of power as portrayed in verses 3b-5, he could become "the rallying point for the nations" without doing harm to him or themselves. And they would proceed to order their affairs, as he has begun to order the affairs of Israel, in accordance with the character and will of Israel's God and theirs.

Read alone, verse 10 could serve as a prop alike for Jewish pride and Gentile envy. But when read in the context of the preceding nine verses, both Jewish and Gentile pride pale into insignificance before a greater glory, the glory of the Lord. For when the Lord comes in all his glory, the nations must cease to glory in all that is theirs.

One thing is sure about Isaiah 11:10's longing for a ruler who will become "an ensign to the people." This desire is today infinitely more widespread in our country and our time than it was in his country and his time. And it runs much deeper among us Americans, as we face the upcoming presidential election, than it did among our founding ancestors. They could choose to have or not to have "entangling alliances" with other countries. The luxury of this kind of choice has long since bypassed us. The choice for us is not whether but how we shall be entangled with other nations. That is why in 1976, for reasons that could not even have been imagined in 1776, we are determined to elect a head of state who will serve both as an example of and a missionary for the kind of political leadership envisioned by our prophet.

A second consequence that will flow from the orientation of the new order in Jerusalem towards the Lord will be termination of the long-standing enmity between humankind and nature (11:6-9). The weakest people and the wildest animals will dwell together in peace and harmony. The resolution of this struggle seems to presuppose the Paradise myth. Just as this hostility originated with man's rebellion against God, it will come to an end in the coming good time because that rebellion itself will be terminated.

Poetic license has doubtless entered into this too neat assimilation of the realms of nature and politics. Yet we must not allow ourselves, in reaction against this oversimplification, to neglect the potential impact of political actions on natural operations. For today, more than ever, it is imperative that we acknowledge this connection. For unless government takes steps to preserve and restore the environment of humankind, the earth will exact its horrible vengeance on our children for the sins of their parents.

Our crimes against nature have already begun to catch up with us. A veritable host of criers in the night, beginning with the authors of *Plundered Planet* and *Road to Survival,* have set the record straight in their indictments. And what a sorry record it is. We have proven that trees, which only God can make, can by any fool be destroyed, and that minerals, which only God can bury, can by any moron be brought to the surface. As if in doubt on this latter point, we have even written into law depletion allowances to reward this rape of nature. "Polluted waters, denuded forests, eroded lands. . .; it is the old story of Adam turning a garden into a wilderness." [6]

Isaiah saw a close connection between the function

102

of government and the friendship of nature. Maybe he drew that connection a little too closely. But there is a connection. And just as surely as Isaiah may have drawn it a little too closely, we have drawn it altogether too loosely.

The Positive Appreciation of Power

As if the kingdoms of God and this world had nothing to do with each other or as though the exercise of power itself were an unspeakable crime, modern church members sometimes decry politics. If only because they both assume and commend a quite different attitude, the dynastic oracles of Isaiah have merited the close attention we have accorded them. Certainly their author, whoever he was, did not seem at all anxious to reduce the power of the chief political figure of his day. What he demanded from him was not the diminution of his power, but for its exercise in a humane and humanizing direction. In short, he bade him to use his power as a force for bringing together the rich and the poor, the powerful and the weak, the greedy and the needy, the realms of society and nature, and, above all, the kingdom of God and the kingdom of humanity.

If the ancestral faith had never been compromised, inasmuch as its most vigorous spokesmen seemed to have rejected the idea of kingship on principle, the institution of kingship would probably never have found a home in Israel. But this alien institution finally did establish a foothold in the land. Yet the king of Israel, unlike many neighboring monarchs, never ceased being reminded that he was a constitutional monarch. In season and out, psalmists and prophets like Isaiah never wearied of reminding both the king and his subjects of his secondary, though nevertheless important, place in the total scheme of things. Not only did they in their dynastic poems and oracles cast him in the role of agent of the divine will, but they proceeded to commend or condemn him solely on the basis of his readiness to play this part. No doubt,

103

the authors of the Declaration of Independence and the Constitution could have taught them a thing or two about the inevitable tendency of such persons to claim the power of God, but we had better never forget or ignore this one thing which these Israelite figures taught the shapers of our democracy: that people, even people in government, can mediate not only the will of God but his power as well.

Many things changed during the interim that elapsed between the coronation of Israelite kings and the inauguration of American presidents. But the need for this use of power was not one of them.

FOOTNOTES

[1] Eugene Carson Blake, *New York Times,* December 28, 1964.

[2] From President Johnson's Inaugural Address, printed in the *Washington Post,* January 21, 1965.

[3] Editorial in *Columbus Citizen-Journal,* January 30, 1965.

[4] R. B. Y. Scott, "The Book of Isaiah: Exegesis," *Interpreter's Bible,* V (1956), pp. 247 ff.

[5] *Ibid.,* 157-60.

[6] J. Wallace Hamilton, *Who Goes There?* (N.Y.: Fleming H. Revell Co., 1958), p. 98.

VI

THE VULNERABILITY OF GOD'S SPOKESMAN

The popular portrait of a great prophet casts him in the role of a tart-tongued, iron-willed and somewhat unfeeling person. Those who dispute this image trace its general acceptance to the nature of the materials we have about him. By and large, these materials consist of reports of his career as a public figure. Relatively few of them deal with his private life. And even fewer of them consist of personal reactions to the demands put upon him by his message and career. Had we more of this kind of personal data, the critics of this conventional interpretation maintain, we would stop looking on him as a sphinx-like paragon of virtue and begin to view him, instead, as a vulnerable human being.

Happily for these humanizers of the great prophet, they have more than an educated guess going for them. There are materials from one such Israelite prophet, namely Jeremiah, that make our knowledge of him an outstanding exception to the above generalization. Not only are they replete with biographical references; they also include personal reactions of the most intimate sort. And they are, fortunately, quite extensive—certainly enough so to justify the strong suspicion that we are more intimately acquainted with Jeremiah than any of the other great prophets of Israel.

We must take care, of course, to resist the temptation to make sweeping generalizations about the great prophets as a group on the basis of our specialized knowledge of only one of them. At the same time, however, we should not minimize the fact that our knowledge of Jeremiah compels us to view him quite differently from the picture of him we get from the exclusive study of his oracles. At the very least, we must concede the possibility that, if we had the kind of intimate personal data about the other great prophets that we have about Jeremiah, we might find them to be as appealing and attractive, personally, as we find him to be. At any rate, since they give a new and surprising dimension to the personality and character of Jeremiah, let us proceed to the examination of these materials with anticipation and imagination.

To the question, "What kind of person do the biographical portions of Jeremiah and his so-called 'confessions' disclose to us?" the loud and clear answer immediately forces itself upon our attention. They reveal a deeply passionate and keenly sensitive human being in the throes of mortal conflict. They reveal a man whose unswerving devotion to God was matched by an equally genuine affection for people. In him the incarnation became real. Jeremiah did not articulate God's stern judgment on a house of rebels with delight; rather, he mirrored the pain and anguish with which the Lord approached this unwelcome task.

By the same token that Jeremiah enlarges our appreciation of the prophet as a model for ministry to humanity, he bids us take a second look at his interior makeup. In what can perhaps best be described as a remarkable anticipation of the higher righteousness displayed by him who was both victor and victim of the cross, Jeremiah demonstrated the singular ability simultaneously to identify with both the author and the recipients of God's judgment. If there is anything more striking than the degree to which he shared Jesus' passion for the will of God, it is the degree to which he displayed Jesus' compassion for human beings.

Under any circumstances, this achievement would have been remarkable, but its accomplishment in the lifetime of our prophet was utterly extraordinary. To appreciate

106

the full truth of this assertion, we have only to take a cursory look at Judah's world at the time of Jeremiah's activity.

The rise of Assyria in the middle of the eighth century to the pinnacle of power transformed the life and politics of the entire Near East. Nowhere was this impact felt more immediately or dramatically than in Syria-Palestine, and nowhere in all Syria-Palestine was this influence more lastingly felt than in Judah. Judahite life had always been subject to the play of international forces, but from this time forward it was destined to be overwhelmingly dominated by the surge of international developments. This terrifying situation framed the background of Jeremiah's entire career.

By letting his life become intertwined with that of Judah, whose life in turn had become inseparable from that of her neighbors, Jeremiah became an actor in a calamitous production on a world stage. He played his part to the tune of shifting empires, with those of Assyria, whose days of glory came to an end within less than half a century of her heyday, and Egypt falling into decline and that of Babylon, in alliance with the Medes, ready to burst into full bloom. This transfer of power from northern to southern Mesopotamia left little unchanged between the Persian Gulf and the Mediterranean Sea, and nowhere was there more immediate or devastating change than in Judah.

Although Egypt suffered a crippling defeat in the 605 battle at Carchemish, where its newly-acquired ally, Assyria, received a mortal blow at the hands of the Babylonians, it was able to come back for more, and it did repeatedly. In fact, 33 years elapsed before the Babylonian armies were able to breach Egypt's borders, and even that invasion failed to produce Pharaoh's acknowledgment of defeat.

As taxing as the shifting fortunes of this struggle must have been for the two nations, its indecisiveness was doubtless even more devastating for the small states of Syria-Palestine. For them the balance of power between

Asia and Africa had become altogether too perfect. They desired nothing so much as to be left alone, yet their only live option seemed to be a choice between two overlords, either of whom, if successful, would likely regard and treat them as bush leaguers. But the temptation to adjust their loyalties with the changing tides of battle, in the desperate hope of improving their bargaining position by anticipating its final outcome, proved to be almost irresistible.[1] In many cases, and especially in that of Judah, this policy turned out to be as disastrous in the long run as it was appealing in the short run.

The death in 609 of Josiah at the hands of Neco put an end to a great deal else besides Judah's last great monarch. For all practical purposes, it likewise marked the end of Judah's hope for the restoration of the throne of David to a position of international prominence and preeminence. Individual kings and their advisers and occasionally even armies could still harbor and pursue imperial dreams, but they could no longer take mass support for granted. At worst so-called national policy became little more than rule by clique, and at best it could scarcely hope for better than a choice between vassalage and conquest.

Although the fall of Judah is normally dated to the defeat of Zedekiah (597-587), he was made king by Nebuchadrezzar, Babylon's powerful head of state, and his reign, if it can be called that, fared well or ill, depending on his readiness to heed or ignore Babylon's will. Zedekiah's downfall began with his decision in 589 to correct this situation. Despite diminished support for revolt against Babylon throughout the small states of Syria-Palestine, Zedekiah and Judah heeded the encouragement and promises of Egypt; they took the fateful and fatal step of joining in open rebellion against Nebuchadrezzar. Less than two years lay between this decision and its frightful climax, but those two years must have seemed like a lifetime to the inhabitants of Judah and Jerusalem. The resisters fought gamely, but the odds were simply too great. In 587, beset on every side by famine and fatigue, the beleaguered natives witnessed a repetition, and worse, of the debacle of Samaria in 721. They saw Jerusalem's walls breached; their fleeing king caught and, in the company of other apprehended fugitives, carried to Riblah to be blinded, before being sent into exile on foreign soil; their ecclesiastical, political, economic and social leaders ticketed for execution; and, as if this were not sufficient, their entire city put to the torch. The land of Judah remained and with it some of her people, but the nation of Judah was finished.[2]

The end of the nation of Judah did not mark the end of Judahite nationalism. Many of the Israelites left behind in Palestine and some of those in exile tended to view their plight as a temporary situation rather than an irreversible condition. Just as the Jews in Palestine read their lot as an interim judgment, those in exile construed theirs as an internment of limited duration. As a consequence, alike in Palestine and Babylon, there were former Judahites who continued to dream and plan and labor in the hope of reconstituting national and cultic Israel on the soil of the Promised Land. So far as we know, they never carried this activity to the point of sedition, but there can be little doubt that it occasionally seduced them into anticipation of the early reversal of their captivity and, perhaps even, the renewal of nationhood through entry into a new anti-Babylonian alliance.

Throughout this turbulent period, both before and after the nightmare of 587, Jeremiah preached against the idolatrous attachment of his countrymen to the land, the church and the state of Israel. (Although some scholars hold that a few of Jeremiah's earliest oracles come from a period when he believed Judah still might be able to avert the loss of nationhood and should, therefore, be read as expressions of hope for Israel's established institutions, I side with those interpreters who question any major shift in Jeremiah's outlook during the course of his prophetic career.) If they did not start subordinating these loyalties to their allegiance to the Lord, he warned

109

them, they would suffer just the kind of calamities that actually were to befall them, whether as a people struggling to remain free or as captives plotting strategy for the recovery of their independence.

Judah's resistance to the prophet's plea proved to be every bit as stubborn as Jeremiah's message itself. The situation was one calculated to drive the prophet to a choice between God and Israel, but Jeremiah refused the bait. He was never quite able to extricate himself from the tension between the pull from above and the push from below. Try as he may, and at times he tried desperately, he could never quite shake himself free of the claim of God, yet he remained as vulnerable as ever to the competing claim of people. He longed for the joy of the prophetic office, but he never experienced its rewards without simultaneously feeling the pain of its burden.

Nowhere do we get surer clues to the prophet's mixed feelings about the demands of his office than in 4:19-22 and 8:18-9:1. In the first of these passages Jeremiah displays his typically ambivalent attitude towards Judah, as he simultaneously offers it words of condemnation and solace. This phenomenon stems from an irrepressible urge to serve, on the one side, as the Lord's spokesman of catastrophic doom, even while, on the other side, voicing the frustration and despair of its victims. Here the prophet displays his remarkable capacity for identifying with both the author and the victims of doom. And this ability is what, above all else, sets him apart from the professional reformer. Although Jeremiah displays a deep attachment to any number of good causes, he never allows it to lull him into personal insensitivity. Quite the contrary, his interest in causes derives from an incurable and passionate concern for persons. In Jeremiah and especially in this passage, we get an anticipation of the kind of righteousness displayed by him who, even while hanging on the cross, retained the capacity to sympathize with those who nailed him there.

The movement in this entire passage marks the outworking of the implicit logic of verse 22, where the prophet traces Judah's imminent disaster to her own rebellion. Jeremiah does not dispute the fact that the people of Judah are still the Lord's children, but neither does he deny that they have been "foolish" and "stupid" children, devoid of true knowledge and understanding, "skilled in doing evil" but unwilling and blind to do good (verse 22). In fact, the preceding sketch of ruin in the wake of an invasion may best be described as the transfer of an analysis of the human situation to a geographical canvas. But his awareness of Judah's guilt notwithstanding, Jeremiah cannot contemplate their demise in Olympian detachment. If nothing else, his use of the first person singular "my" with "collapsed, disheveled, and torn tents," a pathetic description of Judah's abject defeat, illustrates the prophet's inability objectively to analyze Judah's plight.

Quite apart from the oft-observed close kinship of our second passage to Jesus' lament (Matthew 23:37) over Jerusalem, 8:18-9:1 deserves attention as another indicator of the anguish with which Jeremiah's office afflicted him. In 8:20, as it frequently does throughout the entire Bible, the "harvest" stands for the judgment. The meaning of the entire passage is suggested in the following comment: "If the grain harvest failed, the people might still look forward to the fruit, but if the fruit also failed, famine stared them in the face." [3] The people of Judah had traveled the path of rebellion too far either to reverse their course or escape the judgment due their disobedience. Their time of opportunity for bringing forth the fruit of repentance had yielded a harvest of shame. Hence Jeremiah had no alternative but to proclaim an end to their prospects for deliverance from calamity. If we should translate verse 22a in the modern idiom, "Is there no penicillin in the hospital?" Jeremiah's answer would probably be, "Yes, but what good will it do you if you should die on the way there?" Completely absorbed, at least for the moment, in his imaginative anticipation of Judah's fall, the prophet joins the be-

111

reaved, and his thunder of indignation turns to tears of sadness.

Jeremiah stood about as distantly removed from the popular caricature of the prophet as any person could get. Far from being an aloof thunderer of indignation, he identified with the people with whom the exercise of his office brought him into conflict. And he did it until it hurt—until their plight became his plight, their pain his anguish, and their loss his cross. He could not proclaim the purpose of God without sharing the pain of its devastated victims. But that pain, though felt by him as deeply as any of his neighbors, never kept him from the relentless use of the surgeon's knife. He was the revealer in life as well as word, and supremely in life, of the purpose and person of God. It is hardly surprising that Christians for whom the incarnation remains a cardinal belief should continue to draw parallels between Jesus of Nazareth and Jeremiah of Anathoth. For if there is anything more striking than the extent to which Jeremiah shared the commitment of Jesus to God, it is the degree to which he embodied the love of Jesus for people.

The Priority of the Divine Claim

The biographical portions of Jeremiah disclose to us a man of conflict. They reveal a man who felt pressure from every side: that wielded by his peers was exceeded only by that exerted by his superiors. Yet Jeremiah never fully succumbed to the sweep of these horizontal forces. Regardless of the claim by which they were triggered —no matter whether it emanated from within, from his colleagues, or from the masses—they were never quite able to submerge or subdue him. Time and again, just when they seemed on the verge of doing so, a counter-vailing vertical pressure (see especially 1:4-19; 6:11-15, 27-30; 10:23-25; 19:1-20:6; 16:1-9) intervened to jerk and to hold the harassed prophet erect.

112

The Claim of Self

The account of the crystallization of Jeremiah's vocational decision (1:4-19)—which may derive from the prophet's own description of his inaugural experience —dramatizes his acute awareness of the priority of the divine claim on his life. It takes the form of a simple dialogue between God and Jeremiah, without accompaniment of a heavenly choir or benefit of a worshipful atmosphere. "Before I formed you in the womb . . . I . . . consecrated you . . . a prophet," says the Lord to Jeremiah. In this account the prophet translates the primacy of the divine-human relationship into temporal terms. The claim of God, the acknowledged priority for faith, is given priority in time. In this fashion the prophet sets the stage for the rhetorical dismissal of his peers who insist that he justify his exercise of the prophetic office to them. Inasmuch as his directions come from a higher source, why should they be allowed to pass on his credentials?

This assurance aside, Jeremiah must still come to terms with his own immaturity and lack of eloquence. Once again the barriers are bridged from the Lord's side. The Lord follows up the symbolic act of touching his hand to the prophet's lips with this declaration: "Behold, I have put my words in your mouth." Since Jeremiah later mouths curses against God for which he repents, this declaration must not be construed literally. It must be seen, instead, as being at once a promise of freedom from human influences and a threat of judgment if he fails to speak at the Lord's direction. One can even imagine that it served as an answer to an anxious relative's question, "How can a young man from Anathoth say such outlandish things in the presence of the leading clerics (the modern United Methodist counterpart would be the college of bishops) of our time?" The answer: "I only spoke the words which the Lord put in my mouth." Apparently Jeremiah learned, and very early, with what venom traditional religious beliefs could resist

113

the demand for a new beginning. The word of the Lord became to him a hammer, at times smashing the hand that held it; at other times, a consuming fire, scorching the heart of its spokesman; or to put it differently, it moved against the grain of his natural inclinations and deeply human emotions. It was the power that enabled him to meet and conquer the temptation both to trim the sails of responsibility to fit the winds of popularity and the urge to join the faceless mass. It gave him courage to become an individual in an other-directed society.

The parable of the almond rod (1:11-12), which makes a play on the similarity in sound between the Hebrew words for almond tree and watchman, reiterates the prophet's confidence in God. Just as a person is prompted by sight of a tree without foliage to wonder where the source of life is, so Jeremiah is moved by seeing a people who sin blatantly to ask where God is. Taking his clue from the experience of having seen the blossoming of other such trees, the prophet asserts his faith in God's readiness to perform his word. Since God always acts in such a way as to reveal the divine character, this vision should be read simply as a guarantee that the divine power and presence will manifest themselves as the situation warrants. That is to say, God will speak his word in grace, if possible; but if necessary, he will proclaim it in judgment. From the ensuing description by Jeremiah of the internal situation in Judah, it becomes clear that God's immediate word will be, indeed must be, a cry of judgment.

A later vision, that of the boiling pot (1:13-16), in which we get a striking combination of memory (sight) and imagination (literary creation), turns a boiling pot, blown upon by a northern wind to the point of overflowing, into a symbol of Judahite destruction at the hands of a mighty foe. Although the traditional interpretation links this prophecy to a particular group of invaders, its emphasis on the identification of the foe blunts Jeremiah's two basic points: (1) that Judah's trouble is self-inflicted, caused by its infidelity to the Lord;

114

and (2) that the Lord's "anger" or "wrath" is the real source of the judgment about to befall Judah. Certainly the question of the foe's identity pales into insignificance beside the prophet's insistence that he will strike at the Lord's bidding and destroy as the Lord's agent.

The narrative of the prophet's call concludes with the identification of himself as the recipient of Judah's enmity against God (1:17-19). His attackers include priests, princes, kings, and even the people of the land. But the strength of the opposition notwithstanding, Jeremiah "girds his loins" (as for a battle or a race), assured that with the Lord on his side he will emerge from the struggle, though sorely threatened, as "a fortified city . . . and bronze walls."

The importance of this assurance in Jeremiah's life, irrespective of whether it be viewed positively or negatively, can scarcely be doubted or exaggerated. For if it explains his embodiment of "the transition from the prophet to the Psalmist," [4] it likewise holds the key to his most serious flaw: an "inability to conceive that what he deems to be necessary for his good can possibly be other than what God wills." [5] His certainty of God, while quickening his sensitivity to idolatry in the hearts of his neighbors, sometimes reduces his ability to see it in himself.

The Claim of Colleagues

Jeremiah's acute God-consciousness betrays itself nowhere more clearly or devastatingly than in the criticism of his colleagues. He flays fellow priests and prophets for failing to bring a vertical yardstick into their measurement of human relationships (6:11-15). In support of his charge of their addiction to mundane standards, Jeremiah notes, in addition to their proclamation of a message of "Peace, peace," that they deliver their glib assurances to moral reprobates, who compound loss of the capacity to blush at idolatry with the practice of unconscionable greed.

Although Jeremiah does not minimize the guilt of Judah's masses, he singles out its priests and prophets for special condemnation. Like doctors guilty of malpractice, they compound a bad diagnosis with a worse prescription. As if Judah's trouble were a slight headache instead of a deadly virus, they prescribe aspirin instead of antibiotics, thus both minimizing the symptoms and aggravating the disease. Unlike Jeremiah, to whom a single act of injustice can become a harbinger of doom, they shrink major calamities to the size of minor nuisances.

The difference between him and them does not lie at all in the observable data, but solely in the perspective from which they view them. Jeremiah evaluates them in light of the demand of God; they, in terms of the capacity of the average person. Jeremiah does not take human transgression and responsibility lightly because he cannot take God lightly; his opponents, on the other hand, cannot take them seriously because they do not take God seriously.

The Claim of the Masses

At times Jeremiah's estimate of the masses seems as unduly severe as his judgment of Judah's leaders. This tendency likewise stems from his God-centered outlook. When he analyzes the whole of Israel in search of precious metal, he does so as the self-conscious agent of God (6:27-30), and his findings are predictably disappointing. His figure of speech, in which he likens Judah to a mixture of bronze and iron, may betray a certain deficiency in metallurgical science, but it leaves no room for doubt that he deems Judah to be guilty of incredible callousness and hopeless corruption. His metallurgical confusion nothwithstanding, the point of his metaphor lies beyond dispute. If there be any precious metal at all left in Judah, it is so slight and corrupt as to defy separation from its alloys. Therefore, the economic thing to do would be to consign the whole sordid mess to the

116

refuse heap. And that, according to Jeremiah, is precisely what the Lord shall do:

> Refuse silver they are called,
>   for the Lord has rejected them.

Whenever a prophet renders such a wholly negative verdict against his people, we have to raise the question of motivation. At times it is hard to avoid the feeling that Jeremiah's barbs are intended more for his own relief than for Judah's transformation. But this suspicion is allayed by his readiness to intercede in its behalf. Just as he has invoked the Lord's intervention for the punishment of his people, so he calls on the Lord to effect their correction (10:23ff.). Despite the prophet's use of the first person singular in this prayer, it should not be construed in narrowly personal terms.[6] Indeed, since Jeremiah can no more conceive of his vocation in individualistic terms than he can leave Judah to its own fate, it makes little difference whether his prayer be viewed as a personal plea or a plea of intercession in behalf of Judah. Since the realization of one's true self, in the case of a people as a person, lies in strict adherence to the Lord's directions, Judah's fate becomes Jeremiah's agony; its destiny and his vocation come wrapped in the same package.

What is being challenged in 10:23—"I know, O Lord, that the way of man is not in himself, that it is not in man who walks to direct his steps"—is not a person's psychological freedom, but one's capacity rightly to direct one's steps while pursuing a self-constructed path. A person cannot choose the path in which he or she should walk until, exercising one's capacity to look at oneself through the eyes of God, he or she criticizes the path in which he or she has been walking from the divine perspective. In other words, if I may personalize the prophet's argument, I can only discover the true meaning of life by shifting "the emphasis from myself to the end which my life and I are called" to serve.[7]

Looking at Judah's life from this standpoint, Jeremiah

117

bemoans its heedless and headlong rush down a path chosen without reference to the Lord's will, but the impossibility of an unredeemed people becomes a possibility for a redeemed people. And Jeremiah envisions Judah's redemption. His "Correct me, O Lord" anticipates Judah's realization, in its dire extremity, of the truth of its existence. Although the revelation will probably not come in time to avoid punishment, the prophet does not abandon hope, at least for the moment, for a new beginning after the chastisement of Judah. Yet his confidence for Judah in the long run, as surely as his despair for it in the short run, is theologically motivated; it has its source and certainty in the character and sovereignty of the Lord of the covenant.

The primacy of the God-man relationship manifested itself in the prophet's life as well as in his message. When Pashhur, the priest in charge of the temple, ordered Jeremiah's arrest for his proclamation of doom on Jerusalem, the prophet redirected his threatening message against Pashhur himself (20:4). Once the will of God became clear to him, no human force or pressure could deter him from its declaration. Then, as if such threats to his life and safety were not high enough premium for him to pay for his allegiance to the Lord, Jeremiah's vocation forced on him the denial to himself of the joys of marriage and a family (16:1-9). While a later editor may well have doctored this passage in such fashion as to turn the prophet's celibacy into a symbol of the catastrophe in store for Judah, it is unthinkable that Jeremiah's bachelorhood should not have been theologically inspired. If his devotion to God left him without time or room for claim of wife and family, that fact should not take us by surprise. We would have ground for surprise only if it had been otherwise. At any rate, Jeremiah's commitment to God left him with little time or room for most of the claims—professional advancement, social preferment, financial security and personal safety—to which we less fully devout human beings devote the bulk of our time and fortune and lives.

The Persistence of the Human Claim

One thing about Jeremiah was more remarkable even than his incredibly audacious identification with the pain and doubt and despair of humankind. For as ready as he was to instruct his neighbors about God, he was no less disposed to teach God what it means to be human. To this fact two groups of passages bear compelling witness. (In addition to the prophet's famous so-called "confessions" or "laments" in 11:18-23; 12:1-6; 15:10-20; 17:14-18; 18:18-23; 20:7-18, mention should also be made of the group of passages—7:16; 11:14; 14:1-9, 11-12; 15:1—in which Jeremiah serves as the mouthpiece of God's prohibition of further intervention in behalf of Judah.)

The Ascription to God of His Own Righteous Indignation

In the latter group of passages the prophet frequently displays the besetting danger of the zealot's righteous indignation: the disposition to ascribe to God one's own disgust for stumbling humanity. Let us take a look, for example, at 7:16. Close on the heels of God's threat, via Jeremiah, of banishment (7:8-15) for the prophet's fellow citizens comes this divine aside (verse 16; cf. 11:14) to Jeremiah himself: "As for you, do not . . . lift up cry or prayer for them, and do not intercede with me, for I do not hear you."

Considering the response of Jeremiah's neighbors to his ministry, we can easily understand his readiness to put such words into the mouth of God. Doubtless it was triggered by a vocational crisis brought on by contemplation of the slight impact of his words on his hearers. It quite possibly marks his secret reply to the question which, though he never can quite bring himself to put it into words, always lies close to the surface of his actual words: How can the man of God, in face of such blatant transgression, sustain or defend the appeal any longer to such hardhearted people?

119

Various defenses have been made of the prophet's claim of divine release from his prophetic commission, yet the suspicion remains that, instead of the foregoing question, he might have asked himself, instead: Until God himself has destroyed the unrepentant, has the spokesperson for God any right to abandon the call to repentance?

Had Jeremiah paused to ask himself this question he might have checked his tendency, now and then, to let his program for the humanization of God get out of hand. At any rate, his failure to put the issue in these terms leaves us with no alternative but to ask if Jeremiah did not occasionally mistake the prophet's mantle for that of God himself.

At times this confusion of roles is the product of self-pity, but not always. In at least one instance (14:1-12) it comes from contemplation of a natural calamity. As if goaded by the terrors of drought into self-examination, the people join in a prayer of repentance, but their confession soon turns into a taunt song against the Lord. That God is in their midst they do not deny, but they cannot decide whether he should be viewed as an indifferent sojourner or a helpless giant. Conceivably, this prayer originated as a parody of a popular prayer, mockingly spoken at a festival in the temple by Jeremiah. Thus interpreted, we have an appropriate and sufficient ground —the total absence of realism—for God's rejection of the people's plea. Yet the absence of pathos from the divine promise of punishment once again betrays a graceless ring. If previously Jeremiah has gone astray in describing people too much from the standpoint of God, here he errs in describing God too much from the standpoint of people.

Jeremiah was the direct opposite of the self-made, self-sufficient man. What he was he became because he fancied himself to be clay in the hands of a divine potter. Yet this fact did not diminish his need for people. He coveted the nearness, the friendship and the support of his relatives and neighbors; he wanted them to become his friends. Whether they reciprocated this desire remains unclear, but there can be no doubt that it went unfulfilled. They denied Jeremiah the companionship for which he longed. They left him alone, alienated and isolated, the victim of his friendship for God, despite his natural preference for the comradeship of human beings.

The Blame of God for His Own Personal Alienation

Jeremiah's enemies would probably have liked nothing better than to see him fade into prophetic oblivion, but the prophet was not about to grant them their wish. As if to heap contempt on their desire for him to make a quiet exit from the public arena, he left for posterity a series of celebrated outpourings in which he vented his inmost thoughts. These laments or confessions, as they have come to be known, have rarely failed to win recognition, if not praise, for their remarkable mixture of the language of blasphemous defiance with that of joyful surrender.

In Jeremiah's first confession (11:18-23) he identifies himself as one of the "persecuted" prophets of whom Jesus speaks in the Sermon on the Mount (Mt. 5:12). He describes himself as the innocent victim of schemes against his life by his friends and relatives in Anathoth.[8] He quotes their plea for his destruction at the height of his life, only to turn their cry for divine punishment against them. This turn of logic may appear to transform a plea for personal vengeance into a bid for the triumph of divine justice, but the transformation is more apparent than real. At any rate, the prophet concludes the case of the prosecution with a demand for a Jeremiah-directed verdict. Here Jeremiah betrays not only the feeling that his convictions hold good for God, but also the presumption that God's feelings are reflected in his own.

In his second confession (12:1-6) Jeremiah conceals his alternately self-righteous, self-pitying posture behind an expression of concern for the justice of God. The ancient, familiar question of the prosperity of the wicked

121

rekindles the prophet's deep anxiety about his vocation. The problem stems from the irreconcilable cleavage between the teaching of his inherited faith that God is sovereign and righteous and the overwhelming evidence to the contrary. Yet the issue, in view of its quick resolution by him, seems to have been more a cause of public than private doubt. In any event, he disposes of the matter in quick order and with devastating effectiveness.

If you have raced with men on foot, and
    they have wearied you,
  how will you compete with horses?
And if in a safe land you fall down,
  how will you do in the jungle of the Jordan?

These words are seldom seen as being in a league with Job 42:1-6 as a solution to the problem of the divine rule of the world, but they surely belong there. That becomes clear, once we translate Jeremiah's question into economic terms and construe it as an inquiry addressed to an ambitious social climber: "If you had trouble competing with the Smiths, what will you do when you come up against the Rockefellers and the Kennedys?"

Or to put the matter theologically, Jeremiah is saying to himself in this dialogue with his soul (for whom God serves as spokesman) that, if one does not believe in God in spite of the evidence, he or she will not believe in God at all. Fellowship with God is not a refuge from rejection but a refuge for the rejected. The best for which one can hope is not how to escape alienation but how to bear it. And, hopefully, how to transform it in the process.

Jeremiah's fellow Anathothites greatly expedited his personal and theological development. By stripping away from his faith all the human props with which he might have secured it, they taught him just how vulnerable one could become by seeking and heeding the will of God without tarrying for human sanction. In short, they taught him that reliance on God could make him a social outcast and, worse, a terror to himself as well as to his neighbors.

In his next confession (15:10-21) Jeremiah reveals the weakness that is his strength. Even while acknowledging the impossibility of satisfying his desire for comradeship with his peers, he nevertheless reproaches the Lord for frustrating his gregarious impulses. In so doing he betrays the tension that has always marked and haunted the great people of God in every age. Although too committed to God fully to identify with his neighbors, he simultaneously betrays the uncertainty and doubt of a person whose humanity is still very much with him. But he is not just another or even an ordinary human being. Jeremiah is deeply aware of the fact that he is a very, very good person. That becomes clear in his recital of the virtues with which he follows up the denunciation of his mother for delivering him into such an imperfect and lonely world. This catalog, which gives us an important clue to the values sought and treasured by his contemporaries, invites comparison with the best descriptions of the ideal human being. Not only has he avoided lending, borrowing and carousing, but he has sought the benefit of his detractors, interceded in behalf of his enemies and consumed the Lord's words in lieu of caviar and vitamins.

And what has he received in return? The rebuke and enmity of all, his relatives not excepted. And Jeremiah is understandably confused and perplexed by these developments. He is moved to wonder if, after all, God has not ordered the world to the advantage of the righteous man's enemies. Unable any longer either to deny or ignore the mounting evidence in support of this conclusion, he asks if the Lord has not turned deceitful like the seasonal brook which, in the dry season, becomes a parched trail. The temptation to view God as enemy rather than friend grows apace. And the more the prophet yields to it, the clearer it becomes that Jeremiah himself is by no means totally immune to the double-mindedness for which he berates his neighbors. This becomes apparent in his plea for divine vengeance on those who scoff at him in order that his righteousness might be publicly acknowledged as such. He is not content merely to be a man of God. He demands to be recognized as a man of God.

But here, as in his earlier confessions, the Lord refuses to let Jeremiah set the terms of their meeting. He confronts the prophet, as Jeremiah in his name has confronted Judah, with a demand that he abandon the roles of prosecutor and sovereign for those of defendant and subject. And he proceeds to seek from the prophet, as Jeremiah has sought from others, repentance and obedience. Once again, but not for the last time, the prophet learns the hard lesson that his stand before his neighbors as a man of God does not alter or diminish the fact that, before God, he stands as a human being and not an equal.

That the moral and spiritual difference between Jeremiah and the members of his audience is one of degree and not kind becomes even more painfully obvious in the lament in 17:14-18. Here the prophet is responding to the charge of rendering a heartless performance in the role of woe-monger. His answer, which lends credence to the notion that he is as hard-pressed to convince himself as his accusers of his innocence, pleads a twofold defense: (1) he has not urged on the Lord the affliction of Judah; (2) he has spoken with his lips only what the Lord first revealed to him as a message from a much higher source. Having thus summarily dismissed the case against him, he proceeds to do for his mockers what he has hitherto refused to do for Judah: he prays for their destruction without delay or mercy!

Various defenses have been made for this display of excessive pique. According to one of the most ingenious, Jeremiah "needs to be proved right that God's truth might be vindicated—this is the element of truth in all his prayers for vengeance." [9] But this explanation overlooks the prophet's tacit substitution of intellectual correctness for personal faith as the test of true prophecy. And it minimizes the danger, if not the blasphemy, inherent in his blithe presumption of a knowledge of God that allows him to speak much too confidently of his own righteousness and rightness. This failure becomes apparent, however, once we reduce the prophet's demand of God in this passage to a modern, though not inaccurate, paraphrase: "You (God) have to bail me (Jeremiah) out of what I got us into for the sake of my reputation." Put in these terms, it becomes clear that Jeremiah, like John Wesley of the eighteenth century, found it much easier to proclaim than to achieve the pure and perfect love of God.

Another of the prophet's prayers for vengeance on his enemies (18:18-23) offers further evidence of his closer moral and spiritual kinship to his peers than to God. But in this instance, to an unparalleled degree, a plea of an excess of provocation could be entered in defense of the prophet for his display of an excess of venom.

His cry of outrage comes in response to a plot against him by the religious leaders of his day. All the three major groups of spiritual leaders, prophets, priests and wise men, join in the campaign to neutralize Jeremiah. "Come," they say, "let us smite him with the tongue, and let us listen to all his words." [10] A modern paraphrase of this plea might read: "Come, let us slander him to his face; then, after we have provoked him to the boiling point, let us make a tape recording of his words for use in the star chamber trial before the House Unjudean Activities Committee." Their scheme works. Jeremiah straightway beseeches the Lord to do unto his enemies as they would do unto him; he calls upon the Lord to cast them into the pit. Then, as if fearful the Lord might relax the pressure, he bids him do the same for all their relatives.

Assuming a basis in fact for this reported experience, this passage drives us to conclude not only that the colleagues of Jeremiah did not believe him to be incapable of a quite human response to their inhumanity to humankind, but also that the prophet's behavior, on more than one occasion, fully justified their realistic estimate of him.

Jeremiah's final confession (20:7-18) finds him kicking holes in the pit of Hades. Too long isolated from human companionship and friendship, he skips the human agents of his affliction to confront their commander-in-chief headon. His despair now out of hand, he attacks God in singularly severe language. He does not deny that a wide gulf separates humankind from God, but humankind's inferiority, he hints, has to do with power and cunning rather than character and goodness. He accuses God of first deceiving and then overwhelming him. His neighbors, whom he has heretofore greeted with threats of terror on every side, mock the distraught prophet. Turning his own prophecy back upon him, they nail him with the nickname of "Terror is on every side." The counterattack moves Jeremiah to reconsider his vocation.

> If I say, "I will not mention him,
> or speak any more in his name,"

it is to no avail, for

> there is in my heart as it were a burning fire
> shut up in my bones,
> and I am weary with holding it in,
> and I cannot.

Try as he may to shed the Amos mantle, it will no more fall from his shoulders than tame words from his lips. Nor can he remain silent. The flames of divine judgment jump from his mouth as tongues of fire. His confidence temporarily restored, the briefly chastened prophet returns to the attack, once again to reiterate his plea with the "trier of hearts" for vengeance on his enemies. And this time, if only for the moment, he gets what he wants, the promise of judgment against his adversaries, with the consequence that their mockery and his lot become bearable again.

But the euphoria quickly passes, and Jeremiah renews the protest against his accursed lot (20:14-18). And he

126

does it in cries of dereliction that take us with him to the very edge of the abyss. Born to a life of "toil" and "sorrow" and "shame," he even turns the herald of his birth into an antagonist. But this enemy is, of course, a mere stand-in for God, for it was the latter who appointed Jeremiah before his birth to the office of prophet, and thereby doomed him to a life of dreadful loneliness and torment.

The choice of enemy here may be taken as an indicator of the severity of Jeremiah's depression. Yet the absence of any hint of suicide compels us to read his complaint as a protest against his vocation and not his life or, to put it more accurately, against the fact that the two have become inseparably intertwined. Indeed, the very remoteness of this enemy betrays a residue of unshakeable, stubborn, defiant faith beneath the abrasive cover of bitter indictment. Just as no person can really achieve liberation by taking vengeance on the announcer of his birth, it is hopeless for Jeremiah to try to undo his commitment. If he could only undo that, he would be home free. But since that is impossible for him, he has no alternative but to keep on exposing himself to "the slings and arrows of outraged fortune."

Aside from the mere fact they exist, which in itself has to be reckoned the most remarkable thing about the prophet's confessions, they are likewise noteworthy on at least two counts for what they reveal about the prophet's deep humanity. They reveal in him, along with the capacity to identify with his neighbors, the ability to put great confidence in them.

The former talent surfaces most clearly in his violent expressions of self-hatred. In allowing himself to get close enough to his neighbors to voice their indignation against himself for bearing their conscience, he displays something besides the capacity to read their minds; he likewise hints at a secret longing for their comradeship— and in the same breath with which he deplores their character. Yet we must not leave such an observation without adding this important qualifier: he never stopped

127

spurning the role of the popular prophet which, had he accepted it, would have secured for him the social approval for which he longed. In other words, he could identify with his neighbors, but never completely; and he could err from God, but not far enough fully and finally to abandon him.

Such errancy on the part of a man of God can scarcely be viewed as a shocking development for those of us familiar with the narratives of David or the Psalms of lament, yet they occupy a unique place in Old Testament piety. They mark the most spectacular instance in which a historical person offers the general public a guided tour of the secret chambers of his heart and mind. Eschewing the sham piety that shields itself from public scrutiny by drawing a blind over its questions, he takes his peers not only into his convictions and certainties but into his doubts and vacillations. Although he takes second place to none of Israel's prophets in the ability to make the targets of his verbal assaults wish that he would attack them, instead, with more lethal weapons, he nevertheless takes the ultimate risk with them. He entrusts to their care the inmost secrets and doubts and fears and hostilities of his terribly restive and sensitive heart. The God who reveals himself to Israel in Jeremiah does so not in spite of but in the midst of the prophet's very real and very insistent humanity.

How to Win Friends and Influence People [11] is a skill in which Jeremiah clearly did not excel. And he seems to have been equally untouched by *The Power of Positive Thinking*.[12] Unable to keep the critical eye he had learned to train on society off himself, he simply lacked the instinct, so highly esteemed in this era of public relations, for the calculating arts. If at times he appeared to be a man in a muddle, it was because he was so often the man in the middle, torn by an internal conflict between the demand of God, which he could neither deny nor disobey, and the claim of humanity, which he longed to affirm but was compelled to resist.

Admittedly, leaders of this disposition do not get a very good press these days. But then, in the political arena no less than in the religious arena, they never have escaped attack by their contemporaries. Yet think of how much poorer we all would be if the impact of their personalities had not left its stamp upon our traditions—if, suddenly, our Christian heritage were robbed of all trace of the influence and writings of its St. Pauls and St. Augustines and Martin Luthers; or if, by some cruel fate, our American heritage should no longer include the life and words of its Abraham Lincolns and Adlai Stevensons.

If nothing else, our look at Jeremiah should prompt us to go beyond the oft-raised question: "Why does God not raise up for us prophets of the type with which he once blessed mankind?" to ask this further question of ourselves: "Could it be that we seek them in vain because we are looking in the wrong places for people cut from the wrong cloth?"

FOOTNOTES

[1] Martin Noth, *The History of Israel,* trans, P. R. Ackroyd (London: A. & C. Black, 1958), pp. 280-89.

[2] John Bright, *A History of Israel* (2d ed. rev.; Philadelphia: The Westminster Press, 1959), pp. 327-31.

[3] A. S. Peake, "Jeremiah and Lamentations," *The New Century Bible, XVI* (N.Y.: Hn. Frowde, 1910), p. 163.

[4] John Skinner, *Prophecy and Religion* (Cambridge: Univ. Press, 1922), p. 222.

[5] *Ibid.,* p. 228.

[6] J. P. Hyatt, "Introduction and Exegesis to Jeremiah," *The Interpreter's Bible,* V (1956), 902 ff., construes this passage as a personal prayer, but Artur Weiser, *Das Buch des Propheten Jeremia* (Das Alte Testament Deutsch 20-21; Gottingen: Vandenhoeck and Ruprecht, 1952), pp. 91ff., interprets it as a prayer of intercession. The writer's view that this distinction holds little importance for interpreting this passage is expressed by H. Cunliffe-Jones, *Jeremiah* (London: SCM Press, 1960), pp. 100ff.

[7] Stanley R. Hopper, "Exposition of Jeremiah," *The Interpreter's Bible*, V (1956), 904.

[8] This is assuming, as I do, that the second confession, like the first, has its setting in Anathoth.

[9] Cunliffe-Jones, *Jeremiah*, p. 136.

[10] The rendering, based on the Septuagint, of Hyatt, "Introduction and Exegesis to Jeremiah," p. 965.

[11] Dale Carnegie (N.Y.: Simon & Schuster, 1936).

[12] Norman Vincent Peale (Englewood Cliffs, N.J.: Prentice-Hall, Inc., 1952).

VII

THE REWARDS OF THE LORD'S SERVICE

The Old Testament—most especially in Deuteronomy, and occasionally even in the prophetic writings—sometimes encourages the expectation of health, wealth and a long life as proper rewards for faithfulness to God. Yet such rewards were only rarely the lot of its chief paragons of loyalty to God, the great prophets. Most of them drove the heads of church or state to look on them with suspicion, and a few of them even moved their leaders to threats, and in a few instances to acts of violence, against their life. And almost none of them fared any better at the hands of the masses than they did at the hands of their rulers. [1]

Yet centuries passed before prophetic theory finally caught up with prophetic experience. While numerous prophets contributed to this development, the members of the school of Second Isaiah (who, as previously noted, are normally credited with the authorship of Isaiah 40-55 and whose principal activity may confidently be assigned to the twenty years between 550 and 530) were the ones who brought it to its climax, but we must take care not to overlook the fact that their work was consolidated and, here and there, amplified by Third Isaiah 55-66. [2]

Second Isaiah and his disciples are of special interest to us Christians for a very compelling reason. Their understanding of the role of the servant of the Lord (42:1-4; 49:1-6; 50:4-9; 52:13-53:12; see also 41:8-10; 42:5-9, 18-25; 43:8-10; 44:1-2, 21-22; 44:24-45:13; 48:20; 50:10) furnished Jesus' foremost interpreters—and perhaps even

131

Jesus himself—with the definitive clues for the assessment of his mission and achievement and ours.[3] Yet this accomplishment does not stand alone, unrelated to the traditions and history of Israel.[4] Quite the contrary, it (i.e., the reflection that turns God's agent from a triumphant sovereign into a lowly servant) marks the climax of an arduous rethinking of Israel's traditions under highly volatile yet hopeful circumstances. It is the joint that connects Second Isaiah's view of the mission of God to his understanding of the task of Israel.

The Mission of God

Isaiah 1-39, the handiwork of First Isaiah and his disciples, may be confidently dated to the period between 742 and 687. Barring late editorial additions of the sort that found their way into every prophetic collection of any length,[5] these chapters are filled with references to the circumstances that prevailed and the people who ruled during the first half century of Assyrian domination in the affairs of Palestine. The account of the prophet's call (6:1-13), possibly the oldest passage in the entire book of Isaiah, dates his commission as the Lord's spokesman to the year of King Uzziah's death (642). Two of the better known passages in First Isaiah (7:1-8:15 and 17:1-6) clearly allude to the Syro-Israelite alliance of 735-734 when these two neighbors of Judah tried to enlist its support of their plan for revolt against Assyria. The first of these references thrice (7:3-9, 10-17; 8:1-4) recalls Isaiah's plea with King Ahaz not to heed their appeal. While the foe through whom the Lord will soon wreak judgment on, first, Ephraim (28:1-4) and, subsequently, Philistia (14:28-32) is not mentioned by name, it is generally agreed that it was Assyria who inspired these prophecies of doom. Another passage (10:5-19) lists six recent victims—Calno (742), Carchemish (738), Hamath (738), Arpad (741), Samaria (721), Damascus (732) —of Assyrian aggression by name. And the concluding section of First Isaiah (36-39)—a long historical appendix duplicated, except for 38:9-20, in 2 Kings 18:13-20:19—relates the story of the engagement of the prophet's services by King Hezekiah. Why? So that Hezekiah might ascertain Jerusalem's chances of escape from the encroaching Assyrian armies. Inasmuch as the account begins with the admission of Assyria's conquest of Judah's fortified cities (this calamity, we know from Assyrian records, befell Judah in 701) and since Hezekiah was the only Judahite king who thus approached First Isaiah, the events encompassed in these chapters clearly date from the years between 701, the date of Judah's close escape from annihilation by Assyria, and 687, the year of Hezekiah's death.

That was the outlook for Judah at the time of the activity of First Isaiah. Since the great prophets tended to style their proclamation to the needs of their hearers in light of the historical realities of their time,[6] we can determine the popular mood by evaluating the direction and tone of the prophet's message. What did he see as he peered through the faces of his people to pick up the writing on the tablets of their hearts? Quite simply, what he saw was a small country of little people clinging to national independence by a slender thread of arrogant presumption. But that was not all he saw. In addition, he saw the great super power of his day, Assyria, overarmed and overbearing, poised for action, ready at the first hint of weakness or defiance to pounce upon any neighbor foolish enough to dispute its power and grind it into helpless bondage. Nor was that all he saw. Besides that, he beheld the Holy One of Israel, his righteousness offended by his covenantal partner's flagrant unrighteousness, prepared to send judgment—quite possibly, with hated Assyria as its instrument—on his disobedient people.[7]

The smug attitude encountered and attacked by our prophet stemmed from a distorted understanding of the covenant. Judah had translated the partnership between the Lord and his people into a contract between equals. Thus viewed, just as the survival of Judah hinged on the

133

gracious rule of the Lord, the rule of the Lord depended on Judah's survival as an independent national state. Confronted by this flagrant idolatry, First Isaiah felt compelled to take drastic action, and he did. He resorted to shock therapy in his bold effort to free his people from their incredible pride. Inasmuch as they had robbed God of his Lordship by making it contingent on the survival and fortune of their nation, he threatened them with the loss of nationhood. They would have to experience the destruction of what they treasured most highly if they did not learn to esteem God more highly.

Admittedly, the prophet's message to Judah reeks with warning and doom. But that is not because of either the desire of God or the power of Assyria to punish little Judah. As our prophet sees it, even though he sometimes fails to make the point absolutely clear, it is because of his people's disregard of the terms of the covenant. Since the Lord cannot bestow the rewards of covenant keepers on covenant breakers, his spokesman can only address his rebellious people in terms of threat and judgment.

Political realism doubtless figured in our prophet's repeated warnings against the challenge of Assyria on the field of battle. But his advice stemmed primarily from an altogether different kind of consideration. For while he was much troubled by Judah's unpreparedness for a head-to-head confrontation with Assyria, he was even more troubled by its unreadiness for a showdown with the Lord. Since that readiness was hindered, above all else, by the blithe assumption that the sovereignty of the Lord could not survive the eclipse of Judah as a sovereign state, First Isaiah turned his heaviest weapons against not the awesome power of mighty Assyria but the insufferable pride of smug Judah. Try as it might to shift the blame onto some other foe, and Judah tried desperately to pin it on both the one on the other side of the Great River (Assyria) and that even more formidable one beyond the Milky Way (the Lord), our prophet would not let Judah off the hook. In season and out, he kept reminding it that the enemy who was doing it in was neither the one without nor the one above but the one within.[8]

Before his people could again serve as the agent of God's mission, they must first feel the lash of divine discipline. So First Isaiah believed. And so he declared, at court and in the marketplace, in the teeth of a skeptical and unheeding audience.

By the time, two centuries later, Second Isaiah appears on the scene, the above circumstances no longer obtain. Jerusalem, harassed and depopulated, lies in ruins (49:14-19; 51:17-20); the temple, now more than ever the scene of all sorts of apostasy, has fallen into the hands of "the uncircumcised and the unclean" (52:1); and the prophet's comrades, "abhorred by the nations" and "the servant(s) of rulers" (49:7), are captives in a foreign land (49:12ff).

And their mood has changed accordingly. Strident arrogance has yielded place to quiet despair, and abject hopelessness has become the order of the day. And there are reasons—good ones, too—for this change. They are not only displaced persons, exiles through no choice of their own, in the land of the successor to Assyria's imperial holdings, namely Babylon, but they are near enough to the center of things to get a close-up of the achievements of a real super power. And they are properly chastened by what they see. Face to face with the military arsenal of Number One of the world's Big Three, they are embarrassed by memory of the pride they once took in the buildings of Jerusalem and the weaponry of Judah.[9] "How could we ever have become so smug," they must have reproached themselves, "about such paltry achievements?"

Should Second Isaiah, under these circumstances, but duplicate the threatening words of First Isaiah, we would rightly suspect him of having turned afflicter of the afflicted. Both the external circumstances and the personal mood of Jewry obviously call for a very different kind of proclamation. Since the impotence of Israel (although the Babylonian exiles came from Judah and

135

have long since ceased to be citizens of an independent state, our prophet does not hesitate to address them as Israel or to treat them as heirs of the faith and task of the covenantal community) is now due to a shortage, not a surplus, of confidence, the people need to hear not a threatening but an encouraging word.[10] And that is precisely the kind of message with which Second Isaiah greets them.

Not only does he promise Israel release from captivity (49:12 ff.), but he assures it of restoration—and soon!—to the land of Palestine and the city of Jerusalem. This happy event will take place close on the heels, and in consequence, of two other salutary developments: (1) the overthrow of Babylon (45:1-7, 14ff.) by a foe from the east whom victory meets at every step; (2) the emergence of Cyrus, the Persian head of state and leader of the aforementioned victorious eastern warrior, as the engineer of both Babylon's fall and the hope of the exiles for turning the table of fortune in Israel's favor (44:24-45:7).

The frequent mention of these developments in Second Isaiah attests to his knowledge of Persia's displacement of Babylon as frontrunner in the game of Imperial Sweepstakes. Such references likewise justify the conclusion that his optimism was not wholly unsupported by recent political developments. Yet political considerations were no more the only than they were the chief ingredient in his proclamation of Israel's restoration and renewal. [11] As in the case of the great prophets before him, most of whom had dispensed the politics of doom, his political pronouncements were derived from his theological convictions, and not vice versa. For while he was obviously both deeply impressed and greatly pleased by the ruler of Persia and his agenda for the nations, what turned this prophet of the exile into a prophet of hope and consolation was not the new politics of Cyrus, but a new appreciation for the mission of the Lord. Cyrus would, in the expectation of Second Isaiah, preside over the reversal of fortune for Babylon and Israel, but he would not work this wonder in his own power or even in his own behalf. He would do it rather as the instrument of the Lord and in behalf of the mission of God.

Apart from this linkage of Cyrus' activity to God's will and power, the enlightened Israelites would likely have written off Second Isaiah's assurances as casually as they dismissed the misleading messages the popular prophets proclaimed to their ancestors. Certainly their recent experience offered slight ground for viewing Persia's military achievement as anything more than simply another episode in the rapidly shifting succession in international politics. Among them there were probably a few left who could recall the tales of their families about the days when Assyria appeared to be unconquerable, yet the end had long since come to Assyria's reign of terror. And many more of them, of course, had been exposed to the stories of Babylonian plunder and invincibility, yet Babylon's day in the sun had set within little more than a half century of its dawn. Why, given these examples, should the Jews have anticipated a different fate for their most recent conquerors? Or that they as subjects of the Persians, unless subject to and supported by a higher power, would not continue to be passed from one foreign overlord to another?

Second Isaiah was much too close to this kind of skepticism to attempt to come to terms with it on the basis of mere conventional Israelite piety. At the same time he was realistic enough to recognize that, if his words of comfort were to have a really consoling effect upon the exiles, they must somehow touch base with Israel's sacred traditions. In short, the situation called for a message embodying a subtle, even delicate, blend of the old with the new—a bringing together of the two in such fashion as simultaneously to reassure the traditionalists and to arouse the innovators.

Second Isaiah rose to the challenge. He linked past and future together through a highly selective appropriation and a keenly imaginative reinterpretation of Israel's traditions. He transformed the key themes in Israelite religion

137

—to mention only those of which we shall take special notice, the Lord's commission of a historical deliverer, the exodus, and the dominion of the Lord—by construing them in a way that focused attention less upon the past than the future deeds of the Lord.

A Persian Agent of the Lord

He retains the emphasis in Israelite tradition on the Lord's use of a historical person to effect the deliverance of his people, but Moses is not the agent of the Lord, the contemplation of whose work leaves our prophet limp with ecstasy. It is, instead, Cyrus of Persia, and his work has not yet been fully accomplished. And it will not be completed until the Lord's servant, Israel, has been renewed and upheld. Thus the work of Cyrus' deliverance, like that of Moses, will have Israel as its object, and it will, instead of canceling God's prior action, demonstrate the fact that God's action cannot be canceled [12] or, to put it positively and in the language of our prophet, that "the word of our God will stand for ever" (40:8). As if to anticipate a dubious response to the assertion of such a connection between the Lord's election of Israel and of Cyrus, Second Isaiah takes an additional bold step in his bid to establish their continuity: not only does he clearly identify the Chooser of Cyrus with the God of Israel's ancestors, but he emphatically subordinates God's choice of Cyrus to his choice of Israel:

Who stirred up one from the east whom victory meets at every step?

. . . .

Who has performed and done this . . . ?

. . . .

I, the Lord, the first, and the last; I am He.

. . . .

But you, Israel, my servant, Jacob, whom I have chosen,

. . . .

saying to you, "You are my servant, I have chosen you

138

and not cast you off"; fear not, for I am with you,
be not dismayed, for I am your God;
I will strengthen you, I will help you,
I will uphold you with my victorious right hand.
(41:2-10)

Thus says the Lord to his anointed (i.e., "his messiah"),
to Cyrus, whose right hand I have grasped, to subdue
nations before him . . ..

"I will go before you and level the mountains,

. . . .
that you may know that it is I, the Lord, the God of
Israel, who call you by your name.
For the sake of my servant Jacob, and Israel my chosen,
I call you by your name, I surname you, though you
do not know me.
I am the Lord, and . . . , besides me there is no God
. . . ." (45:1-5)

The Exodus From Babylon

Our prophet further underscores both the similarity
and the difference between the redemption wrought
under Moses and that about to be effected through Cyrus
by describing the upcoming deliverance in terms of
Israel's escape from Egypt (40:3-5, 41:17-20; 42:14-16;
43:1-3, 14-21; 48:20f.; 49:8-12; 51:9f.; 52:11f.; 55:12f.).
Thus Israel's awe-inspiring origins become in his hands a
type of even more wonderful things to come.[13] Yet he
takes pains to free his hearers of the fear that the exodus
from Babylon will be a mere repetition of the exodus
from Egypt, with its all too rapid decline from glorious
independence into hopeless encirclement into abject
bondage. Despite his description of Israel's imminent
rescue from Babylon under the imagery of its release
from Egypt, Second Isaiah nevertheless calls attention to
the discontinuity between the two exoduses.

After drawing an invidious comparison between the
"former things" (the exodus from Egypt) and the "new

things" (the exodus from Babylon), he calls upon Israel to forget the "former things" (46:8-11). Yet he proceeds to make it impossible for Israel to heed his counsel. He keeps reminding Israel of its exodus from Egypt as if there were no other way of nourishing confidence in its exodus from Babylon. And, of course, there is no other way of achieving this end. For while the splendor and grandeur of the second exodus may dwarf that of the first into seeming insignificance, it will exactly duplicate the escape from Egypt in this most important particular: this act of redemption, like its prototype, will have the Lord as its subject.

The God of Creation

Were our prophet to leave off his theological reconstruction with the foregoing assertion, we would be justified in describing him as an echo—to be sure, a rich and lively echo, but nevertheless an echo—of Israelite tradition. But Second Isaiah does not drop the matter with the establishment of the Lord's identity as the author of both exoduses. He proceeds to swell the boundaries of the Lord's domain. Just as he celebrates his control over the history of Israel (41:17-20; 43:16-21; 48:20-22; 55:6-13), he likewise calls attention to his rule in the affairs of Africa (45:14-17), of Babylon (43:14 f; 47:1-15; 52:11 f.) and of Persia (40:1-7; 44:24-28; 45:1-13; 48:12-16). And even more importantly, he identifies this sovereign Lord of all history with the sovereign Lord of all creation.[14]

We can fully appreciate this development only if we recall the circumstances in which Second Isaiah achieved his understanding of God. He was exposed, in addition to the traditions of his people, to those of the Babylonians. The latter included, among other items, a myth called the Enuma Elish,[15] the widely influential Babylonian tale of creation. It details the story of how a quarrel among the deities resulted in the transformation of formless matter by Marduk into an ordered universe. Babylonian worship was directed towards Marduk, who spread forth the earth and stretched out the heavens, lest he relax his vigilance and allow a rival deity once again to reduce order to chaos.

The Persian defeat of Babylon sullied the claims of Marduk's worshipers, but the influence of Enuma Elish continued to be felt among the Jews. Genesis 1:1-2:4a, the first of the biblical stories of creation, derives from the activity of exiled priests who borrowed extensively from the Babylonian account of creation. And, of course, Second Isaiah reflects its influence repeatedly (40:21 f.; 42:5; 44:24; 45:12; 48:13, 51:13, 16; cf. 42:10-17; 51:9-11).

But our prophet has no interest in the doctrine of creation as a theological abstraction. He is not in any sense a philosophical, historical or even systematic theologian. Insofar as the professional label of theologian applies at all in his case, the appropriate qualifier is pastoral. His concern for what God is in himself is strictly secondary to his interest in God's availability to human beings and his significance for human life. If he could relieve Israelite anxiety without the consideration of questions of this sort, he might very well forego them. But he cannot console the people of Israel, on either his terms or theirs, without asking them. For better or worse, the question of Israel's destiny has become intertwined with that of the origin of the world.

Second Isaiah repeatedly grounds his message of comfort for Israel in his claim for the Lord as the God of creation. For example, he has the Lord preface his reassuring words to Israel, "I am the Lord, I have . . . taken you by the hand and kept you" (42:6), with the ringing declaration:

Thus says God, the Lord
    who created the heavens and stretched them out,
    who spread forth the earth and what comes from it,

> Who gives breath to the people upon it
>   and spirit to those who walk in it: . . .
>   (42:5)

Here it is almost as if our prophet had taken a leaf out of the Babylonian Psalter and substituted the name of the Lord for that of Marduk. We can only guess at the reason for this usage, but it was very likely prompted by misgivings on the part of those to whom he addresses his bold words about the victorious rise of Cyrus and the imminent restoration of Israel. "Why," they lament, "should we take your promises seriously? For granted the will of the Lord of Cyrus to trigger a new exodus, why should we believe that he has the power to accomplish his mission?"

"You should believe that the Lord will accomplish his mission," answers the prophet, in effect, "because the Lord of Cyrus is the God of creation." Or, to employ the prophet's own words, "you should believe because 'The Lord is the everlasting God, the Creator of the ends of the earth. He . . . gives power to the faint, and to him who has no might he increases strength.' " (40:28 ff.).

Just as earlier he has subordinated the Lord's choice of Cyrus to his election of Israel, so now he invokes the work of God in creation to inspire confidence in his impending act of redemption (42:10-17). The pastoral motivation of the prophet's celebration of the Lord's power becomes even clearer in 51:9-11. In this remarkable passage he assimilates the themes of the creation, freely employing elements drawn from both the Enuma Elish myth (vs. 9), and the Israelite accounts of the exodus from Egypt, with special emphasis on the crossing of the Reed Sea (vs. 10), to that of the future deliverance from Babylon (vs. 11). Even without this last verse, whose authenticity has been questioned, there is no mistaking the purpose of the prophet's cry to Israel. He recalls the mighty acts of God in order to rekindle his people's faith in God's mission—and Israel's.

142

The Mission of Israel

Second Isaiah deserves special credit for turning Israelite theology back onto a global course, but he does not effect this achievement at the expense of belief in Israel's election. At times it almost seems as if he is at pains to intensify the notion that Israel holds a special place in the divine affection. Not only does he also refer to "The Lord, who created the heavens and . . . spread forth the earth" (42:5) as "the Creator of Israel" (43:15), but he repeatedly hails him as Israel's king (e.g., 43:15) and Redeemer (41:14; 43:14; 44:24; 47:4; 48:17; 49:7, 26; 54:5, 8). And, even more strikingly, he employs familiar language to describe the Lord's care for Israel. He has borne Israel as a father from the womb, and he will continue to bear it until gray hair crowns its old age (46:3). "For," declares "the Holy One of Israel, your (i.e., Israel's) Savior" to the people of Israel:

> Because you are precious in my eyes, and honored, and I love you,
> I will say to the north, Give up, and to the south, Do not withhold; bring my sons from afar and my daughters from the end of the earth. . . .
> (43:3-6)

But forgiveness and not merit is the ground of Israel's hope for renewal. For while our prophet can once bring himself to say that Israel has received "double for all her sins" (40:2), what he typically emphasizes on this score is not the excess of Israel's punishment, but the enormity of its transgressions and guilt. Even the foregoing word of pity is prefaced with a reference to its iniquity. The Lord will restore Israel for his sake, not its own, and will forgive the people despite their sinfulness, and not because they are innocent. All these points are driven home in a highly luminous and meaning-ladened passage:

143

Thus says the Lord, your Redeemer, the Holy One of Israel:

. . . .
". . . you did not call upon me, O Jacob;
  but you have been weary of me, O Israel!
You have not brought me your . . . burnt offerings,
  or honored me with your sacrifices.

. . . .
But you have burdened me with your sins,
  you have wearied me with your iniquities.

"I, I am he
  who blots out your transgressions
  for my own sake
  and I will not remember your sins." (43:14-25)

The contrast between the Lord's indictment of Israel at the beginning of this utterance and his words of consolation at the end is almost startling, yet "it is also deliberate. The sole reason for making the proclamation is given in the words, 'for my own sake.' The proclamation is the execution of the God-given task of comforting: 'Say to her that her iniquity is pardoned.' " [16] "Tell Israel," in other words, "that, thanks be to God—and to no one else, least of all Israel herself—her election as God's people still stands."

The Lord's pardon of Israel, already attested in Cyrus' triumph over Babylon, through whom God has disciplined his people, is doubtless the most crucial element in Isaiah's message of consolation to Israel, yet it but sets the stage for the prophet's assurance of Israel's imminent restoration to its homeland.

When Israel laments that its present humiliation confirms its abandonment by the Lord, Second Isaiah again turns to the family for figures of speech with which to enforce his consoling words. Not only does he assure Israel that the Lord's love for it exceeds that of a mother for her unweaned child (49:15), but he denies, invoking the marriage metaphor employed so boldly by Hosea, that the Lord has granted Israel a bill of divorcement. Even though Israel is in exile because it abandoned the Lord, the Lord has not abandoned—and he will not abandon—Israel in its exile. Neither will he leave Israel to its own devices or, for that matter, to the consequences of its own devices. Its rebellion against him has not altered his intention for it. Just as temporarily its disloyalty for him has nullified his loyalty for it, ultimately this situation shall be reversed, and the Lord's faithfulness will cancel the effects of Israel's faithlessness.

As if to acknowledge the tameness of this domestic analogy, the prophet dredges up a figure more likely to kindle the interest of brokers in power politics (54:16 ff.). After casting the Lord in the paradoxical roles of sovereign over the world's leaders in the arms race and tender protector of Israel, he proclaims the Lord's intention of blunting the weapons and thwarting the aims of Israel's enemies. The Lord, he declares, will redeem Israel from the tyrants who now hold it captive (49:22-26). Yet the impact of his redemptive action will not be confined to Israel. Just as he shall pave the way for its return to Palestine, it will prepare the way for him to extend his rule over the nations. Then Israel, now the servant of the nations, will again become the servant of the Lord (49:7-13; cf 41:8, 42:19). And Zion, bathed in beauty and righteously governed, will dwell in peace with both God and its neighbors (54:11-17).

Yet the happy consequences of Israel's restoration to Zion and its environs will not be confined to Israel alone. God's redemption of Israel will have a transforming impact on the outlook not only of the nations but also of Israel. Just as the nations' contempt for Israel will be replaced by astonishment at its elevation (49:7-13), Israel's preoccupation with its own privileged status will yield place to concern for its mission to the nations (42:5-9, 14-16; 43:8-13; 44:3 ff.; 45:22 ff.; 49:1-16; 51:4 ff.; 55:1 ff.). "It is too light a thing," declares the prophet as spokesman for the Lord,[17] for my agent simply to restore "the preserved of Israel; I will give you as a light to the nations, that my salvation may reach to the end of the earth" (49:6).

The similarity of the language in this description of Israel's mission to that in the prophet's description of God's role in creation is not accidental. He has merely redrawn the scope of Israel's mission to fit the extended boundaries of the Lord's realm (42:1-9; cf. 49:1-6, the last verse of which is quoted above). Yet it will not do to say that Israel's mission in the view of this great prophet is exactly what it was in the estimate of his preexilic predecessors. For while it is true that he follows them in cutting the cloth of Israel's mission on the pattern of God's mission, his acute awareness of the Lord's role as Creator compels him to redefine Israel's mission in universal terms. Thus while Israel continues to be one with the preexilic Israel of promise, the boundaries of that promise have been greatly enlarged.

The unity of Israel's mission with the Lord's becomes most explicit in 42:7-16. At the beginning of this passage the Lord commands Israel "to open the eyes that are blind"; it concludes with a promise from the Lord that he himself "will lead the blind." Not only has Israel become interchangeably with God the subject of action designed to alleviate life's burdens (blindness, as employed in this context typifies the "human suffering . . . due to man's creaturely status" [18]), but Israel has adopted the target of God's reconciling work as the beneficiary of its own redemptive action. "God has designated Israel to be a light to the world and to mediate salvation to it; she is to bring enlightenment and liberation to others." [19]

The remarkable thing about this enlargement of the scope of Israel's work is that our prophet effects it without at all impairing its quality. In fact, the task of God's people, as he defines it, envisions much the same goals— genuine compassion (e.g., 42:7), social justice, (42:1, 7, 15; 51:4) pure and enthusiastic worship (49:5-7; 55:4)— as those to which the great prophets of the preexilic period directed Israel's attention and energies. Only now, instead of pursuing these ends for the benefit only of itself, Israel, the servant of the Lord, names the whole of God's creation as the target and beneficiary of its service.

Actually, this version of the nature and dimensions of Israel's mission does not originate with Second Isaiah. It goes back at least to the period of the JE historian, whose summons to Abraham and his descendants calls upon them not only to become a blessing but also to serve as the vehicle of God's blessing to "all the families of the earth" (Gen. 12:1-3); which, being translated into modern terms, means that they are called of God not only to receive his love for themselves, but to share it with the whole of humankind.

The introduction of this universal note at the very beginning of the story of salvation was doubtless intended as a warning to Israel that it could remain the object of God's love only by becoming its bearer to others. And, at the same time, it stood as a reminder to Israel that, "right from the first," as Westermann observes, "God had the whole world in view in his special activity with this nation (namely, Israel): it is in this nation that God journeyed with the nations of the world . . . in all stages of its history up to the collapse of the state and the uprooting of the nation." [20]

At the time and in the place—the period of the exile in Babylon—where, for many Israelites, the world has come to an end, second Isaiah rediscovers the world as the proper field and focus of Israel's mission. As a consequence, his version of the prophetic summons of Israel to embrace its destiny as the people of God reflects this highly significant, if not entirely new, development: the call for its enlistment as the servant of God becomes, at the same time, the call for its commitment to the service of humankind.

The Method of the Servant

Second Isaiah's message of comfort is motivated not by personal sympathy but by theological conviction. That is clear from the way he organizes his prophecies. They are set within the framework of a structure that is held together, at both ends, by affirmations concerning the word of God.

The prologue highlights the contrast between the transciency of all things human and the indestructibility of God's word. When the prophet, called to serve as Israel's comforter, asks what he is to say, he is told to cry:

. . . All flesh is grass,
    and all its beauty is like the flower of the field.
. . . .
The grass withers, the flower fades;
    the word of our God will stand for ever. (40:6-8)

The words in verse 7, identifying "the people as grass," may be a later addition to the text, but they exactly capsule our prophet's recognition that the divine purpose does not vary with the fortune of this or that group of human beings.

"The 'word of God' spoken to Israel in her past history is not part and parcel of the inevitable (or, we might add, of the not so inevitable) decay: it stands, it persists, it abides. . . . Nothing in existence has the power to make it void, not even the desperate plight which was Israel's." [21]

In the epilogue to his prophecy Second Isaiah adds to this assurance concerning the durability of God's word the further consolation that it shall achieve the end for which it was spoken.

For as the rain and the snow come down from heaven,
    and . . . water the earth,
making it bring forth and sprout,
    giving seed to the sower and bread to the eater,

so . . . my word . . . shall not return to me empty,
but it shall accomplish that which I purpose,
    and prosper in the thing for which I sent it. (55:10 ff.)

The exile may have put the divine purpose out of Israel's
reach, but it has not put Israel beyond God's reach. And
God is still determined that his purpose, somehow, shall
be accomplished through Israel.

But how? That now becomes the question at which we
must take a closer look. At the outset, it can be said,
considering the way Second Isaiah redefines the nature
and scope of the mission alike of God and Israel, we
should hardly expect from him and his disciples a conventional solution to this problem. In fact, we would
have occasion for surprise only if they should fail to
confront us with a demand for the radical rethinking of
this whole issue. Even so, were it not for the fact we have
heard so many sermons on the theme of vicarious suffering, we would still probably be shocked by the limits
to which they push this doctrine as the key to Israel's
lot and destiny.

To be sure, this idea is carried to an unparalleled
degree in the famous servant songs (the passages, 42:1-4;
49:1-6; 50:4-9; 52:13-53:12, previously identified as the
songs of the servant of the Lord), but it is approximated
elsewhere (e.g., in the explanation of Israel's punishment
in 42:18-25 and 48:17-19; cf. also 44:21-23; 55:1-5). Even
if, suddenly, the servant songs should be removed from
Second Isaiah and the problem of the servant's identity
in relation to Israel should go away, we would still be
struck at the difference between Israel's role as it is
typically depicted, on the one hand, and as it gets reflected in Second Isaiah, on the other. Certainly the
difference between the role of the servant as depicted
in the four servant songs and that of Israel as seen elsewhere in Second Isaiah is one of degree rather than kind.
And the degree is not so great but that we may legitimately treat the two groups of passages as a theological,
if not quite a literary, unit. At least we are justified in

149

so viewing them in determining Second Isaiah's view of Israel's method of accomplishing its mission or, to put it more exactly, of enabling God to achieve his mission through Israel.

If nothing else, the above-cited passages dealing with Israel's punishment disprove the popularly assumed irreconcilability of the divine election of Israel with its liability to suffering. While conceding that Israel's exile does not mark the fulfillment of God's intention for it, our prophet nevertheless construes it as a witness to the righteous rule of God (48:17-19). In other words, God will not compromise his character for the sake of his elect, but he will, if need be, chasten his elect for the sake of his honor. In fact, that is precisely how Second Isaiah interprets the ordeal of Israel's captivity in Babylon: for ignoring his teaching and refusing to walk in his ways, the Lord himself delivered Israel into the hands of robbers and plunderers (42:18-25). Quite clearly, since this Israel is one with the Israel whom the Lord has "chosen . . . and not cast . . . off" (41:9), the notion of Israel's glorification of God in its extremity can hardly be reckoned an idea that is totally alien to the mind of our prophet.

Now we turn our attention to two passages outside the servant songs which cast Israel in the role of the Lord's servant. While neither of these oracles speaks of the servant's self-debasement, the subject of the redeeming action whereby Israel becomes witness to the nations is the Lord himself.

In the first (44:21-23) of these passages, God's redemption of Israel becomes an occasion for a celebration of unprecedented proportions. When the Lord redeems Israel, despite its manifold sins and transgressions, the whole of the created universe joins in a hymn of praise to Israel's God. Here Israel's servant status is dramatized by the fact that what evokes this response is not an act of Israel in behalf of the Lord, but an act of the Lord in behalf of Israel. True enough, it does not play a demeaning role, yet it is nevertheless the case that Israel serves

150

the cause of God and neighbor at the will not of itself but of another.

Despite a shift in the subject matter of the second passage (55:1-5), the roles of both God and Israel remain pretty much what they were in 44:21-23. The Lord plays host to a banquet to which Israel is invited to bring nothing save a hearty appetite for food and celebration, and Israel comes to the feast on God's terms. Moreover, it becomes witness among the nations to the grace and providence of God. If here the servant becomes the guest and the host the servant, it is still a fact—and, in all probability, the main point of the passage—that the guest serves the host's purpose by calling the attention of the nations to the room at his table for other guests.

The first of the servant songs (42:1-4) portrays Israel as God's agent in the establishment of justice. Yet his almost passive manner belies his revolutionary function. For if persistence and faithfulness are hallmarks of his style, so also are meekness and quietness. It is almost as if he had determined to call attention to God by not calling attention to himself.

The spokesman in the next servant song sounds very much like the personification of the prophetic movement throughout the period of the great prophets, from Amos to Second Isaiah (49:1-6). Addressing the nations, he recalls that his original commission, echoing the mission of the great prophets of the preexilic period, entailed work among the people of Israel that God might be glorified through them (verses 1-3, 5). In this effort, by his own admission, he failed, but the Lord vindicates him and his work by broadening his commission. God now appoints him—the same servant, mind you, who, by all recognizable standards of success, has so miserably failed—to glorify the Lord by carrying his salvation to the ends of the earth. If we are startled here by the movement from a little paradox, the Lord's reckoning of failure as success, to a bigger paradox, the Lord's entrustment of the mediation of salvation to all the world by one who could not even mediate it to all Israel, there is no excuse for it. After all, the task to which the prophet is commissioned, originally as well as later, involves the biggest paradox of all, one "that no one could ever have imagined —a servant is to glorify his master!" [22]

The third servant song (50:4-9)—in which, incidentally, God's agent is called not servant but disciple, though cast in a clearly prophetic role—further accentuates the paradoxical character of the servant's work as mediator of God's purpose and mission: though faithful in the extreme in both receiving and declaring God's word, he is made the target of unending abuse and insults by the people to whom he proclaims it; and though convinced that his suffering is willed by God, he nevertheless looks forward to his vindication at God's hands (50:4-9). Here it is broadly hinted that a positive relationship exists between the servant's experience of affliction and God's gift of salvation, but that connection has yet to be spelled out.

In the final servant song (52:13-53:12), this connection does get spelled out, fully and clearly; in fact, the terms are almost as difficult to misunderstand as they are to accept. This effect is achieved by heightening the contrast between the servant's fate at human hands and his impact on human destiny.

Shame and rejection and contempt hound him from the cradle to the grave (53:1-9). His life consists of a dreadful brew of illness and persecution, and his death, lonely and unmourned, does not come until after he has been mercilessly flogged and disfigured. Not even the cemetery brings relief from his troubles, for he is buried with disbelievers and evildoers. Quite clearly, if ever any person could have moved us to question his creation by God, he would have been the one. But look at what happens to him and, even more importantly, through him!

The servant's disfigurement and ignominy nothwithstanding, God does not join the ranks of his enemies, but quite the contrary (53:10-13). Not only does he take pleasure in his life, but he intervenes in his behalf after his death. And he exalts him by appointing him to make "intercession for the transgressors."

Following this reversal, an equally remarkable transformation overtakes the nations (52:13-15). Their astonished kings acknowledge the Lord's exalted one to be none other than the humiliated servant at whom they have scoffed and on whom they have poured their abuse. Now they are ready to receive the light from him whom, formerly, they were ready to consign to the outer darkness.

Even more remarkably, the servant's neighbors are now ready to accept the blame for his sorry lot. "Surely," they confess, "he has borne *our* (not his) griefs and carried *our* (not his) sorrows; . . . he was wounded for *our* (not his) transgressions, he was bruised for *our* (not his) iniquities" (53:4-6). Yet all this does not transpire without divine approval: "the Lord . . . laid on him the iniquity of us all" (verse 6); "it was the will of the Lord to bruise him" (verse 10). Nor does it fail to advance his purpose: "by his knowledge shall the . . . servant . . . make many to be accounted righteous" (53:11). Just as the servant relieves others of their guilt by taking it upon himself, he frees them from the punishment due their sin by suffering in their stead. He delivers them from the penalties of justice by absorbing the pains of injustice.

The servant stands Israel's—and, for that matter, most—traditional thinking about suffering squarely on its proverbial head. Israel had been taught to view suffering as punishment for one's sins. But the servant was suffering not for his but others' sins. And our prophet, instead of pondering the question of why God should permit this travesty of justice, simply asserts that God has used the servant's suffering "to break through the stubborn wall in a sinful (humanity's) heart and to open their eyes to his truth." [23] Onlookers "taste his redemption in the way he suffers." [24]

Second Isaiah and his disciples cast Israel in a new role—that of servant rather than master—in the drama of redemption. They abandon the vision of Israel as striding conqueror among fallen subjects for that of Israel as willing sufferer in the service of God's mission.

They do not promise good will and fair treatment at human hands to those who surmount the genealogical and geographical barriers to God's kingdom. In fact, they warn them of the possibility of quite the opposite. They offer them no gain at all, save the knowledge of doing God's will and extending his reign. Not only do they extol "purity of heart" [25] as defined by Kierkegaard—"to will one thing," namely God's will, "alone"—but they encourage us to believe that the servant of the Lord neither seeks nor needs any other reward than this.

That is why, in their summons of Israel—and, through Israel, of us—to a decision for destiny, they link together the mission of the Lord and his people with the method of his servant. For if we, as the Lord's people, cannot separate our mission from his, neither can we separate the decision for destiny from the decision for service. On this point the greatest of all the commentators on Second Isaiah left no room—none at all—for doubt: "And Jesus called and said to them, 'You know that . . . whoever would be great among you must be your servant, and whoever would be first among you must be slave of all' " (Mk. 10:42-44).

FOOTNOTES

[1] What is more, John H. Otwell, *A New Approach to the Old Testament* (London: SCM Press, 1967), p. 76, wryly observes: "Few of us would welcome them as friends or would want one as a pastor."

[2] See Claus Westermann, *Isaiah 40-66*, trans. D. M. G. Stalker (Philadelphia: The Westminster Press, 1969), pp. 295-308, for a discussion of Third Isaiah, with special attention to the relationship of chaps. 40-55 to 56-66.

[3] As evidenced, e.g., in a recent book of Holy Week sermons by Carlyle Marney, *The Suffering Servant* (N.Y.: Abingdon Press, 1965).

[4] Gerhard von Rad, *Old Testament* Theology, II, trans. D. M. G. Stalker (N.Y.: Harper & Row, 1965), pp. 276ff., notes that this theme is not as "isolated . . . in the prophetic message as it has often been supposed to be."

[5] For an indication of the scope and character of such additions, see Otto Kaiser's two vols., *Isaiah 1-12 (1972)* and *Isaiah 13-39* (1974), both trans., R. A. Wilson (Philadelphia: The Westminster Press).

[6] Abraham Heschel, *The Prophets* (N.Y.: Harper & Row, 1962), p. 76, says of Isaiah of Jerusalem, e.g., that "his primary concern is not Judah's foreign policy, but . . . the inner state of the nation."

[7] Bright, *A History of Israel,* pp. 288-91.

[8] The God of the prophets "set a plumb line in the midst of Israel," writes Levi Olan, "The Stone . . . the . . . Builders Rejected," *Interpreting the Prophetic Tradition* (Harry M. Orlinsky, ed.; Cincinnati: Hebrew Union College Press, 1969), p. 129, "and his eyes are on the sinful people to destroy it. . ."

[9] For a description of the Jews in exile, see Curt Kuhl, *The Prophets of Israel,* trans. R. J. Ehrlich and J. P. Smith (London: Oliver and Boyd, 1960), pp. 136-52.

[10] The prophet's message of "comfort . . . is consistent," observes James Muilenburg, "Isaiah 40-66: Introduction and Exegesis," *The Interpreter's Bible,* V (1956), p. 424, "with (his) message of an imminent redemption."

[11] *Ibid.,* pp. 398-413.

[12] Westermann, *A Thousand Years and a Day,* p. 237.

[13] Bernhard W. Anderson, "Exodus Typology in Second Isaiah," *Israel's Prophetic Heritage* (B. W. Anderson and W. Harrelson, eds.; N.Y.: Harper & Row, 1962), pp. 177-95.

[14] Lindblom, *Prophecy in Ancient Israel,* pp. 376ff.

[15] Pritchard, *Ancient Near Eastern Texts,* pp. 60-72.

[16] Westermann, *Isaiah 40-66, p. 133.*

[17] Admittedly, this description comes at the climax of one of the songs of the servant of the Lord, a group of passages often denied Second Isaiah, but I agree with those many writers who hold that the views expressed in these songs accurately mirror the thoughts of our prophet. See, e.g., G. von Rad, *Old Testament Theology,* II, p. 251, who thinks these songs have so much in common with the rest of Second Isaiah that we have no reason to ascribe them to a different author.

[18] Westermann, *Isaiah 40-66,* p. 100.

[19] *Ibid.,* p. 101.

[20] *A Thousand Years and a Day,* pp. 240ff.

[21] Westermann, *Isaiah 40-66,* p. 42.

[22] *Ibid.,* p. 208.

[23] James D. Smart, *Servants of the Word* (Phila.: The Westminster Press, 1960), p. 86.

[24] Marney, *The Suffering Servant,* p. 37.

[25] Title of a work by Kierkegaard translated by Douglas V. Steere (rev. ed.; N.Y.: Harper & Bros., 1938).

155

VIII

THE LEGACY OF THE GREAT PROPHETS

The great prophets were the heirs of a noble tradition. And we, thanks in no small measure to them, are the heirs of a nobler tradition. For while they may more aptly be called restorers than reformers of Israel's ancestral faith, they nevertheless transformed that faith in the process of restoring it.

Yet, given its source and essential character, it could scarcely have been otherwise. Inasmuch as it was rooted and centered in the living and sovereign and surprising Lord of history, they really had but one alternative to joining the ongoing dialogue between their inherited faith and contemporary culture. That was to deny the faith itself. For just as the "former things" led them to anticipate the "new things," once the "new things" had come to pass, they could no longer fully understand or explain the "former things" without one eye on the "new things." Then, as these "new things" took their place among the "former things," they could not avoid the anticipation of still additional "new things." In short, the more they practiced the ancestral faith, the less content they were merely to praise the faith of their ancestors. They were too busy investing the spiritual capital of their forebears to think about hoarding it.

If we would do justice by their legacy to us, we can scarcely do better than take our cue from their treatment of the legacy of their ancestors. We must take time to criticize our heritage with the same kind of zeal and respect for the personal revelation of the living God as they exhibited in passing judgment on their heritage. And that, as we have seen, is a tall order, indeed. If we have any doubt on this point, we have but to consider the ways, noted below, in which they altered the stands of their ancestors. In fact, since the frontiers on which they labored have yet to be fully explored and occupied, we cannot indicate their achievements in their situation without, at the same time, suggesting their relevance for us in our situation.

This would not be the case, of course, if their legacy to us consisted of a series of neat answers to religion's standard questions, but this is not at all the stuff of which their bequest is made. For while they were by no means short on answers, it is not because of their positions—rather, it is because of their posture—that they provide us with exactly the right point of departure in handling the call to our God-appointed destiny. Not only do they bring us hard against the requirement of having to make "ever new decisions as conditions change and experience grows," [1] but they do it under circumstances of instructive significance for us in our ongoing struggle with the competing claims of apparent contradictions. That is why, in the first half of this final chapter of our study, we shall take a close look at the combination of apparent opposites in their revision of the Mosaic faith. Following that, we shall briefly recall its personal cost to those who drafted it.

The Combination of Apparent Opposites

The list of such combinations could be extended indefinitely. Those of which we shall take note are surely among the most obvious and the most relevant, but they do not exhaust the possibilities.

Before proceeding, I should point out that, since I look on this portion of our discussion as a way of summarizing my findings without repeating the language of earlier chapters, the elaboration of these pairs will be minimal. I will, in each instance, after briefly indicating the resolution of the paradox in question by the great prophets, call attention to the direction in which they seem to be pointing us. This summons may take the form either of suggesting implications or raising leading questions. In no case will it take the form of specific directives. For just as the application to life of what the great prophets learned from their mentors in the faith required of them ever new decisions to meet the changing circumstances and experiences of their life, so the application to our life of what we learn from the prophets will require ever new decisions of us.[2]

1. *The One and the Many*. The JE historian's assimilation of world to Israelite history was matched by the extension of the Lord's dominion to the uttermost limits of creation. That in itself was no mean achievement. What made it doubly significant is the fact that he effected this transformation without seriously breaching or diminishing God's concern. By setting the election of Israel's ancestry within the context of the history of humankind, he kindled the suspicion of a cause-and-effect relationship between the failure of the line of Adam and the call of the line of Abram. He not only made it perfectly clear that this shift did not mean God's abandonment of his purpose for persons in the mass, but he left his successors with the question whether Israel would have been elected at all had not humankind defected. After him, the role of Israel could no longer be settled solely on the basis of its old election traditions; henceforth, Israel's destiny in relation to God could not be determined without consideration of his relation to other peoples, and most especially those with whom Israel came into immediate contact.

Yet it was only gradually that the prophets evolved the wider implications of the JE writer's equation of the Lord of Israel with the God of creation. Amos abetted the process by giving the Lord credit for the exodus not only of the Israelites but also of the Syrians and Philistines; Hosea, by asserting the Lord's control over nature

158

as well as history; Isaiah, by asserting the Lord's use of the Assyrians as his instrument for the chastisement of Israel; and Jeremiah, by interpreting Judah's exile to Babylon as the Lord's work. Then Second Isaiah and his disciples climaxed this development by greeting Cyrus of Persia as God's agent in the new exodus of Israel. In so doing they raised radically new questions for their readers by portraying the Lord's servant as the worker of redemption for the nations through voluntary suffering. Among these questions we would have to include the following: Can particularism ever be anything more than a provisional and temporary strategy for the advancement of true universalism? Is it not the case that God, instead of electing Israel in place of others, elected Israel for the sake of others?

Few of the modern heirs of the biblical tradition, whether Jewish or Christian, European or American, have been able to sidetrack this inquiry. And, by and large, they have answered it in the affirmative. To be sure, we Christians, having spiritualized Israel into the New Israel, and we Americans, having substituted the nation of America for that of Israel, have had to rephrase the question as follows: Is it not the case that God, instead of electing the American and Christian communities— assuming that God did, indeed, elect them at all—in place of other peoples, elected them for the sake of other peoples?

We Christians have answered this inquiry with an emphatic affirmative. Our late great world-encompassing and ever-expanding missionary movement removed all room for doubt on this point. And our response as Americans has been much the same. To that fact our now-defunct colonies once bore eloquent witness, for invariably, in our defense of these holdings, we rationalized them by pointing to the benefits they stood to gain from us.

If this answer does not come as easily as previously, there are reasons why. For one thing, there is the changing—if not *changed!*—attitude of the citizens of the

159

Third World. To put it bluntly, it will no longer wash in their eyes. They are tired of being patronized by those who come among them in the name of him who became the servant of all, and they are weary of being developed to the great profit not of themselves but of their self-appointed benefactors. And there is, in addition to this external pressure, a growing conviction within the Christian community that in this whole area a break-through on the order of that made by Second Isaiah is long overdue. If the God of the great prophets is one with the God of Jesus of Nazareth, who has not left himself without a witness in any place or time, why should others not feel as compelled to bear witness to God among us as we among them? In short, is not Missionary Boulevard—or, to put it politically, the promotion of the self-development of the peoples of the world—a two-way street, and must not the traffic move in both directions?

It will take great courage, possibly greater courage than we can muster, to face up to this challenge. Perhaps we would rather leave it to the next generation. If so, that is a sure sign that we would rather admire the mantle of the great prophet than wear it.

2. *Faith and Culture*. The culture in which the Mosaic faith took root stood centuries away from that of monarchic Israel during the heyday of the great prophets. The culture of the former period was nomadic-pastoral; that of the latter, agricultural-commercial. Hand in hand with each of these cultural types went a predisposition toward a certain style of life and a matching system of values. Accordingly, the most ardent adherents to the Mosaic faith held that the two cultures could at no point be combined without the ancestral faith itself being compromised. Judging by the measure of their sensitivity to the inevitable link between faith and culture, the great prophets must have been tempted by this response to the cultural challenge of their day, but if so, they successfully resisted this temptation. For like the JE historian, their mentor and model in the faith, they construed the

160

reduction of the conflict between Mosaic faith and commercial civilization to a simple either/or as a gross oversimplification. They accepted it, instead, as an invitation for a fresh and thorough examination of each from the standpoint of the other. Instead of merely heaping praise on the reformers of yesteryears, they paid them the supreme compliment of adopting their posture. By refusing uncritical acceptance of the faith of the fathers, they demonstrated their belief that the Lord is a living God. By the same token, in withholding blanket endorsement of the prevailing culture, they bore witness to their belief that the living God is the truly sovereign Lord.

The significance of this solution to the problem of the relationship between faith and culture can scarcely be exaggerated. That it helped forestall both the eclipse of Mosaic faith and its premature calcification there can be little doubt. But even more importantly, it confirmed the Israelite people's commitment to the way of dialogue as the course to follow in meeting the challenge of change. This is not to suggest that their descendants did not sometimes reduce this challenge to a sham battle, yet their dialectical view of the relationship between faith and culture finally won the day. And the quest for alternative solutions to the hard problems that emerged in this conflict went ahead, despite the vigorous efforts of partisan spokesmen for each side to call a halt to the debate.

Undeterred by past failures, culture's partisans are still hard at it. We Christians have fallen upon difficult days in our efforts to keep this dialogue going. "What," we are asked, "can a faith cradled in a stable possibly have to say to this generation to which moon-walking has become so commonplace that network television no longer feels obliged to give it continuous coverage?" Should we answer, "About as much as the desert-born faith of the Mosaic traditions had to say to monarchic Israel," we would probably get the same kind of brushoff as that to which Jereboam I and Amaziah subjected

Amos. And we would probably be as right in thus analyzing our situation as Amos was in his analysis of Israel's.

3. *Divine Sovereignty and Human Freedom.* The solution of the great prophets to the problem of this relationship was thoroughly anticipated in the JE history of Israel. But this central fact about their resolution of this paradox merits renewed emphasis: Even though they treat the two with equal respect and seriousness, they do not deal with them as if they moved on the same level. As is most clearly revealed in the Babylonian conquest of Judah, God can shrink the freedom of human beings, but human beings cannot reduce the sovereignty of God. The benevolent design of God triumphs over the wicked design of his malevolent children. They may temporarily frustrate the grace of God, but they cannot finally thwart his power or his purpose. They can, by their rebellion and disobedience, cut themselves off from the fruits of life, the joys of faithfulness, the gifts of obedience. But they cannot undermine the sovereignty of God by the simple expedient of disregarding his commands. When people thus abuse their freedom, and this is precisely what they do when they defy God, they neither cancel nor neutralize the divine sovereignty. They simply turn it from an instrument of blessing into a vehicle of wrath. They mock the prophet's call to decision by electing for themselves—and others, as well—a destiny other than that which God intended for them.

There are those who feel that the oil-rich nations, by their price-gouging tactics; the food-rich nations, by their refusal to feed the hungry; the textile-manufacturing nations, by their refusal to clothe the naked; and the nuclear arms-making nations, by their fear-mongering politics, are on the verge of converting the grace of God into his judgment. Perhaps you share this fear. If you do, you are probably a greater debtor to the great prophets than you think.

162

4. *Human Heritage and Divine Demands.* Israelite traditions become something more in the great prophet's hands than mere connecting links between past and future generations. They do not relate them for the sake of awakening in their fellows an overweening feeling of dependence on their ancestors. They transmit them, rather, from the perspective of the faith to which they seek to win their hearers.

This is not to deny the influence of tradition in the shaping of their faith, but to assert the influence of their faith in the shaping of tradition. Instead of accentuating the dissimilarity between the situation of their ancestors and that of their contemporaries, the great prophets stress this one thing the two groups share in common: both occupy a common status before a common judge, the selfsame judge who defines the law by his demands and acquits or convicts those charged under it by his deeds. He is, of course, the Lord of heaven and earth, the God with whom Israel had—and has—finally to come to terms.

The great prophets' story of Israel does not become a part of "sacred" history because of the special sanctity of the people of whom they write. They do not ignore or downplay the fact that many Israelites, like Jacob, the patriarch from whom Israel gets its name, frequently display a singularly secular and even selfish bias. It is "sacred" history because "the people who work and suffer in it work and suffer as they do in virtue of their relationship to God." [3] And it is "sacred" history because the great prophets do not suppress the repeated efforts of the fathers to deny or mute this relationship. By telling it like it was, they leave their hearers without excuse for failing to see that it is with God and his demand alone that they, in the final analysis, must reckon.

Many readers of the Bible feel that the great prophets not only leave us exactly where they left their contemporaries, before God, but also precisely as they left their contemporaries, without excuse. Perhaps this is the feeling with which they leave you. If it is, then rejoice, for this is how they should leave us all.

An Example in Involvement

Who were these men who leave us in the throes of the divine-human encounter? What was a great prophet like? What can we learn from such a one? While he has much to teach us about how to cope with life's paradoxes—the list could easily be extended by noting how he related the sacred and the secular, privilege and duty, continuity and change—through the exercise of reason, his most important lesson to us comes at the point where the exercise of reason gives way to the exercise of risk. He was the decision for destiny to which he summons us.

If now we should ask what it was that he risked for the sake of his calling, the answer would give us a personal profile in bold relief of the great prophet. This is not to suggest that, if as much could be said for us, we would be justified in pressing for recognition as their modern counterparts, but it is a safe bet, nonetheless, that prophetic religion would experience smoother sailing in our society than it now does.

1. *An Authentic Individual.* He dared to be an individual in a world intolerant of individuality. One institution after another volunteered to do his thinking for him. But he insisted on his inalienable right to liberty of conscience, freedom of speech and devotion to the truth. As an individual responsible only to God, he scorned the attempt of smug society to exact from him the tribute of conformity and compromise. That bit of defiance won for him the opposition of heads of state and church alike, but his courage kept pace with the increase of his opponent's rank.

Nathan's rebuke of David (although we do not normally number Nathan among the great prophets, in this instance he gives us the classic illustration of the classical prophet) marks a striking case in point. Upon learning that Bathsheba, a woman whom he wants to add to his harem, has Uriah, a faithful soldier in his army, for husband, King David orders that Uriah be sent into the front line of battle (2 Samuel 12:1-6). Her husband now safely out of the way, David woos and wins the favor of the "mourning" widow. Later when the attendant announces Nathan's entrance, he arises to receive the congratulations of his guest. But they never come. Instead, the prophet relates a parable in which a wealthy farmer expropriates a poor tenant's only lamb, the pet of the entire family. His anger blazing, the indignant king declares, "As the Lord lives, the man who has done this deserves to die." Nathan charges the atmosphere electric with his explanation of the parable. "Thou," he says to the king, "art the man."

Great prophecy begins exactly as the confrontation between Nathan and David ends—with the single individual "standing in the presence of God, so wrought upon by Him that he comes away ready . . . to declare in the teeth of all opinion and all persecution, 'Thus says the Lord.' " [4]

2. *An Optimistic Democrat* (in the lower case of course; not to be confused with the major U. S. political party by this name). The great prophet did not build the first democracy, but he helped to lay the foundation— in his lofty view of human beings—on which others did. To be sure, we do not draw this conclusion from his public statements concerning the achievements of his fellows, for these seldom elicit an approving remark from him. We base it, instead, on the fact that only creatures of dignity could hope to perform the arduous task, which invariably involves a commitment to personal transformation and social reform, for which he serves as recruiter.

He derived from the discovery in his own soul of humankind's basic kinship to God tremendous implications for the whole of human life. If the real medium of encounter with God be the surrendered heart and attentive mind, then religion can survive the collapse of the altar sacrifice, all the pious protests to the contrary notwithstanding. If the covenant between man and God depends more on moral and spiritual than on national ties (Jeremiah 3:31-34), then the children of Israel can sing the Lord's song on foreign soil and among strange people. If nothing but the rebellious heart can effect estrangement between humanity and God, then nothing but human stubbornness can perpetuate that separation (Jeremiah 29:12 ff.).

Perhaps the best proof of the great prophet's commitment to the democratic ideal appears in his readiness to champion the cause of the downtrodden and oppressed. Of all the leaders of that part of the ancient world, he was one of the few to espouse the cause of the common people. With passion and conviction he pleaded the case of the exploited masses against the privileged few. By so doing he gave structure to his belief in the intellectual and moral competence of the ordinary human being, without which democracy degenerates into hollow mockery. To this faith belongs the credit for many of the humanitarian pieces of legislation embodied in the books of Deuteronomy and Leviticus. These extend special new benefits to slaves (Leviticus 25:1-7), the poor (Leviticus 19:1-18), and other groups likely to become victims of oppression and discrimination.

The search for a suitable description of the great prophet has yielded a veritable host of intriguing candidates. Of all these possibilities, "man for others" would get my vote as the one that most aptly and accurately tells us who he was and what he was about. That is, of course, unless you should prefix a qualifier and make it "God's man for others."

3. *A Committed Actor.* The great prophet's knowledge of God was no theoretical matter. It did not begin as an intellectual exercise, but as an act of the will. A confession of surrender, "Here I am! Send me" (Isaiah 6:8), was the first step towards its achievement.

As a rule, that step marked the beginning of a stormy life, for it implied the willingness to make enemies and run risks. But that did not deter him. As the bearer of Israel's conscience, the seer had to become a sayer. Though his words left status quo society all broken out in a rash of indignation, he kept right on translating his insights into sermons. The only way his enemies could ever still him was to kill him.

His life was no serene and calm affair, but a deeply disturbing and terribly dangerous venture of faith. And his lot was not made easier by contemplation of a here-after in which life's inequities would be fully adjusted. Unfamiliar with the hope for a bright and happy future in some faroff "sweet bye and bye," he set himself, almost impatiently, to the task of helping God set aright the terribly disjointed here and now.

Without any thought of recording the events of his time for ours, he gave himself to the task of shaping those events in such a way as to pass on a better world than the one to which he fell heir. Unlike the rank and file prophet, he continued to be a reformer after the reformation became a dangerous possibility. In fact, had it not been for him, there would probably have been no reformation.

4. *A Holy Adventurer.* Above all else, the great prophet was an adventurer with God, a pioneer blazing trails on as yet unexplored frontiers. Only rarely could the questions confronting him be settled by appeal to well-established precedents. This was true for a variety of reasons, but chiefly because the issues with which he dealt, as often as not, were raised not by troubled comrades but by a troubled conscience, his own. Although he was the heir of a rich past, he used its achievements not as the rule of progress, but as a guide to progress. As servant of the living God, whose lordship embraces the future as well as the past, he appealed all questions to the bar of the Judge to whom no time is a stranger and from whose control no time is exempt. Sometimes

these appeals produced verdicts that must have taken even their spokesmen by surprise. One illustration stands out. Whereas popular prophecy had reduced foreigners to servants of Israel, the last of the great prophets casts Israel in the role of servant to foreigners (Isaiah 42:1-4; 49:1-6).

One searches the ancient past in vain for a real parallel to the great prophet of Israel. He was truly God's representative of his time and place, for the problems with which he struggled were the monumental, yet practical, problems—political, social, economic, religious—of his own day and circumstances. For example, how should Israel meet the approaching horde of Assyrians? By entering into a mutual defense pact? If so, with whom, Egypt or Babylon? Or by remaining neutral? Or, to shift attention away from international to domestic politics, what about the widening gap between the haves and have nots? Did that reflect the will of Israel's God of justice?

Israelite tradition offered no prefabricated solutions to these problems. Undismayed by this fact, the great prophet sought answers to such questions in the only way left open to him—by exposing them to the judgment of his own God-enlightened conscience. That was how he worked to keep the stream of tradition open and fresh. And that is how he managed, at the same time, to nourish Israel in the hope that "the kingdoms of (this) world" would one day become "the kingdom of our Lord" (Revelation 11:15; while this is the language of the New Testament, the idea originated in the Old).

Their Decision and Ours

By thus incarnating the destiny to which God summons all humanity, the great prophet confronts us with the demand to purge ourselves of all purposes that compete with God's in the arena of decision.[5] Admittedly, that is a staggering challenge, but he does not leave us to our own resources—or, more to the point, without benefit of his—in meeting this challenge. For if, by his analysis of the paradoxes facing us, he spotlights the hurdles blocking the path to obedience, by his example of personal and total involvement, he shows us how to leap them.

FOOTNOTES

[1] R. B. Y. Scott, *The Relevance of the Prophets* (Rev. ed.; N. Y.: Macmillan Publishing Co., Inc., 1973), p. 217.

[2] Paul Minear, *Eyes of Faith* (St. Louis, Mo.: The Bethany Press, 1946), pp. 193-214.

[3] Gordon D. Kaufman, *Systematic Theology* (N. Y.: Chas. Scribner's Sons, 1968), p. 14, uses these words of truth, but in my view (and Kaufman's, too) they apply also to God.

[4] H. Wheeler Robinson, *Record and Revelation* (Oxford: Clarendon Press, 1938), p. 314.

[5] A rough paraphrase of Minear, *Eyes of Faith*, p. 92.

Appendix I

JE MATERIALS IN GENESIS—NUMBERS

Although many scholars find traces of the J and E authors and their redactor continuing into Deuteronomy and beyond, the following list includes nothing beyond Numbers, since all the essential articles of the Mosaic faith get clearly articulated— or reflected—in the JE portions of the first four books of the Old Testament.

The assignment of materials in this listing is patterned after Walter H. Harrelson's adaptation of Martin Noth's division of the sources of the Pentateuch (first five books of the Old Testament).[1] You might find it useful to underline the JE material in your Bible. Where JE material interrupts another source in the middle of a verse, the first or last words, depending on where they come in the text, of the JE source are given in parenthesis. After you have finished underlining the text, try reading only the underlined portions as a continuous narrative.

Genesis 2:4 ("In the day . . .")-25; 3:1-4:24; 6:1-8; 7:1-5, 7-10, 16 ("and the Lord . . .")-17, 22-23; 8:2 ("the rain . . .")-3 (". . . continually."), 6, 8-12, 13 ("and Noah . . ."), 20-22; 9:18-27; 10:8-19, 21, 24-30; 11:1-9, 28-30; 12:1-4 (". . . with him."), 6-20; 13:1-5, 7-10, 13-18; 15:1-16:2, 4-14; 18:1-20:18; 21:1, 7-34; 22:1-24; 24:1-25:6, 21-26 (the last 9 words of vs. 26—"Isaac was sixty years old when she bore them."—belong to another source), 27-34; 26:1-33; 27:1-45; 28:10-35:5 (the last 16 words of 33:18 belong to another source); 35:7-8, 16-22 (". . . heard of it."); 37:3-46:5 (the first 15 words of 41:46 belong to another source); 46:28-47:26; 47:29-48:2, 8-22; 49:2-50:11, 14-26.

Exodus 1:8-12, 15-22; 2:1-23; 3:1-6:1; 7:14-18, 20 ("In the sight . . .")-21 (". . . from the Nile"), 23-25; 8:1-4, 8-15, 20-32; 9:1-7, 13-35; 10:1-11:9; 12:21-23, 29-39; 13:17-22; 14:5-7, 10-14, 19-21, 24-25, 27 ("and the Egyptians . . ."), 30-31; 15:1-26 (the first 17 words of 15:22 belong to another source);

170

17:1 ("and camped . . .")-18:27; 19:2 ("they encamped . . .")-24:14; 32:1-34:35.

Leviticus contains almost no clearly identifiable JE material.

Numbers 10:29-12:16; 13:17 ("and said to them . . .")-20, 22-24, 26-33; 14:1 ("and the people . . ."), 4, 11-25, 39-45; 16:1-2, 12-15, 25-34; 20:14-21; 21:1-24:25.

FOOTNOTES
[1] Interpreting the Old Testament (N.Y.: Holt, Rinehart and Winston, Inc., 1964), pp. 487-92.

Appendix II

THE DETECTION OF SECONDARY ADDITIONS TO A PROPHETIC BOOK

Isolation of later additions to a prophetic book must await discovery of the approximate setting of the primary material. In the case of Amos, which illustrates the process by which each of the prophetic books came to be what it is, this determination can be made rather quickly. Neither the style nor the date nor yet the setting of his activity leaves us with many unanswered questions.

The book of Amos divides readily into three principal sections: oracles of judgment against the nations bordering Israel (chapters 1-2); oracles of judgment against Israel (chapters 3-6); and the report of five visions, climaxed with further threats and promises (chapters 7-9). Save for a few minor exceptions, all three parts exhibit sufficient similarity in style and circumstance to be the work of a single prophet within a relatively brief span of time. They likewise offer decisive clues to the time and place of his activity.

Aside from the dating of Amos' career to the reigns of Uzziah of Judah and Jeroboam II of Israel in the dubious superscription (1:1; all superscriptions should be viewed with suspicion; they were supplied, for the most part, by persons many years after the proclamations of the original prophets, but who lacked the critical tools for ascertaining the date of the material in question), at least three quite casual and, for this reason, quite probably authentic references to Jeroboam II appear elsewhere in the book (7:9, 10, 11). Except for mention of the fact that Amos prophesied "two years before the earthquake," which so far has gone both unidentified and undated, we have no precise indication of the period during this king's long reign in which the ministry of Amos fell. Yet the prophet's consistent assumption of Israel's favorable international position, economic affluence, and social stratification points to the later years in the reign of Jeroboam II, after he had happily resolved Israel's differences with Syria. Any time during the fourth and fifth decades of the eighth century B.C. would seem to fit the assumed circumstances of his extremely limited public career. The completeness of the reports of his public activity may be questioned, but they suggest a prophetic career of brief duration and limited geography. These reports record one appearance, for sure, in the royal sanctuary at Bethel (7:13) and they yield a veiled hint of a visit to the capital city of Samaria (4:1). Assuming with most scholars that Amos delivered most of his oracles to the assembly at Bethel on the occasion of his one visit to that city's royal shrine, we may trace the bulk of all three sections of his book to that appearance, though each may have been embellished by subsequent additions of various sorts. Actually, such additions to the book are rare in the extreme; the authenticity of few passages in Amos has ever been challenged. Yet a few passages are quite generally regarded as secondary. A look at these passages, and more especially at the grounds for disputing them, should indicate to us both the need for and the difficulty of identifying the secondary passages in prophetic literature.

The vague and generalizing character of the oracle against Judah (2:4-5) can scarcely fail to arouse suspicion. Both the oracles against other foreign nations (1:3-2:3) which precede it and that against Israel (2:6-6:14) which follows it detail the offenses of each transgressor in vivid specifics, And they spotlight the kinds of infractions, "crimes against humanity," [1] against which Amos most repeatedly and most vehemently inveighs. Measured against these indictments, the charge against Judah, that it has "rejected the law of the Lord, and . . . not kept his statutes," sounds both too tame and too pious for Amos. In fact, it so closely resembles the kind of formula met in the Deuteronomic history of Israel that one is tempted to view this entire oracle as the product of a Deuteronomizing editor's effort to update the message of Amos for a Judahite audience. Yet we have to concede not only that the silence of Amos against his own country, given the intensity of his attack against the northern kingdom, does seem strangely out of character, but that he did have access, in all probability, to the cultus from which the Deuteronomists derived their standardized formulas of indictment. Consequently, despite the surprising vagueness of his alleged attack against Judah in the context of his bills of particulars against other nations, he could have had plausible reasons for rendering his indictment against Judah in terms of a legal formula. Certainly this oracle should not be labeled "secondary" without reservation.

Among other oft-questioned passages in Amos, three Psalm-like doxologies (4:13; 5:8-9; 9:5-6) continue to arouse widespread critical doubt as to their authenticity, mainly on stylistic grounds. Alike in language and thought, they bear striking resemblances to the doxological portions of Second Isaiah and Job, both of which are dated by most scholars to the post-exilic period. They likewise exhibit a marked kinship to the Psalms of the Lord's enthronement, also normally interpreted as products, most probably, of the post-Amos era. Yet these Psalms are increasingly recognized to have been derived from Near Eastern originals of quite ancient vintage. And these originals, many would hold, constituted an important element in the cultic heritage of both the people and the prophets of Israel. Certainly no one could challenge the authenticity of any one of these hymnic fragments on the ground of its inappropriateness to the context. Not only do they all identify the Lord as the God of creation and the cause of its violent upheavals and terror-awakening tempests, but each follows immediately in the wake of a proclamation of doom against Israel. How else, one might ask, could the prophet have more effectively underscored the seriousness of his warning or the alarm with which Israel should have reacted to it than by following it up with a well-known quotation from a hymn of praise to the Lord of creation? Assuming the use of such hymns in Israelite worship during the time of Amos, we have ample explanation not only of their inherent appeal to the prophet, but also of his employment of them as sanctions for his grim message. In fact, granted this background, one could argue that their dissimilarity from the prophet's own style would have lent credence to his warning. From this we may safely conclude that, barring the discovery of proof of the post-Amos origin of all such liturgical pieces, the case for construing the Amos doxologies as secondary additions to the prophet's work is no better than that for giving Amos himself the credit for having incorporated them into his message.

Of all the contested passages in Amos, 9:8b-15 marks the one with the fewest claims to genuineness. Yet even it is

174

clearly not a literary unit, and no less clearly, its different parts do not by any means stand at an equal distance from the time or outlook of Amos.[2] For example, 9:9-10, assuming that what is portrayed here is an imminent sifting of Israel among the nations in a judgment from which no Israelite shall escape, may be read as a simple variation of the prophet's gloomy forecast in 9:1-4. The latter half of verse 6, which holds out hope to at least a part of "the house of Jacob," would then come under strong suspicion. Certainly it would be totally out of place between two such passages of inescapable and un-qualified doom. On the other hand, one can readily under-stand why the person responsible for assimilation of the hope-ful pronouncement in 9:11-15 would have sought to lend credibility to his conclusion to the book of Amos by reading a hopeful note back into the prophet's own oracles; hence 8b may be viewed as the contribution of an editor with a friendly bias towards the happy and quite inappropriate con-clusion that has been appended to the book of Amos. The Paradise myth underlying the promise in 9:11-15 of prodigal fertility and lavish prosperity doubtless predates Amos, but the passage's apparent presupposition of the destruction of the temple (verse 11), the Edomite plunder of Judah following the defeat of Nebuchadrezzar's armies (verse 12), and the removal of the Israelites from their land (verse 15), compels us to assign it a post-exilic date.[3]

Hopefully, this discussion of the secondary material in Amos has impressed on you the inequality of the grounds for pinning the label of "secondary" on passages from the prophets. Yet one needs to bear in mind the atypical character of Amos in this regard. Certainly other Old Testament books, among them certain of the prophetic collections, would more quickly stir your suspicion of multiple hands at work in their creation. Confronted by their display of the absence of logical sequence, not to mention abrupt shifts in both style and theme, you would hardly be overwhelmed by mention of the possibility that, instead of the unified work of a single author, you were reading an editorial compilation of the words of many authors.

The admission of secondary material into the text of biblical books can scarcely be termed surprising. The conditions of producing books in antiquity—not only without benefit of printing press or copyright laws, but also without author's royalties or pride of authorship—virtually foredoomed them

to unpredictable, if not irreconcilable, additions and altera-
tions. Add to these considerations the fact that none of the
prophets or their earliest disciples were conscious of producing
"Sacred Scripture," and you can readily appreciate the freedom
with which compilers and redactors put words into their
mouths. During the five centuries between Amos and initiation
of the canonizing process, the prophets' interpreters sometimes
became their editors, and not always from sinister motives,
either. Their additions were frequently intended merely to
update ancient writings or to harmonize their outlook with
the current view.

While scholars frequently dispute the status, whether
primary or secondary, of particular passages in the prophets,
few scholars would contest the presence in most prophetic
writings of some secondary material. Despite their fallibility,
various helpful criteria have been evolved by biblical critics
for distinguishing later additions and embellishments. These
include the familiar literary canons of vocabulary, style, continuity of theme, literary relatives, theological posture, social
outlook, and historical allusions. Quite often, although we did
not find this to be the case in Amos, several of these criteria
will converge in such fashion as to overwhelm the claim of
a particular passage—or, in some instances, even a long series
of passages—in a prophetic book to authenticity. When this
happens, we can ill-afford to dismiss that passage, or group of
passages from further consideration. Isaiah 40-55, which most
scholars ascribe to an anonymous prophet of the time of
Cyrus of Persia, offers ample proof of the fact that a secondary
writing need not be either inferior to or less important than its
original. The designation of a passage as secondary does not
represent a judgment as to its quality or significance. It represents, rather, an opinion concerning its probable author and
its approximate date, and this is all that it represents.

FOOTNOTES

[1] Harrelson, *Interpreting the Old Testament,* p. 344.

[2] R. S. Cripps, *A . . . Commentary on . . . Amos* (London: S. P. C. K,.
1955), pp. 67-71, divides the passage into two parts, and he contends
for the secondary origin of both parts.

[3] H. E. W. Fosbroke, "Amos: Introduction and Exegesis," *The
Interperter's Bible,* VI (1955), pp. 774-75.

THE ABSENCE OF PROPHETESSES
FROM THIS STUDY

The reason for the exclusion of prophetesses from this work, despite mention in the Old Testament of three prophetesses by name, is quite simple. None of the "writing prophets" (see Chapter 2 for my discussion of the special meaning of this term) whose works won canonical status in the Hebrew Scriptures was a woman. I have also paid little attention to the male prophets whose disciples, if they had such, failed to transmit canonical collections of their sayings and activities. Certainly my concentration on the words and works of those prophets whose disciples did honor them with such collections has not been arbitrary. It was dictated by the fact that the accounts of the speech and actions of the other prophets, whether male or female, have been so overlaid with legend in the historical writings of the Old Testament—and we have no Old Testament references to prophetesses outside these writings—that we cannot, with confidence, reconstruct either the events of their lives or the key elements in their proclamations.

The real issue does not concern the question of why female prophets occupy so small a place in this study. It has to do, instead, with the question of what it was in the character of ancient Israelite society that predisposed it to discourage women from full participation in the prophetic movement. This is the question for which Phyllis Bird, in her essay, "Images of Women in the Old Testament," which appears in the book edited by Rosemary Radford Ruether, *Religion and Sexism* (N.Y.: Simon & Schuster, Inc., 1974), pp. 41-88, searches for an answer. And I would say that she has given us as clear and accurate an answer as we could hope to find. Although the whole of her article merits careful study, her most immediately relevant comments to the issue under discussion are contained in the following quotations (page references are given in parenthesis at the end of each paragraph):

> . . . the Old Testament is a man's "book," where women appear for the most part simply as adjuncts of men, significant only in the context of men's activities. (41)
> . . . female prophets . . . in Israel . . . were . . . rare. No collections of their words have survived among the prophetic books of the Old Testament—at least none identified by a woman's name. . . . Most likely, female prophets were always few in number, and presumably not associated with guilds and disciples who might have collected and preserved their oracles. Their exercise of their calling must have been at best part-time, at least during child-rearing years, and may not even have begun until later in life. For the Israelite woman such a profession could only have been a second vocation. Early marriage, with its demand upon women of a primary vocation as wife and mother, would have excluded the early cultivation of the gift of prophecy. (68)
> It is with that same understanding of the dynamic character of history that the prophets speak of God's continued action in their own day, an action portrayed typically as judgment upon a people who had replaced theological norms with sociological ones (security, status, wealth, etc.). Neither the prophets nor the theologians, such as J and P, succeeded in wholly escaping the culturally determined understanding of male and female roles that they had inherited. . . . But distinctions of all types lend themselves to exploitation and to the creation of differential ethical standards. The historians of the Old Testament look behind the present state of division and alienation to an original and intended equality and harmony in creation, while the prophets focus upon the existing state of inequality and exploitation, addressing it with a concept of justice manifested in judgment—justice understood as a new act that God will perform to purge his creation, an act of retribution and rectification. The proud will be abased (Isa. 4:17), and the "men of distinction" will head the exile train (Amos, 6:4-7); but she who is now an outcast in men's eyes will not be punished for her sin (Hos. 4:14). (76)

Some among the prophets saw beyond the present day . . . to a new order with new possibilities for human existence, radical possibilities that would abolish the present alienation and exploitation based on distinctions of species, age, sex and social status. . . . (76)

. . . That Israel rarely lived up to this vision is all too apparent, but the vision should not be denied. (77)

Of all people, we Christians should be the last to deny the validity of this prophetic vision. Since the point of departure for Christian existence is the conviction that God in Jesus Christ has already ushered in the age to come, we are left without excuse for any delay in enlisting our energies in the bid to guarantee all persons, without regard for race or sex or economic status or any such thing, full access to the justice and equality and dignity due them as God's children and our siblings in the human family. The denial of such service would be an act of brazen heresy. It would be a refusal of the destiny to which God, through the events of our history, is now calling us, as once through the events of Palestinian history, he called Israel's prophets. When the Lord bade them take his place beside the oppressed poor, they took him at his word, and later generations rose up to praise them for the liberation of their father and sons. In addition to the oppressed poor, who still, to our shame, surround us on all sides, we can put the descendants of today's Blacks and women in our debt. And they will rise up to praise us if we will but heed the Lord's summons to take his place today beside their aunts and mothers and grandmothers.

The day of the male prophet has not yet ended, but that of the female prophet has finally begun to dawn. However, if she does her job as her masculine counterpart in ancient Israel did his, her monopoly of the spotlight at high noon will be shortlived. She will have to share it with female managers and executives, female elders and bishops, female professors and deans, and even, let us hope, female cardinals and . . . !

When this happens, let us not forget to thank the great prophets for their signal contribution to this development. For despite their birth and death in a patriarchal society, they made its achievement all but inevitable when they grounded their plea for justice and righteousness in the character and will of God.

STUDY GUIDE

Introduction

The great prophets were actors in a historical drama (the very same one, by the way, as the drama whose cast we are now being asked to join: the drama of redemption) of uncertain outcome, but this is not the popular view of them. Inasmuch as they have long since become our prompters in the faith, prodding us in our search for the right lines with which to respond to God's call to us, we tend to envelop them in a romantic cloud. We think of them as persons who, if they had a past on which they drew, could have fared quite well without it; who, if they met opposition, did not take it seriously because they and God were on the same wave length and, despite all the evidence to the contrary, were confidently shaping events to their own design; and who, in the teeth of royal and pious opposition, squeezed from reluctant Israel two of the world's great religions, Judaism and Christianity. By this picture we are understandably intimidated into awed silence.

We might be able to dismiss this caricature if the only issue at stake were historical accuracy. But we cannot ignore it, for what it calls into question is the humanity of both the great prophets and ourselves. It raises this challenge by wrongly shifting our attention away from the process to the product of their activity, and thus encouraging us to assess their relevance for us in terms of neatly transferable conclusions instead of the decision-making process by which they arrived at them.

180

If we would surmount this temptation, and thus maximize the relevance of these great Israelite figures for our time and situation, we must close the gap between their humanity and ours. We must be able to show, as I believe we can and must, not only that they had access to no power to which we cannot likewise lay claim, but that they were as vulnerable as we are to the vagaries and miscarriages of human reason, emotion and history. But how, you ask, can we effect this demonstration? By bringing into clear and sharp focus, I would answer, the two contexts—those of the writer and reader—with which all serious Bible study must concern itself.

In the eight chapters of this study book I have sought to reconstruct the first of these two contexts. To what extent have I succeeded in this enterprise? Only to the degree that I have enabled you to feel yourself into the crisis—supported by the faith that sustained them, torn by the pressures that troubled them, and troubled by the doubts that vexed them—that pushed the great prophets into a corner, forcing them to make decisions whose consequences they could neither foresee nor escape. Or to put it negatively, I have failed to achieve the end for which I wrote this book unless, as you have perused its contents, you have become convinced that, had you been in their audience, you too would have been catapulted into the throes of a destiny-shaping decision; that you, seeing the same facts as those at which they looked and analyzing them from the same motives as those by which they were moved, might have taken different actions from those which they took; and that, had you done so, you would have produced a very different history from that to which we have fallen heir.

The achievement of this kind of rapport with the great prophets in their setting marks the first step enroute to appreciation of the radical difference between their context and ours. We cannot really come to know them thus without sensing the deep cleavage between their world and ours. To achieve empathy with them in the peculiarities of their circumstance is to acknowledge the uniqueness of their situation. For by the same token that their faith and ours are at least a Testament apart, so too our overwhelming pressures and besetting doubts are at least a world apart from theirs.

As in the time of the great prophets, God's word to humankind today is unique. It is personal communication in the fullest and most complete sense. For just as God spoke to them in light of their peculiar circumstances, he speaks to us in terms of our culture and background. But his aim is not to take us backward to some bright yesterday, but to lead us forward towards a brighter tomorrow.

To declare that the life of humankind, from the standpoint of the great prophets, has no meaning apart from God's word is a mere truism. But it is no less a mere truism to say that they bear witness to no other word of God than that which is spoken and heard in human experience. Therefore, if we would make a decision for the destiny to which God, through them, is now summoning us, we must take our stand where they took theirs—at the feet, not of God's spokesmen, but of the God who spoke and still speaks. We must worship the Lord over history by heeding his direction within history—by listening for and acting upon his word about life as he proclaims it to us in the midst of the living of it.

The study of the great prophets in either their or our historical context is a guide for action. But the tense of the action depends on our choice of contexts. To focus on their context might enable us to discover the guide to where the action *was*. But if we would discover the guide to where the action *is*, perhaps we should focus more heavily on our context. By the same token, if it is our aim and responsibility to chart a course of action for the future, we would probably be best advised to think ahead, with one eye trained on each of the aforementioned contexts. From this dual focus should come a keen appreciation of both our live possibilities and our very real limitations. And we sorely need an acute consciousness of both these things. Otherwise we are apt to fall victim to either unbridled messianism or fatalistic despair, and it is difficult to say which would be more disastrous.

We have many aids to assist us in our quest for this kind of meaningful dialogue. Hosts of good books on one or more of the Bible's great prophets, several of which consciously explore the implications of their message for today, have been published in recent years. And there is a growing and significant, even if as yet quite modest, number of books that attempt to update their message for our day. The bibliography contains a list of books for each of these approaches.

You should feel free to contract or expand both the number and the length of sessions for this study in line with the special needs and interests of your own particular group. While most of the bibliographical entries can be counted on to suggest to you several possibilities for departing from my outline, two such plans, one for reducing and the other for increasing the number of sessions, are discussed below.

Let's suppose, for example, that you would like to do this study in five sessions. You could combine chapters I and II for an exploration of "The Heritage (I) and Character (II) of Israelite Prophecy." "The Horizontal (III) and Vertical (IV) Dimensions of the Covenant" would be a suitable theme for tying together the third and fourth chapters. Chapters six and seven could be joined under the title of "The Obligations, the Temptations (VI), and the Rewards (VII) of the Prophet." If you should employ the lecture method in presenting the contents of this volume in line with this suggestion, you would need to rearrange the major heads in my outline; in most instances, however, the subheads would require no alteration.

Should you wish to increase the number of sessions, the possibilities are virtually endless. A session on "The Individual Prophets (e.g., Nathan, Micaiah, Elijah, Elisha) before the Great Prophets" could be inserted between the second and third chapters. Some phase of the thought or work of one of the great prophets not included in this study (e.g., Micah, between chapters V and VI; or Ezekiel, after chapter VI) might be explored in another additional session. Further additional sessions might be devoted to the exploration of some phase of the thought or work of Amos, Hosea, Isaiah, Jeremiah, or Second Isaiah outside the scope of this study. Then, of course, the possibilities are simply endless for contemporizing the message of the great prophets. "Amos' Address to the 1976 General Conference" (see Amos 1:2-2:16 for a point of departure), "The Faithless Bride of Christ" (Just as Hosea treats Israel under the figure of the bride of the Lord, the New Testament at times labels the church the bride of Christ. Employing Hosea as a model, draw up an indictment of modern Christendom.), "Isaiah Goes to Dinner with Henry Kissinger," "Jeremiah, the Counselor; Jeremiah, the Counselee" (after describing Jeremiah's analysis of a typical psychiatrist, summarize what you think the latter would have to say about Jeremiah), and "Second Isaiah's Proposal for Peace between Israel and the Arabs" mark a few of the intriguing possibilities for updating the prophetic witness for a late twentieth-century audience.

This study book focuses attention on the message of Israel's great prophets as a way of sensitizing us to God's summons to a decision for our and mankind's destiny as members or his family. Needless to point out, the aim of the great prophets was not simply to get a hearing, but rather to bring their hearers to the point that they could clearly understand and would diligently seek to perform God's will for their lives and society. Our ultimate purpose must likewise reach beyond the intellectual comprehension of prophetic faith in search of help for its faithful practice. Accordingly, I shall not hesitate to offer suggestions for turning ideas for analysis into a program for action.

This study guide provides for eight sessions, any or all of which may be abbreviated or lengthened as your situation may dictate, by the selective use of the proposed helps for teaching the course. These proposals are offered for each session under the headings, respectively, of *Resources,* which may be either somewhat general or quite specific; *Goals,* setting forth both the basic aim and the specific objectives; *Questions,* not only for individual reflection but also for group discussion; *Suggestions,* for class participation and, occasionally, social action as well as effective communication. Supplementary helps may also be offered from time to time under other appropriate headings.

Since my proposals are viewed simply as possible aids for assisting you in developing and enriching your own approach to the presentation of this study, they will not be organized into a neatly constructed, airtight set of lesson plans. It is my hope and expectation that you will rely heavily on your own creative and imaginative powers and resources in the design of a program for presenting these materials.

Since the number for each session of this study guide will be the same as that of the chapter for which it is offered, the titles of the chapters will not be repeated.

Session 1

Chapter I introduces this study of the great prophets by rejecting out of hand the popular view of them as innovators who neither had nor needed forerunners to blaze the trail of faith for them. It then offers an exposition of the Mosaic faith as it was articulated in the JE history of Israel. It holds that this formulation of Israelite religion not only spared God's spokesmen the necessity of having to launch their calls to repentance from scratch, but that it also provided their audiences with a clearer understanding of the divine summons that was being mediated to them than they were ready to heed. In short, it dates the end of Israel's age of innocence to the period before the rise of its classical prophets.

A. Resources

Appendix I contains a list of JE passages in Genesis-Numbers. Do the exercise suggested in the last line of the second paragraph of this appendix. If you cannot find time for this assignment, the next best thing would be to study one of the great creedal expressions of ancient Israelite faith with the help of recent commentaries. These capsule summaries appear in Deuteronomy 6:20-25 and 26:5-10 and Joshua 24:2-13. Either *The Interpreter's Bible* or *The Interpreter's One-Volume Commentary on the Bible* may be employed for this exercise.

The American heritage, though much less explicitly theological in tone, is also held together by a certain quite definite and fairly consistent body of beliefs. Since these articles of faith are perhaps nowhere more clearly reflected than in The Declaration of Independence and The 1787 Constitution (Including Amendments) of the United States, you should take a close look at these two documents. Inasmuch as these and subsequent documents like them (the text of all of which appears in *Basic American Documents*) have spawned the unifying faith of this country, aptly called "American civil religion" by Conrad Cherry, it would be well to read Cherry's account of this religion. It appears in his introduction to the 1971 volume, edited by him, whose striking title, *God's New Israel*, accurately suggests its contents. Magazine and newspaper clippings, personal interviews, films (especially of the type done on our American heritage by Alistair Cooke in his television series, first done, I think, in 1973; some of the Luther films do an equally effective job in giving us a capsule version of the abiding elements in our Protestant heritage), would also be informational.

B. Goals

1. Basic Aim: To achieve an understanding of the controlling elements in the religious heritage to which Israel's great prophets and their contemporaries fell heir.

2. Specific Objectives: The form for the presentation of this session may vary, but it ought to be used in such a way as to enable the students to restate in summary fashion the chief concern of each of the four headings of the outline. Such mastery will greatly facilitate appreciation of both the urgency and reasonableness of the message of the great prophets. It will also assist us in drawing parallels—and this we shall be doing constantly, I hope—between Israel's situation and our own.

C. Questions

1. What does the author mean by his description of the Old Testament account of the exodus as a "liturgical historical narrative"?

2. If Deuteronomy 7:7-8 be an accurate description of the God of all creation, must not the exodus story be stripped of all its national and ethnic overtones before we can apply it to our situation today? In other words, to what extent is the symbolic value of this narrative dependent on its historical facticity?

3. How does "the Old Testament Gospel," to recall the author's label for the Passover narrative, resemble the New Testament proclamation of the Gospel? In what way does the good news about God in the latter version differ from that presented in the JE story?

4. Which of the terms, king or president, more accurately describes God's relationship to Israel within the framework of the covenant in its classical formulation?

5. Why did the Israelites *rejoice* when they understood the requirements of the law?

6. Does the transformation of the belief that Palestine is Israel's God-appointed home into a "motivational myth" (see the text for the meaning of this term) represent an extension or distortion of the theology of the JE writer?

7. Ponder the questions raised in the first paragraph on page 14 (beginning "In case of . . .). How would the JE writer have answered each of these questions?

D. Suggestions

1. *For Effective Communication:* Have the group (hereinafter known as the Civiltarians) of three or four students

whom you have previously assigned to list the three or four major ingredients of American civil religion either as it is reflected in the Declaration of Independence or as it is defined by Cherry, *God's New Israel,* pp. 8-21, to present their outline to the class. When this has been done, explain that the Israelites to whom the great prophets addressed themselves also had a religious angle of vision from which they looked at life, and that it will be the goal of this first session to discover just what constituted its chief characteristics. Call the group's attention to the above questions, noting that the presentation of the materials of this chapter will provide them with the data for answering them. It may be well to make specific assignments of responsibility for answering these questions before launching the formal presentation. The presentation itself may take the form of a lecture or of a panel discussion. If you choose the latter route, the moderator could do the introductory and concluding sections of the chapter and each of the other panel members one of its four major divisions. After completion of the presentation, give the students some time to write down their answers to the questions for this session before opening the floor for discussion.

2. *For Class Participation:* After the assigned questions have all been adequately explored, you might assign a small group (hereinafter known as the Ecumenists) to draft an outline of "ecumenical Christian faith," which would pinpoint the four or five principal beliefs that today's major Christian bodies share in common.

Now appoint a third small group (hereinafter to be known as the Renewists) to draft an evaluation of American life and society on the basis of the JE theological outlook.

Ask the Civiltarians and the Ecumenists to do the same from the perspectives, respectively, of American civil religion and ecumenical Christian faith.

Before having the spokespersons for these three groups report back to the entire assembly, ask all members of the latter body to jot down any suggestions that might occur to them as they listen to these reports for renewing American life and society. When the reports are completed, appoint someone to record 15-20 of these proposals on a blackboard or a sheet of newsprint. Then lead the class in the refinement of this list into a five-point program for the renewal of American life and culture.

3. *For Social Action:* Ask each of the three groups named above—the Civiltarians, the Ecumenists, the Renewists—to select the one item in this program that could best be implemented from its perspective. This means, of course, that the Renewists would settle for an item calling for deep religious insight and equally great personal commitment and, therefore, likely to evoke the interest of only vanguard Christians; the Ecumenists, for one that would attract broad Christian and perhaps even interfaith support; and the Civiltarians, for a cause demanding strong commitment to the principles of human decency and justice but without requiring special theological sophistication. Once these selections have been made, challenge each of the groups to accept its choice as its Social Action project for this course. Although work on these projects may extend beyond the duration of the course itself, opportunity for reports of progress in these undertakings should be offered at least two or three times during the class sessions themselves.

Session 2

On what basis are we able to distinguish the Israelites who were prophets from those who were not? Chapter II, after exploring the clues that have produced some of the more traditional and less satisfying answers to this inquiry, ends up by discounting its importance. It contends that, inasmuch as only a few of the many persons accorded the title of prophet in ancient Israel were responsible for the high esteem in which it has come to be held, we should look, instead, for the characteristic that both bound these great prophets to each other and, at the same time, forces us to distinguish between them

189

and the rank-and-file prophets. This search did not prove fruitless. What it turned up as the ultimately decisive mark of the great prophets was their simultaneous openness to tradition and change. Yet this openness was at all times both derived from and subject to their overpowering commitment to the person and will of God. From this finding two questions force themselves upon us: (1) Must we not narrow the number of Israelite prophets on whom we pin the label of great? (2) May we not quite legitimately look for successors to the great prophets among our contemporaries?

A. Resources

Most of the standard introductions to the Old Testament, as well as most of the survey works on the prophetic literature, have a chapter on the prophets before Amos. You might also consult a good dictionary (such as McKenzie's one-volume *Dictionary of the Bible* or *The Interpreter's Dictionary of the Bible*). The film, "Heritage to Destiny," and the filmstrip, "Frontiersmen of Faith," and the slides in the set on "The Prophets" that portray the prophets before Amos. See also "Portrait of the American as Reformer," *Living Ideas in America,* edited by H. S. Commager, pp. 466-72.

B. Goals

1. Basic Aim: To develop the kind of appreciation for the style and stance of the great prophet that will enable him to trigger a crisis of faith for us. Hopefully, this encounter will not come to an end until we have received a call to decision for our God-appointed destiny not only as the people of God but, and more particularly, as heirs of "the pilgrim faith" on the eve of our bicentennial celebrations.

2. Specific Objectives: At the end of the session the students should be able to distinguish between the merely traditional marks of great prophecy and its indispensable requirements. They should also be prepared to make

190

the same kind of distinction vis-à-vis the various contemporary expressions of Christianity.

C. Questions

1. Does the etymological approach emphasize the infant or mature phase of the prophetic movement?

2. Was susceptibility to ecstatic seizure more likely to secure immediate or long-range endorsement of a prophet's words?

3. Did membership in a band of prophets disqualify one for consideration as a legitimate spokesman for God?

4. What was the connection between the ancestral faith and religious experience in the development of the prophetic movement in Israel?

5. In what way may the activity of the collectors of Hebrew prophecy be compared to that of the prophets themselves? See Appendix II.

6. Given the view of prophecy espoused in the concluding section of this chapter, who are some of the twentieth-century figures to whom we might justifiably apply the title of prophet?

D. Suggestions

1. *For Effective Communication:* The contents of this chapter may very well be presented as a panel discussion. In addition to the moderator, the panel might include either three or six other members; if three, each panel member would assume responsibility for two of the six major divisions of the chapter. Before the formal presentation begins, assign each of six small groups the responsibility of listening for the answer to one of the above questions. Before the appointed spokespersons of these groups report to the entire assembly, give them 5-10 minutes in buzz sessions, so that they can double-check with their colleagues.

2. *For Class Participation:* Ask a member of each of the three groups (Renewists, Ecumenists, Civiltarians) to which we were introduced in the opening session to serve on a symposium for discussing the topic, "What

the Prophetic Movement in Israel can Teach Us about
How to Deal with the Current Charismatic Movement,"
from the standpoint of that group's special bias. You
should set a time limit for this discussion, but you ought
to allow at least 15 minutes for it.

Session 3

Chapter III focuses on the radically different theological interpretations of Israel's ancestral faith that prompted
Amos and his contemporaries to anticipate exactly opposite outcomes for Israel's near future. It raises some
knotty problems for those of us who believe that the
issues of religious and national loyalty can be easily
tested and judged. It surfaces the question of our motives
for participation in public worship, and it compels us to
ask if they can possibly be valid if they do not issue in
human service.

A. Resources

The book of Amos, Chapter 2 of study book, the
articles and commentaries on Amos listed in the bibliography, the film on "The Founding of Jamestown," and
the filmstrip, "Amos, God's Angry Man."

B. Goals

1. Basic Aim: To discover the contemporary relevance
of Amos' insistence that the acid test of religion is to be
found, not in what it does for the feelings of those who
practice it, but in what it moves them—in response to
and in imitation of God—to do for their neighbors.

2. Specific Objectives: To ask ourselves whether we
Christians in this country do not need to probe our rather
uncritical appropriation of biblical faith from Amos' angle
of vision. This means, of course, that we must pay less
attention to the muscle of other power blocs and greater
heed to what, under God, is just and right; that, while
we can defend the notion of America's election, we must
take care to define it in terms of responsibility for the
whole family of mankind; that piety without humanity

is a form of Godlessness; that human justice and divine worship, while not identical, nevertheless bear an inseparable connection; and that God's character and purpose may, if his chosen people should betray the cause for their election, compel him to reject them in favor of some other people as the instrument of his will.

C. Questions

1. If we would understand Amos' criticism of Israelite life, what else do we need besides knowledge of the domestic economic situation and the state of international politics?

2. What was the source of Amos' theological convictions?

3. What would you say to the assertion that, in Amos' view, "religion was both the disgrace and hope of Israel"?

4. Which type of considerations, theological or humanitarian, weighed more heavily in Amos' plea for social reform?

5. If we push the implications of Amos' doctrine of election to its logical limits, what happens to the idea of special treatment at God's hands?

D. Suggestions

1. *For Effective Communication:* Before presenting the materials of this chapter, regardless of the format you may choose for the presentation, ask the class to listen to it with the possibility of doing an update of Amos' Bethel message (see especially Amos 1:2-2:16) for a contemporary American audience. At the end of the presentation, give the group an opportunity for discussion of all the suggested questions and any others which you may have triggered, then ask a member of each of the three groups, the Renewists, the Ecumenists, and the Civiltarians, respectively, to role play the proclamation of Amos' updated message for the following groups: the Renewist, for an assembly of civil rights leaders; the Ecumenist, for a conference of the officers of the World

or National Council of Churches; the Civiltarian, for a Washington gathering of American business and political leaders for one of their Prayer Breakfasts. (Lest they be intimidated by this assignment, remind them that Amos was "*only* a layman" from the hill country of Judah.)

2. For Class Participation: Assign three members of your group to lead the entire class in a depth Bible study, using commentaries and other aids, on the meaning of election for us in light of Amos 3:1-2 and 9:7. Ask the other members of the class, as they listen to this discussion, to be thinking about the answers to the following questions: Were the founders of our country justified in thinking of Americans as a chosen people? Would America's treatment of the underprivileged in this country and abroad meet Amos' requirements for an elect people? Are other countries justified in thinking of themselves as God's newly elected peoples? Does a people's concern for its status as God's elect community assist or retard its capacity for the discharge of its divine mission?

3. For Social Action: Ask three socially aware members of your class to constitute themselves a committee for rewriting some portion of the last printed report of the Annual Conference's Board of Church and Society from the standpoint of Amos' convictions about religion and the common life. Next week, as a sort of review of this session, have the two versions—first, the one prepared by the Conference Board; then, the rewrite done by your Amos committee—read, paragraph by paragraph, before the entire class. Perhaps the Renewists, the Ecumenists, and the Civiltarians would like, in light of this presentation, to devise a program for working an Amos-like reform through their special contacts in one specific area of our common life. At any rate, pass along the suggestion, and request that they report back to the class on its progress at a later session.

Session 4

Chapter IV focuses attention on the close connection

between beginning and end in Israelite theology. It traces Hosea's hope for Israel's ultimate renewal, despite his hopeless outlook for its immediate future, to his contemplation of the current situation in light of the origin and early history of the covenant between the Lord and Israel. It goes on to point out that Israel's only hope of restoration after judgment lies not in its disposition to change, but in the creative power of the Lord's redemptive love to transform her disposition.

A. Resources

The book of Hosea, Chapter 4 of study book, the commentaries on Hosea by Mays and Ward (see bibliography), and the filmstrip, "Hosea, Prophet of God's Love."

B. Goals

1. Basic Aim: To reassess the popular understanding of Old Testament religion in legalistic terms from the perspective of Hosea's emphasis not only on the priority of love over law, but on the outgoing love of God as the source and inspiration of human goodness.

2. Specific Objectives: By the end of this session the students should be able to distinguish between personalistic and legalistic understandings of the covenant; indicate how God's "faithfulness" can both punish and renew Israel; explain why Israel's faithlessness can move God to chasten but not abandon it; and show why God—on account of and not in spite of his righteousness —can kindle hope in the midst of despair and bring obedience out of disobedience.

C. Questions

1. How does the Christian view of the church's origin differ from Hosea's account of Israel's creation?

2. How does Hosea reconcile the relationship between the love and justice of God?

3. To one who explains the failure to love as God

loves by saying, "After all, I'm only human!" how would Hosea respond?

D. Suggestions

1. For Effective Communication: Have a symposium of three persons (not including the moderator) discuss Abraham Lincoln's interpretation of the Civil War in terms of the three elements of "The Message of Hosea" as presented in the last major division of Chapter 4 in the study book. The first speaker would show how that God, despite his love for America, had forced the Civil War upon it; the second, how that America, even though it had brought this affliction upon itself, would not be totally destroyed by it; the third, how that justice, though it could not be trodden underfoot with total impunity, would nevertheless yield place to mercy. Wolf's book, *The Religion of Abraham Lincoln,* would be an excellent resource for the presentation of Hosea's message as it became enfleshed in the words and deeds of Abraham Lincoln. If you like this idea, the contents of the introduction and of the first two major divisions of Chapter 4 may be presented either as a panel discussion or in a lecture.

2. For Class Participation: Stage a formal debate on the question: "Resolved that Hosea's message holds the key to discovery of a solution to the problems of crime and delinquency." Those on the affirmative side would be helped by the books included in the bibliography of *The Crime of Punishment,* by Karl Menninger; those on the negative, by the books of the late J. Edgar Hoover and those authors to whom he refers with approval. Care must be taken, however, lest Hosea's understanding of love be reduced to mere sentimentality.

Session 5

Chapter V casts Isaiah in the role of a meddler in politics. It traces the prophet's activity in the political arena to an understanding of the covenant that forbids the neat separation of life into the watertight compartments of sacred and secular. It even hints that the popular belief a person can separate one's political activity from one's religious convictions represents an expression of atheism.

A. Resources

Chapter 5 of study book, the book of Isaiah, the filmstrip, "Isaiah, Statesman for God," the commentaries on Isaiah listed in the bibliography, and most especially, "Isaiah — A Wise Statesman for Our Modern Era," in *The Prophets of Main Street*, by J. Elliott Corbett.

B. Goals

1. Basic Aim: To develop an appreciation of Israelite prophecy's irreconcilable union of religious responsibilities and political duties.

2. Specific Objectives: By the end of this session the students should view the prophets as opponents not of the use but of the abuse of politics; as agitators not for the surrender of power but for its imaginative enlistment on the side of justice; and as forerunners of the current clamor for seeking peace between the natural environment and humanity.

C. Questions

1. How does the interpretation of Isaiah underlying Corbett's updated version of the prophet's message in "Isaiah — A Wise Statesman for Our Modern Era" compare with that presented by the author of the study book?

2. Has Christianity suffered or prospered from its tendency to adopt more of a hands-off attitude towards politics than that reflected in the dynastic oracles?

3. Are today's champions of concern for the environment justified in enlisting Israelite prophecy in support of their cause?

4. Did Isaiah provide the American revolutionaries with a precedent for rebelling against the British monarchy?

D. Suggestions

1. *For Effective Communication:* Present the materials of this chapter as a panel discussion or in a lecture.

2. *For Class Participation:* Have a member of the class who writes well to draft an eyewitness account in the present tense of a coronation ceremony in ancient Israel, paying special attention not only to the contents of the dynastic oracle but also to its central place in the celebration. R. deVaux's, *Ancient Israel,* 2d ed. (London: Darton, Longman & Todd, 1965), pp. 100-14, contains all the necessary data for depicting this scene.

Have a second good writer to draft a 10-minute address for use by the President of the United States on the occasion of his inauguration on January 20, 1977. The dynastic oracle may serve as a model for this production, but the writer should bear in mind that the speech is being written for use in a twentieth-century A.D. democracy and not in an eighth-century B.C. monarchy. Recent inaugural addresses by American Presidents might be of help in this project.

3. *For Social Action:* Call for reports of progress from representatives of each of the three groups—the Renewists, the Ecumenists, the Civiltarians—on their social action projects (adopted in the first session). After these reports have been received, ask them how they would like, each group from its special perspective, to design an action program for effecting a more harmonious relationship between the natural and human environments. If they respond positively to this idea, tell them that they will be given an opportunity to report on this undertaking.

Session 6

Chapter VI introduces us to the interior makeup of Jeremiah. And we are surprised, to put it mildly, by the kind of person he turns out to be. As expected, he consistently displays the kind of commitment to God that enables him to put all the Lord's would-be rivals in their place. But, and for this discovery our popular notion of God's spokesman had not prepared us, his triumphs do not come easily. His enemies are real enemies, and that is particularly true of his most severe foe, the enemy he beholds only when he looks in the mirror. And his battles are not sham battles, not even when God is on the other side. Having successively resisted the claims, respectively, of self, of colleagues and of the masses, we would expect Jeremiah to rejoice. But, instead, we find him blaming God for his isolation and alienation. In short, on close inspection, he reveals enough of the humanity with which we all are much too familiar, flawed as it is by nagging doubts and lingering resentments, both to amaze and challenge us by his faithfulness and devotion to God. Far from intimidating us into a feeling of awed helplessness before God's call, he moves us, instead, to wonder if, after all, even we might not be capable of service to God's mission in the world. The God who reveals himself to us in Jeremiah discloses himself to us "not in spite of but in the midst of a very real and terribly insistent humanity."

A. Resources
Jeremiah 1:4-19; 6:11-15, 27-30; 10:23-25; 11:18-23; 12:1-6; 15:10-20; 16:1-9; 17:14-18; 18:18-23; 19:1-20:18, with the help of the commentaries; Chapter 6 of the study book; the filmstrip, "Jeremiah, The Reluctant Rebel"; the slide, from "The Prophets," of Michelangelo's painting of Jeremiah; the biographies of such stalwart historical figures, in church and out, as St. Augustine, Martin Luther, Abraham Lincoln and Adlai Stevenson, all of whom, despite their lofty reputation, were often torn by self-doubt and personal insecurity.

B. Goals
1. Basic Aim: To see the great prophets as an illustration of God's capacity to advance his mission through persons of widely varied inclinations and personalities.

2. Specific Objectives: By the end of this session the members of the class should be able to draw the connection between Jeremiah's stormy world and his moody disposition; to identify both the claims that threatened God's hold on the prophet's affection and the commitment that enabled him, finally, to shake himself free from their tyranny; and, in addition, to read his mixture of prayers for divine vengeance against his human enemies with impudent cries of reproach against God as an indispensable element in the development of incarnational theology.

C. Questions

1. What hope did Jeremiah have for the survival of Judah as an independent political entity?

2. Were Jeremiah's neighbors justified in looking on him as a traitor to his country?

3. Did Jeremiah get his kicks from proclaiming oracles of doom?

4. What does Jeremiah's expression of hostilities and doubts and feelings of guilt suggest to us about the way we should respond to those who are always telling us how to achieve peace of mind and soul?

5. Would Jeremiah believe us to be entitled to a life of calm repose in a world where God has so great difficulty in bringing neighbors in need to our attention?

D. Suggestions

1. *For Effective Communication:* The materials of this chapter may very effectively be presented as a panel discussion. A moderator, who would present the introductory material that sets the prophet in his historical context and the concluding remarks concerning his contemporary relevance, and two other persons might constitute the membership of the panel. One of these other panel members would tell the Jeremiah story in such fashion as to spotlight "The Priority of the Divine Claim"; the other, in a manner that would focus attention on "The Persistence of the Human Claim."

2. *For Class Participation:* At one of the first sessions of this course, have your class select the one book that offers the most trustworthy guide to the development of

a religious personality. Now on a sheet of newsprint have the person whom you have long since asked to read this book for today's session write a four-point description of the ideal person from the standpoint of this book. Once this description has been completed, have the other members of the class to identify the four main elements in Jeremiah's character. After thoroughly exploring the contrasting pictures, you might wish to follow up this exercise with a discussion of "The Constants and the Variables in the Personal Make-Up of God's Servants."

Session 7

Chapter VII focuses attention on Second Isaiah's challenge of the dogma of retribution. Earlier Israelite teachers had given tacit support to this idea—which says, in effect, that people get pretty much that to which, by moral right, they are entitled: if they fare well, that may be taken as evidence of their basic goodness, and vice-versa—by interpreting imminent or recent natural calamities and national disasters as divine punishment for rebellion against God, and by hinting that these misfortunes could be averted through repentance. Second Isaiah calls this logic into question with his portrait of the Lord as the sovereign God not only of all creation, but also of all the conditions and circumstances in which people find themselves. And that means, according to our prophet, not only that affliction may be out of all proportion to the offender's transgressions, but that God can and, in fact, does work his redemptive will through voluntary self-giving, even if unsought and at first resisted, in behalf of others. In the formulation of this idea Second Isaiah does more than merely give us the clue that comes as close as any ever yet unearthed to enabling us to make sense of Israelite history. He gives us at the same time, at least from the standpoint of Christian faith, not only the key for unlocking the mystery of the life and death of Jesus of Nazareth, but also an important angle of vision from which to view our destiny as human beings.

A. Resources

Chapter VII of study book; Isaiah 40-55 (with special attention to 42:1-4; 49:1-6; 50:4-9; 52:13-53:12), with the help of the previously suggested commentaries; the filmstrip, "Prophet-Poet of the Exile"; "Second Isaiah and the Problem of the Future," in *The Old Testament in Dialogue with Modern Man*, by James D. Smart, pp. 104-17; and "Second Isaiah: His Time and Ours," *The Prophets on Main Street*, by J. Elliott Corbett, pp. 135-55.

B. Goals

1. Basic Aim: To explore the potential values and possible dangers that may derive from use of the servant motif in Christian teaching and preaching.

2. Specific Objectives: By the end of this session the students should be able to trace Second Isaiah's hopeful attitude towards Cyrus to a basically theological and not merely political analysis of his role in Judah's history; to see the prophet's enlargement of Israel's mission as the by-product of his enlarged understanding of the rules and character of God, and not vice versa; and to appreciate the fact that the validity of the servant motif begins and ends at precisely the point where the mission of God—and, by the same token, the mission of God's people—begins and ends. In short, while it may quite properly be invoked as a symbol of the divine-human relationship, its use as a sanction for the oppression of some human beings by other human beings can only be described as a piece of monstrous blasphemy. When Second Isaiah thought about Israel's destiny under God and its decision for service to humankind, he was not thinking about two things but one. To see and appreciate this fact: that is the thread that enables us to tie together all the specific objectives of this session into one central purpose.

C. Questions

1. Why would Second Isaiah have been ill-advised to have simply repeated the message of Isaiah to Jerusalem?

2. What is the connection between Second Isaiah's view of Cyrus and his understanding of Israel's mission?

3. Are WASPS justified in appealing to the oppressed for patience and forebearance and self-effacing service in imitation of the servant of the Lord?

4. What does Second Isaiah's rejection of older motifs for that of the servant in defining Israel's role as God's agent suggest to us about the connection that must obtain between symbol and history?

D. Suggestions

1. For Effective Communication: The Christian has been called "the most free lord of all, and subject to no one, and the most dutiful servant of all, and subject to everyone" (a paraphrase of the famous paradoxical description of the Christian person by Martin Luther). This paradox must be kept clearly in mind in presenting the contents, however done, of Chapter VII. Otherwise we can easily twist Second Isaiah's message into a plea for us to become other-directed patsies of anybody with the gall thus to dehumanize us. To do that would be to overlook the fact that, from the prophet's viewpoint, we are to serve our neighbors only in consequence of our commission by God as agents of his will. As such, we are as prohibited from doing their bidding as we are from seeking our own pleasure, save as their good pleasure and God's are one.

2. For Class Participation: Have each of three of the more socially aware members of the class do a role play of Second Isaiah addressing each of the following groups concerning its duties as the Lord's servant in relationship to the indicated second party: (1) America, in relationship to the countries of the Third World; (2) white American Protestantism, in relationship to American blacks; (3) the black Christians of America, in relationship to the world's blacks in other lands. See Corbett, pp. 135-55, for suggestions on how to perform this assignment.

203

Session 8

Chapter I of this study book summarizes the religious heritage of Israel's great prophets, while Chapter II traces the history of the prophetic movement in Israel. Each of the following chapters, III through VII, isolates a group of passages from the collection of some one of five of Israel's great prophets that bear on a contribution of his of special significance for getting a comprehensive picture of the ongoing contribution of Israelite prophecy to the faith and life of mankind. In Chapter VIII these diverging emphases are fitted together: first, in such a fashion as to produce a digest of the theological contribution of the great prophets; and secondly, in a way designed to clarify their contribution as persons.

A. Resources

The last chapters, respectively, of the study book and of *Prophetic Religion,* by J. Philip Hyatt; the filmstrip, "In the Fulness of Time"; the films, "The Cardinal" and "From Montgomery to Memphis" (a documentary on the life and work of Martin Luther King); and the set of slides on "The Prophets."

B. Goals

1. Basic Aim: To tie together the various strands of the previous chapters in such a way as to obtain a coherent picture of the personality and thought of Israel's great prophets.

2. Specific Objectives: This chapter should clearly indicate the relevance of Israel's great prophets for us as we face the challenges of our terribly complex world (1) by revealing them to be persons capable of entertaining quite complex solutions to the problems thrust upon them by their times and, even more to the point, (2) by pointing up their ability to achieve a clear personal identity in a society where numerous groups were working hard to remake them in the image of their own special interests.

C. Questions

1. How did the great prophets reconcile the traditional emphasis on Israel's election with their existence in a world where Israel's survival could not be separated from the health of other nations?

2. Were the great prophets opposed to culture on principle?

3. Did the great prophets view the freedom of God and of human beings as co-equal forces?

4. How do the great prophets help us in our efforts to distinguish between the demands of God, on the one side, and those of society, on the other?

5. Does our emphasis on the *writings* of the great prophets aid or retard our discovery of them as human beings?

D. Suggestions

1. *For Effective Communication:* Today's lesson may easily be presented as a panel discussion. A moderator and eight panel members would constitute the membership of the panel. As usual, the moderator would introduce the session and the panel members and, at the conclusion, briefly summarize the findings of the group. Each of four of the panelists would present one of the points under "The Combination of Apparent Opposites," which briefly recapitulates the significance of the great prophets as our models in coping with social and theological issues of a complex sort; and each of the other four panelists would do the same for one of the points in the second half of the chapter, "An Example in Involvement," which should be of special help to us in our search for a God-centered sense of identity in a society that scarcely encourages us in this quest.

2. *For Class Participation:* Give the Renewists, the Ecumenists, and the Civiltarians an opportunity to give a final report on the progress on their projects to date.

3. *For Social (or, as the case may be, Continuing) Action:* Appoint a committee of strongly committed and motivated volunteers (hereinafter to be known as "The

Propheteers") to assume responsibility for drafting a program, to be given shortly after the first of the year, for a general assembly of the UMW (at the local church, district, or conference level, as you wish). Imitating the format of the President's annual "State of the Nation" message, the title of this presentation might be "The State of the Church in Prophetic Perspective." Who knows? This production might become Chapter I of The Now Prophetesses or, better yet, a step en route to turning all United Methodist Women into prophetesses.

BIBLIOGRAPHY

An Arabic numeral in parenthesis after an entry indicates the chapter for which it has special value.

No asterisk before an entry indicates that its value has to do chiefly with the biblical writer's context.

*A single asterisk before an entry indicates that its value has to do chiefly with our context.

**Two asterisks before an entry indicate that its contents are more important for teaching methodology than it is for biblical or theological interpretation.

BOOKS

Anderson, Bernhard W. *Understanding the Old Testament,* 2d ed. Englewood Cliffs, N.J.: Prentice-Hall, Inc., 1966.

————, and Walter Harrelson, eds. *Israel's Prophetic Heritage.* New York: Harper & Bros., 1962.

**Anderson, Frances M. *Team Teaching in Christian Education.* Chicago: Evangelical Covenant Church of America, 1967.

Baly, Denis A. *Geography of the Bible.* New York: Harper & Row Publishers, Inc., 1974.

**Bowman, Locke E. *Straight Talk About Teaching in Today's Church.* Philadelphia: The Westminster Press, 1967.

Bright, John. *A History of Israel,* 2d ed. Philadelphia: The Westminster Press, 1972.

————. *Jeremiah.* Anchor Bible. New York: Doubleday & Co., Inc., 1965. (6)

Brown, R. E., S.S.; Joseph A. Fitzmyer, S.J.; and R. E. Murphy, O. Carm; eds. *The Jerome Biblical Commentary,* Englewood Cliffs, N. J.: Prentice-Hall, Inc., 1969.

Buber, Martin. *The Prophetic Faith,* trans. Carlyle Witton-Davis. New York: The Macmillan Company, 1949.

Buttrick, George A., ed. *The Interpreter's Bible* (Vols. 5 and 6 contain the commentary on all the great prophets who come in for individual treatment in this study book). New York: Abingdon Press, 1956.

Case, Harold C. *The Prophet Jeremiah*. New York: Woman's Division of Christian Service, Board of Missions of The Methodist Church, 1953. (6)

Chase, Mary Ellen. *The Prophets for the Common Reader*. New York: W. W. Norton & Company, Inc., 1963.

*Cherry, Conrad, ed. *God's New Israel*. Englewood Cliffs, N. J.: Prentice-Hall, Inc., 1971.

Clements, Ronald E. *Prophecy and Covenant*. Naperville: Alec R. Allenson, Inc., 1965. (1)

*Commager, H. S., ed. *Living Ideas in America*. New York: Harper & Row, Pubs., Inc., 1951.

*Commager, H. S. *The American Mind*. New Haven: Yale University Press, 1950.

*Corbett, J. Elliott. *The Prophets on Main Street*. Richmond, Va.: John Knox Press, 1965.

*————. *Christians Awake*. New York: Harper & Row Pubs., Inc., 1970.

*de Huszar, G. B., H. W. Littlefield, and A. W. Littlefield, eds. *Basic American Documents*. Ames, Ia.: Littlefield, Adams & Co., 1956.

*Faramelli, Norman J. *Technethics*. New York: Friendship Press, 1971.

*Gasser, Elaine, and Hilda Lee Dail, eds. *The Now Prophets*. New York: Joint Commission on Education and Cultivation of the Board of Missions, The United Methodist Church, 1969.

**Gettys, Joseph M. *How to Teach the Bible*. Atlanta: John Knox Press, 1961.

Gottwald, Norman K. *All the Kingdoms of the Earth: Israelite Prophecy and International Relations in the Ancient Near East*. New York: Harper & Row Pubs., Inc., 1964.

Heschel, Abraham J. *The Prophets*. New York: Harper & Row Pubs., Inc., Vol. 1, 1969, Vol. 2, 1971.

Hillers, D. R. Covenant: *The History of a Biblical Idea*. Baltimore: The Johns Hopkins Univ. Press, 1969. (1)

Hyatt, J. Philip. *Prophetic Religion*. New York: Abingdon Press, 1947. (8)

————. *Jeremiah: Prophet of Courage and Hope*. New York: Abingdon Press, 1958. (6)

Johnson, Aubrey R. *The Cultic Prophet in Ancient Israel*, 2d ed. Cardiff: University of Wales Press, 1962. (2)

208

**Jones, Clifford M. *The Bible Today: For Those Who Teach It.* Philadelphia: Fortress Press, 1964.

Kaiser, Otto, *Isaiah 1-12,* trans. R. A. Wilson. Philadelphia: The Westminster Press, 1972. (5)

—————. Isaiah 13-39, trans. R. A. Wilson. Philadelphia: The Westminster Press, 1974. (5)

Kapelrud, Arvid S. *Central Ideas in Amos.* Boston: Universitetsforlaget, 1971. (3)

Kelly, Balmer H., ed. *The Layman's Bible Commentary* (Vols. 11, 12, and 14 contain the commentary on all the great prophets who come in for individual treatment in this study book). Richmond, Va.: John Knox Press, 1964, 1959, 1960.

Knight, George A. F. *Deutero-Isaiah: A Theological Commentary on Isaiah 40-55.* New York: Abingdon Press, 1965. (7)

*Kuhn, Margaret E. *Get Out There and Do Something About Injustice.* New York: Friendship Press, 1972.

Laymon, Charles M., ed. *The Interpreter's One-Volume Commentary on the Bible.* New York: Abingdon Press, 1971.

Leslie, Elmer A. *Isaiah.* New York: Abingdon Press, 1963. (5)

—————. *Jeremiah.* New York: Abingdon Press, 1954. (6)

**Leypoldt, Martha M. *40 Ways to Teach in Groups.* Valley Forge, Pa.: Judson Press, 1967.

Lindblom, Johannes. *Prophecy in Ancient Israel.* Philadelphia: Fortress Press, 1972.

**Little, Sara. *Learning Together in the Christian Fellowship.* Atlanta: John Knox Press, 1956.

McKenzie, John L., S. J. *Dictionary of the Bible.* Milwaukee: Bruce Publishing Company, Inc. 1965.

Mays, James Luther. *Amos: A Commentary.* Philadelphia: The Westminster Press, 1969. (3)

—————. *Hosea: A Commentary.* Philadelphia: The Westminster Press, 1969. (4)

**Miles, Matthew B. *Learning to Work in Groups.* New York: Teachers College Press, Columbia University, 1959.

**Miller, Donald E., Graydon F. Snyder, and Robert W. Neff. *Using Biblical Simulations.* Valley Forge, Pa.: Judson Press, 1971.

**Minor, Harold D., ed. *Techniques and Resources for Guiding Adult Groups.* Valley Forge, Pa.: Judson Press, 1973.

Napier, B. D. *Prophets in Perspective.* New York: Abingdon Press, 1971.

209

*Nathan, A. G. *How to Plan and Conduct a Bicentennial Celebration*. Harrisburg, Pa.: Stackpole Books, 1971.

North, Martin. *The World of the Old Testament,* trans. V. I. Gruhn. Philadelphia: Fortress Press, 1964.

Orlinsky, Harry M., ed. *Interpreting the Prophetic Tradition*. New York: Ktav Publishing House, Inc., 1969.

Otwell, John H. *I Will Be Your God*. New York: Abingdon Press, 1967.

Phillips, J. B. *Four Prophets*. New York: The Macmillan Pub. Company, Inc., 1963.

**Rood, Wayne R. *The Art of Teaching Christianity*. New York: Abingdon Press, 1968.

Rowley, H. H. *The Servant of the Lord and Other Essays on the Old Testament,* 2nd. ed. Naperville: Alec R. Allenson, Inc., 1965. (7)

*Scherer, James H. *Global Living Here and Now*. New York: Friendship Press, 1974.

Schilling, S. Paul. *Isaiah Speaks*. New York: Woman's Division of Christian Service, Board of Missions of The Methodist Church, 1968. (5)

*Scott, J. A. *Trumpet of Prophecy*. New York: Alfred A. Knopf, Inc., 1969.

Scott, R. B. Y. *The Relevance of the Prophets,* rev. ed. New York: Macmillan Publishing Company, Inc., 1969.

Smart, James D. *History and Theology in Second Isaiah: A Commentary on Isaiah 35, 40-66*. Philadelphia: The Westminster Press, 1965. (7)

————. *Servants of the Word*. Philadelphia: The Westminster Press, 1961.

————. *The Old Testament in Dialogue with Modern Man*. Philadelphia: The Westminster Press, 1964.

Smith, George Adam. *Jeremiah*. London: Hodder & Stoughton, 1923. (6)

Vawter, Bruce C. M. *The Conscience of Israel*. New York: Sheed & Ward, Inc., 1969.

von Rad, Gerhard. *The Message of the Prophets,* trans. D. M. G. Stalker. New York: Harper & Row, Pub's. Inc., 1972.

*Ward, Barbara. *The Lopsided World*. New York: W. W. Norton & Co., Inc., 1968.

*————. *The Rich Nations and the Poor Nations*. New York: W. W. Norton & Co., Inc., 1962.

Ward, James M. *Amos and Isaiah: Prophets of the Word of God*. New York: Abingdon Press, 1969. (3, 5)

————. *Hosea: A Theological Commentary.* New York: Harper & Row Pubs., Inc., 1966. (4)

Westermann, Claus. *Basic Forms of Prophetic Speech,* 2nd ed., trans. by Hugh K. White. Philadelphia: Westminster Press, 1967.

————. *Isaiah 40-66,* trans. D. M. G. Stalker. Philadelphia: The Westminster Press, 1969. (7)

Wolf, Wm. J. *The Religion of Abraham Lincoln.* New York: Doubleday & Co., Inc., 1963.

Wright, George E. and Floyd V. Filson. *The Westminster Historical Atlas to the Bible,* rev. ed. Philadelphia: The Westminster Press, 1956.

Zimmerli, Walther, and J. Jeremias. *The Servant of God.* Studies in Biblical Theology, No. 20. London: SCM Press, 1957. (7)

ARTICLES AND TABLOIDS

Buchanan, G. W. "The Old Testament Meaning of the Knowledge of Good and Evil," *Journal of Biblical Literature,* 75 (1956), 114-20.

Crook, M. B. "A Suggested Occasion for Isaiah 9:2-7 and 11:1-9," *Journal of Biblical Literature,* 68 (1949), 213-24. (5)

Eichrodt, Walther. "The Holy One in Your Midst: the Theology of Hosea," *Interpretation,* 11 (1957), 269-73. (4)

Gehmann, H. S. "The Ruler of the Universe: The Theology of the First Isaiah," *Interpretation,* 11 (1957), 269-81. (5)

Gordis, R. "Hosea's Marriage and Message: A New Approach," *Hebrew Union College Annual,* 25 (1954), 9-35. (4)

Gray, J. "The Kingship of God in the Prophets and Psalms," *Vetus Testamentum,* 11 (1961), 1-29. (5)

Light in the Steeple: Religion and the American Revolution. New York: Ecumenical Task Force on the Religious Observance of the Nation's Bicentennial of the National Council of Churches, n.d.

McCullough, W. S. "Some Suggestions About Amos, *Journal of Biblical Literature,* 73 (1953), 247-254 (3)

McKenzie, J. L. "Divine Passion in Osee," *Catholic Biblical Quarterly,* 17 (1955), 287-99 (4)

————. "Knowledge of God in Hosea," *Journal of Biblical Literature,* 74 (1955), 22-27. (4)

May, H. G. "The Fertility Cult in Hosea," *American Journal*

of Semitic Languages and Literature, 48 (1931/32), 73-98.
(4)

Rignell, L. G. "A Study of Isaiah 9:2-7," *Lutheran Quarterly,* 7 (1955), 31-35. (5)

Ritschl, Dietrich. "God's Conversion: An Exposition of Hosea 11," *Interpretation,* 15 (1961), 286-303. (4)

Rust, E. C. "The Theology of Hosea," *Review and Expositor,* 54 (1957), 510-21. (4)

Rowley, H. H. "The Marriage of Hosea," *Bulletin of the John Rylands Library,* 39 (1956), 200-33. (4)

Stinespring, W. "Hosea, Prophet of Doom," *Crozer Quarterly,* 27 (1950), 200-7. (4)

Stone, P. F. "The Temple Sermons of Jeremiah," *American Journal of Semitic Languages and Literature,* 50 (1933-34), 73-92. (6)

Stuhlmueller, Carroll, C. P. "The Theology of Creation in Second Isaias," *Catholic Biblical Quarterly,* (1959), 429-467. (7)

Thomas, D. Winton. "The Age of Jeremiah in the Light of Recent Archaeological Discoveries," *Palestine Exploration Quarterly for 1950,* 1-15. (6)

Whitley, C. F. "The Call and Mission of Isaiah," *Journal of Near Eastern Studies,* 18 (1959), 38-48. (5)

Wolff, H. W. "Guilt and Salvation: A Study of the Prophecy of Hosea," *Interpretation,* 15 (1961), 274-85. (4)

AUDIOVISUALS

FILMS

The Cardinal. 16mm/175 minutes. Rental $37.50. (8)
The story of a prophetic Roman Catholic priest who becomes personally involved in the struggles against racism and a church that compromises with tyranny. Available from Brandom Films, Inc., 221 West 57th Street, New York, N.Y. 10019.

The Founding of Jamestown. 16mm/18 min./color. Rental $6. (2)
A film that depicts the impact of the Christian heritage on the development of the first permanent settlement in America. Produced by the Executive Council of the Episcopal Church. Available from Roa's Films, 1696 North Astor, Milwaukee, Wisconsin 53202.

Heritage to Destiny. 16mm/30 minutes. Rental $7. (1)
Although this film tells the story of the Disciples of Christ,

the appeal of this film crosses denominational boundaries. It closes with the reminder that each generation of God's people hears the call to decision at the place where heritage opens the door to destiny. Available from the producer: United Christian Missionary Society (Disciples of Christ), Office of Audio-Visual Services, 222 So. Downey Avenue, Indianapolis, Indiana 46219.

Prophet from Tekoa. 16mm/30 minutes. Rental $10.50. (3)
A presentation of Amos' message in its original setting, with some attempt to relate it to the American scene. More valuable for its power to stimulate discussion than for its theological interpretation. Produced by the Southern Baptist Convention. Available through Baptist Bookstores.

FILMSTRIPS

(Available from the producer: Cathedral Films and Filmstrips, 2921 W. Alameda Avenue, Box 1608, Burbank, California 91505. Cost of each filmstrip, $9 with record, $6 without record. Also consult your conference film libraries.)

Amos, God's Angry Man. 46 frames, flipside of recording for *Frontiersmen of Faith.* (3)

Frontiersmen of Faith. 54 frames. Introduces the roles and times of the prophets. (2)

Hosea, Prophet of God's Love. 52 frames. It highlights the danger and power of the prophet's discovery of God's love, but it errs in putting too great stress on the prophet's domestic experience as the key to his theological development. (4)

In the Fullness of Time. 44 frames, flipside of recording for *Prophet-Poet of the Exile.* Traces the connections between the prophetic movement and the emergence of Christian faith. (8)

Isaiah, Statesman for God. 59 frames, flipside of recording for *The Vision of Isaiah.* (5)

Jeremiah, the Reluctant Rebel. 54 frames. (6)

Prophet-Poet of the Exile. 52 frames. Second Isaiah is interestingly portrayed in this filmstrip, although it too casually labels him "the greatest of the prophets." (7)

(All of the filmstrips listed above belong to the 10-filmstrip series on "The Story of the Prophets," issued in Parts I [consisting of 6 filmstrips, which sell for $40.50 per set with records] and II [consisting of 4 filmstrips, which sell for $27

per set with records]. Available from denominational film libraries and other Cathedral dealers.

SLIDE SETS

The Prophets. 15 slides, color, script. Sale $6.50, rental $1. Consists of reproductions of original paintings by Michelangelo and Sargent. Utilization resources and suggestions are provided. Produced by Yale University Divinity School. Available from Instructional Materials for Church and School, Oberlin, Ohio 44074. (2, 8)

GLOSSARY

AHAZ. King of Judah (735-715 B.C.) who, in the teeth of Isaiah's strong insistence that he not do so, solicited Assyrian help in warding off the threat from an alliance of the Israelites and Syrians.

ALLEGORY. A literary type in which characters and events and qualities represent veiled references to something other than what is written. Such literature is, therefore, to be interpreted figuratively, not literally. *The Pilgrim's Progress*, by Bunyan, is one of the best known allegorical writings.

AMAZIAH. Priest at the royal shrine in Bethel who opposed Amos.

AMOS. A prophet from Judah who, late in the reign of Jeroboam II (786-746), journeyed into the Northern Kingdom of Israel to prophesy there. The oldest of the prophetic books of the Bible, it contains the traditions of his oracles and activity.

ANCESTRAL FAITH. Another designation for the classical religion of Israel, elsewhere called the Mosaic faith.

APOCALYPTIC WRITINGS. Interpretations of history in which the writers present their works as revelations by visions, cast in highly symbolic language, to ancient worthies who bespeak the authors' own views. Typically, they construe their own present as the prelude to the transition from this age to the age to come.

APOSTASY. A serious breach of the faith.

BAALISM. Designation for the nature religion of the Canaanites. It is so named because Baal, the god in the Canaanite family of deities in control of the weather cycle, played the lead role in this fertility cult.

BICENTENNIAL CELEBRATION. Observance of two-hundredth anniversary. 1976 marks the bicentennial of the Declaration of Independence from England by the American colonies.

215

CANAANITES. The name of the pre-Israelite inhabitants of Palestine.

CANON. This term comes from the Greek word for reed, as of cane. Since the regular joints of the cane reed qualified it for use as a measuring instrument, by means of logical extension, it came to mean "standard." Applied to the Old Testament Scriptures, it refers to the writings employed by Jews as the standard for deriving and defining their faith.

CARCHEMISH. An important city on the trade route between Assyria and Asia Minor. In 605 B.C. it was the scene of the defeat of the Assyrian-Egyptian alliance by Nebuchadrezzar's Babylonian armies in one of antiquity's most important battles.

CF. "Compare."

CHARISMATIC FIGURE. One who acts under what is perceived to be, by himself or others, the immediate influence of the divine spirit.

CONFESSIONAL HISTORY. A popular narrative via which a people simultaneously tells the story of its past and articulates its faith.

CONFESSIONS. Another name for the "laments" of Jeremiah. The prophet's confessions have frequently been compared with the laments of the Psalter.

COURT PROPHETS. Prophets attached, usually in a body, to the staff of a king. Outstanding exceptions to this description—e.g., Nathan—have raised doubt as to whether all the prophets who prophesied at court may be dismissed as mere "court prophets."

COVENANT. An Agreement between two parties. The covenant discussed most often in this book is that of the suzerainty (involving unequals) and not the parity variety. The partners are God and Israel, and the great prophets uniformly recognize the former as the Lord of the covenant.

CULT PROPHET. A prophet with a special relationship to and some responsibility for the conventional means of communication between God and his people. Normally such a person would be tied both to a specific shrine and to other such functionaries.

CYRUS. The Persian monarch (550-530 B.C.) who, in 538, issued the edict permitting Israel's return from exile (see Isaiah 44:28; 45:1ff.; 2 Chronicles 36:22ff.; Ezra 1:1-4, 7; 6:3-5.).

DISCIPLES OF THE PROPHETS. The admirers or associates of

a prophet who assumed responsibility for collecting, expanding, editing, updating and transmitting their master's words.

DYNASTIC ORACLE. The deliverance of a prophet or priest from the Lord concerning the role of the king at the time of his coronation.

E. Symbol for the second of the four Pentateuchal (pertaining to the first five books of the Bible) documents. It approaches the style and theology of J closely enough at times to make the separation of the two documents both impossible and meaningless. The work of theologians with a North Israelite background and bias, it originated between the appearance of J and 721.

ECSTASY. It may refer to a state of intense excitement in which one loses control over bodily movements and behaves in an erratic, even bizarre manner. It may also describe the complete absorption of one in contemplation of God to the point that a person becomes oblivious to his or her environment.

E.G. "For example."

ENTHRONEMENT CEREMONY. An annual celebration of the kingship of God at the turn of the year. The earthly ruler was simultaneously confirmed as the bearer of God's blessing and power.

ENUMA ELISH. The ancient name of the Babylonian epic of creation.

EPHRAIM. The name of a son of Joseph and one of the tribes of Israel, Ephraim also became a poetic designation for the Northern Kingdom of Israel in the prophecies of Hosea, Isaiah, Jeremiah and Ezekiel.

EXODUS. The second book of the Old Testament. It relates the story of Israel's escape from Egypt. This account furnishes Israel with a prototype of the description of its deliverances, future as well as past.

FEAST OF UNLEAVENED BREAD. An old Canaanite agricultural festival that the Israelites assimilated to their observance of Passover.

FERTILITY CULT. A form of nature worship that has as its major focus and goal the increase of one's harvest through the adoration and appeasement of the god(s) in charge of the weather cycle.

GIBEAH. The home of Saul, Israel's first monarch. Hosea's

hostile references to Gibeah (9:9; 10:0) may best be construed as reflections of his negative estimate of the kingship.

GOMER. Daughter of Diblaim and wife of Hosea (1:2-9). The author of *Decision for Destiny* attaches little significance to Gomer's role in interpreting Hosea's message.

GOSPEL. When applied to the Old Testament, it refers to the story of the divine initiative in effecting Israel's deliverance from Egypt.

HEZEKIAH. King of Judah from 715 to 687/686, he demonstrated greater religious fidelity than political foresight.

HOSEA. A younger contemporary of Amos, Hosea came from the Northern Kingdom of Israel to which he also addressed his oracles about 750 to about 721. He is often pointed to as the opposite of Amos, but he places hardly less emphasis on divine judgment than does his fellow prophet from Tekoa.

IBID. "The same reference."

ISAIAH. A prophet of Judah during the heyday of Israelite splendor, he lived through Samaria's exile and Judah's drastic fragmentation, but he remained hopeful in spite of these tragic developments. His stature may be inferred from the fact that the longest of all the Bible's collections of prophecies bears his name.

J. Symbol for the earliest of the four Pentateuchal (pertaining to the first five books of the Bible) documents. Its style is vivid; its theology, at once concrete and sublime. The work of theologians from the Southern Kingdom of Israel, it originated in the 10th or 9th century B.C., quite possibly shortly after Solomon's death.

JEDP. Code letters employed by scholars to designate the four principal documents, none of which is regarded as a literary unit, which have been edited to produce what appears to the casual reader to be a running narrative of Israelite beginnings. This narrative includes at least the first five books of the Old Testament.

JEHU. King of Israel from 842 to 815. He enjoyed the support of certain contemporary prophets, but the prophet Hosea declared that the Lord would wreak judgment on him for his blood-letting.

JEREMIAH. A prophet of Judah during the last decades of its turbulent life, from the reign of Josiah until well after the fall of Jerusalem in 587, he both acted as the nation's conscience and became a symbol of its tragedy.

JEROBOAM II. One of Israel's most successful kings (786-746 B.C.), despite the failure of either of the great prophets contemporary with him, namely Amos and Hosea, to look with favor on his administration.

JE THEOLOGY. Since the central theological concerns of the J and E documents are basically the same, they may be treated as a theological unit, even though certain literary and cultural differences continue to manifest themselves.

JOSEPHUS. A Jewish historian, who lived from 37/38 until 110 A.D., Josephus' works undertake demonstration of the greatness of Jews and Judaism. Although he traced the history of the Jews all the way from creation, his main, if often dubious, importance is confined to those periods for which he is our only source.

JOSIAH. King of Judah from 640-609 B.C. Though admired by Jeremiah, the extent of the prophet's support for his reform activity, rooted in the imposition of a new law (2 Kings 22-23; cf. 2 Chronicles 33-34), continues to be a matter for debate.

JOTHAM. King of Judah from 742-735 B.C., Jotham's reign witnessed a shift in Judah's fortune from the glory days of Uzziah, and it was decidedly for the worse.

KNOWLEDGE OF GOD. As used in the Bible, especially in Hosea and the great prophets, this term refers to an interpersonal union between the deity and persons in which the latter increasingly internalize the feelings and concerns of God.

LAW. System of requirements believed by the Israelites to have been disclosed by God to Moses and his successors and, therefore, to be obeyed without question or qualification. Such demands were formulated in consequence of reflection upon the divine will.

LEGALIST. One who puts heavy stress on the formulation of God's will into specific requirements and insists on literal compliance with their demands. Such a person is usually thought of as one who puts the letter before the spirit of God's demands.

LITURGICAL HISTORICAL NARRATIVE. The ordering of the story of a people's experience in a fashion suitable for use in a service of worship. Many scholars regard the Exodus accounts of what transpired in the exodus and at Sinai as examples of this literary type.

MARDUK. The god of the city of Babylon whom Hammurabi (about 1728-1686 B.C.) invested with the titles and attributes of other gods and elevated to the headship of the Mesopotamian pantheon.

MESSIAH. Literally "an anointed one"—such as a king, priest or prophet. In the Old Testament it comes to refer to the one who will act as agent of God in effecting the fulfillment of God's hope for his people.

MOSAIC FAITH. Shorthand for the religion of Israel as it took shape under the impact of the work of and traditions about Moses.

MOTIVATIONAL MYTH. An understanding of history's purpose that has penetrated one's subconscious to the point that the person under its influence cannot respond to any strong stimulus, emotional or rational, without revealing its powerful hold on one's life.

MYTH. A traditional narrative account of natural or historical occurrences that simultaneously mirrors an understanding of reality and encourages the appropriation of this insight at the levels of emotion and action.

NAHUM, HABAKKUK AND JOEL. Three Old Testament prophets who used literary forms from the rituals of Israel's cultic celebrations as vehicles for the communication of their message.

NATHAN. A prophet at David's court whose rebuke of the Israelite king for his abuse of Uriah and Bathsheba (see 2 Samuel 12:1-25) spotlights the danger of lumping together all the prophets before Amos as unworthy bearers of the prophetic mantle.

NEBUCHADREZZAR. King of Babylon from 605/604 until 562 B.C., he turned his capital city into one of the wonders of the ancient world, in addition to engineering the defeat and exile of Judah.

NECO. The Egyptian Pharaoh who murdered King Josiah in 609 B.C. in a meeting of the two heads of state at Megiddo.

NOMADS. People without a fixed habitation who wander from place to place in search of pasture for their herds and flocks.

ORACLE. A communication from a divine being to its people through someone, such as a prophet, commissioned to act as its spokesperson.

OSTRACA. Pieces of broken pottery. Because of the expense of writing materials in the ancient world and because of the durability of pottery, occasional writing was often done on ostraca. Some of the most important literary finds in Palestine were inscribed on ostraca.

PARITY COVENANT. A solemn ritual agreement between equals.

PASHHUR. The priest in charge of the Jerusalem temple who had Jeremiah flogged for prophesying that sanctuary's fall (see Jeremiah 20:1-6).

PASSOVER. An Israelite festival in celebration of the exodus.

PRIMARY MATERIAL. That portion of a document which may confidently be attributed to the person with whose name it has traditionally been linked.

PROPHETESS. In the Old Testament it is not always clear whether a person is so designated because she is married to a prophet or because she functions as the prophet's female counterpart.

PROPHETIC BAND. The organization of a group of prophets around a common shrine (e.g., the cult prophets) or a common function (e.g., the court prophets).

PROPHETIC FAITH. Israelite religion as it was refined under the impact of the stress of the prophets on the otherness, the righteousness and the universalism of the divine sovereignty.

PROPHETISM. The beliefs, actions and rituals associated with the exercise of the prophetic office.

ROYAL PSALM. A psalm composed for use in connection with the coronation or enthronement ceremony for a king.

SAMARIA. A royal city of the Northern Kingdom of Israel built by Omri in the 9th century B.C., it became a symbol of Ephraimite corruption, quite possibly because it continued to be heavily populated with Canaanites.

SECONDARY MATERIAL. That portion(s) of a document which cannot be credited to the person with whose name it has been traditionally linked.

SECOND ISAIAH. Name given to the anonymous prophet, active between 540 and 520 B.C., mainly responsible for the collection of the oracles in Isaiah 40-55. His work has been distinguished from that of the First Isaiah on historical, theological and literary grounds.

SEER. An early designation for those who came to be known as prophets. The seer's tendency to major in visions and other practices of a semi-magical sort suggest some of the primitive elements in the background of biblical prophecy.

SINAI. Because this was the name of the mountain on which Moses, according to tradition, received the Ten Commandments, it has become a symbol for religious law.

SINAITIC HISTORY. The cluster of narratives detailing the events of Israel's history from the time of its enslavement in Egypt to the disclosure of the Ten Commandments through Moses.

UZZIAH. King of Judah from 783 to 742 B.C., the achievements of his reign were as impressive as its length (see 2 Kings 14:21-15:7).

VISION. That which appears, whether to the eyes or the mind, to the seer and becomes to him a vehicle for the communication of a very special, usually deeply personal and, more often than not, quite private meaning.

ZEDEKIAH. King of Judah (597-587 B.C.). Although installed as king by Nebuchadrezzar of Babylon, it was his revolt against the Babylonians that set the stage for the fall of Jerusalem and the exile of Judah.

THE AUTHOR

This study of representative passages from selected Old Testament prophets, *Decision for Destiny,* springs from the conviction that these Israelite prophets have the power to do for us what they did for their ancient neighbors: precipitate that crisis of faith in which the claims of God and society become so clear that a choice between the two becomes inescapable.

Dr. Tilson is the author of other books, including *The Conscience of Culture* and *Segregation and the Bible.* He has also been a contributing author to a number of other volumes, including *Christian Mission in Theological Perspective, Theological Perspectives of Stewardship,* and *The Pulpit Speaks on Race.* Earlier this year, Abingdon Press published a resource book by him and two of his colleagues, *Ways the Bible Comes Alive in Communicating the Faith.* Articles by him have appeared in such journals and periodicals as *Religion in Life, Interpretation, Christian Century, British Weekly, motive, Journal of Religious Thought* and the *Journal of Bible and Religion.*

223

Before coming to the Methodist Theological School in Delaware, Ohio, where he is Professor of Old Testament in the James Ralph Riley Chair of Biblical Studies, Dr. Tilson taught Biblical Theology for eight years in the Divinity School of Vanderbilt University.

In 1957 Dr. Tilson served as chairman of the Conference on Christian Faith and Human Relations that called on President Eisenhower to join forces with those Southerners, black and white, who were working for the implementation of the Supreme Court's desegregation decision of 1954. He served as president in 1958-60 of the King College Alumni Association and, in 1960-61, of the Southern Section of the National Association of Biblical Instructors.

Born in Virginia, Dr. Tilson received his higher education, including a Ph.D. degree from Vanderbilt University Divinity School, from the following institutions: Marion College, King College, Scarritt College, Garrett Theological School, Vanderbilt University, Hebrew Union College, Yale University Divinity School and Heidelberg University. An ordained United Methodist minister, he has served congregations of The United Methodist Church, the United Church of Christ and Presbyterian Church, U.S., in Tennessee as well as the congregation of the United Presbyterian Church in Spencertown, New York.

Mrs. Tilson, who holds the M.A. degree in English from George Peabody Teacher's College, teaches third grade in the Delaware, Ohio, public schools. The Tilsons have three sons and a daughter: Stephen, an attorney-at-law; Lee, a graduate student in philosophy; Joseph, an undergraduate student, majoring in political science; and Hazel Tilson Lilly, a student in the Riverside Hospital School of Nursing in Columbus, Ohio.

THE COVER

The Prophet by Gregory Ridley

Using a technique known as repousse, where the artist hammers or presses a design on the reverse side of metal, Mr. Ridley has created a striking and compelling figure that reflects what must have been the strength and verve of the prophets of Old Testament times and of today.

Mr. Ridley, a Tennessean by birth, is internationally known as a professor, painter, sculptor and repousse artist, having perfected the repousse technique. He frequently lectures on art history, art education, art appreciation and Afro-American art. He studied at Fisk University, Tennessee State University and the University of Louisville. He has taught at Alabama State University, Grambling College (Louisiana), Elizabeth City State College (North Carolina), Brooklyn College (New York), Tennessee State University, Fisk University (Tennessee) and Lehman Medgar Evers College and Nassau Community College (both in New York).

He has a number of commissions to do work in repousse on the life of "Great Blacks," "The Life of George Washington Carver," and "The Life of Christ." Mr. Ridley has won many prizes and awards during his 20-year career, and his work may be found in many public and private collections as well as in publications.

Mr. Ridley is married to Gloria Louise Brooks; they are the parents of five children. They currently live and work in Brooklyn, New York.

The Prophet hangs in the collection of Elliott and Juanita Wright in New York City.

225

Prepared for the

Women's Division

by the

Education and Cultivation Division
Board of Global Ministries
The United Methodist Church

Order from

Service Center
7820 Reading Road
Cincinnati, Ohio 45237
Price, $1.45
JBW 2/75